"Sam Renihan has served the church
ly—one historical and the other bibli
dissertation, *From Shadow to Substanc*
the development of seventeenth-centu
covenant theology. His most recent w

senses, is a biblical presentation of the issues covered in his dissertation.
The Mystery of Christ is well-written, displays ample knowledge of issues
discussed concerning covenant theology by Baptists and paedobaptists,
grounds its arguments in scriptural exegesis and theology, recovers old arguments for a new day, presents a cohesive map of the covenants of Scripture, and exalts our Lord Jesus Christ, the last Adam, throughout. Schol-
arly but never dry; exegetical but never pedantic; pastoral and practical but
never trite; this is a fine work."

Richard C. Barcellos
Pastor of Grace Reformed Baptist Church, Palmdale, CA, and Associ-
ate Professor of Exegetical Theology at IRBS Theological Seminary,
Mansfield, TX. He is the author of *Getting the Garden Right: Adam's
Work and God's Rest in Light of Christ* and *The Lord's Supper as a Means of
Grace: More than a Memory.*

"What is this book good for?

It establishes a clear linear understanding of the biblical text in its purpose
of driving the reader to see how faithfully God executes His purpose in
creation. The covenantal framework from Adam to Christ, from creation
to consummation is a most apt way of seeing the flow of the entire biblical
text. One is lifted into the journey to see the entire scope of divine provi-
dence work out the divine decree from generation to generation, book to
book, event to event, person to person.

This book serves for an excellent and rich primer on covenant theology
and demonstrates how it leads from the Covenant of Redemption to the
final claiming and purifying of the people given by the Father to the Son.
Profession of faith, baptism, Lord's Supper, and church discipline all are
practiced as an expression of consistency with the eternal purpose of God
in covenant. In this book one may come to a firm and clear grasp of such
important ideas as continuity and discontinuity, positive law in relation
to natural/moral law, Covenant of Works in relation to the Covenants of
Redemption and Grace, and the finality of Christ as the one who consum-
mates all the covenantal arrangements by His person and work.

This book is delightful to the point of entertainment to see how fittingly biblical texts open their meaning in the context of these covenantal discussions. How pertinently both biblical exposition and theological synthesis tie together the microcosm and macrocosm of Scripture finds the point of integration in the theme of covenant.

Renihan's writing also adds to the charm of this seriously theological work. Some of the most powerful points of synthesis have a literary lilt that gives memorable power to the overall argument: "God swept Israel off its feet as their redeemer, their husband, here to take her home to safety and blessing and prosperity, ready to shower her with good gifts." "Egypt's religion was… ancient, beautiful, artistic, creative, and tangible…. It is no surprise, then, that Israel broke the covenant only days after its pledge to keep the same. You can take Israel out of Egypt. But you can't take Egypt out of Israel." "God was so very kind to Israel, as seen in its history. But Israel was utterly faithless." "They failed to realize just how much the New Covenant would not be like the Old Covenant, and why that was such a blessed reality." "[T]he study of the mystery of Christ, His covenant, and His kingdom is a devotional experience. It is a way of wonderment, a path of praise. It is a balm, a salve, a nepenthe, a panacea, a cordial, a precious remedy, a sweet medicine, 'a sure and steadfast anchor for the soul' (Hebrews 6:19)."

Indeed, it is so; and Renihan's organization, insight, and style gives the reader every opportunity to see this."

Tom Nettles
Retired Professor of Historical Theology at The Southern Baptist Theological Seminary, Louisville, Kentucky

"The themes of covenant and kingdom have always been crucial to Reformed thought, and Reformed theologians will surely be pondering and debating these issues until Christ returns. In this new volume, Sam Renihan offers a clear and engaging study that should help to keep this conversation going. One of the most useful things Renihan does—which readers across the Reformed spectrum should appreciate—is keep covenant and kingdom together, not as independent themes but as themes that absolutely depend on one another. While I am in no position to say how confessional Reformed Baptists should regard Renihan's work, I know that I, as a Presbyterian theologian, will from now on look to his book as a prime resource for Reformed Baptist covenant theology."

David VanDrunen
Robert B. Strimple Professor of Systematic Theology and Christian Ethics, Westminster Seminary California

"In *The Mystery of Christ* Samuel Renihan offers a compelling narrative arguing that the biblical witness coheres in the covenantal kingdom of its central character, Jesus Christ. While Renihan capably contributes to the growing literature of "progressive covenantalism," he smoothly evinces a truth heretofore largely downplayed: Covenantal theology was the major biblical theology paradigm for Baptists at their beginnings in seventeenth-century England. This sharp young theologian is also to be commended for preserving a high view of Scripture while taking the historical nature and literary aspects of divine revelation seriously."

> **Malcolm B. Yarnell III**
> Research Professor of Systematic Theology, Southwestern Seminary, and author of The Formation of Christian Doctrine, Royal Priesthood in the English Reformation, and God the Trinity: Biblical Portraits

---

"Sam Renihan has written a clear, concise and forthright account of the covenants, their history and their theological and religious significance. This has required skills in theology, exegesis and biblical history, including the study of the place of typology in the Old Testament as this was made plain in the anti-types of the New Testament. It is not surprising that these topics, viewed together, are of some complexity, and without careful attention, the seeds of misunderstanding will quickly grow and entangle. So, a reliable guide, such as the author has provided, is indispensable.

Another emphasis of the book is on the Mystery of Christ. Not only in the culmination of the Father's covenantal purposes and in the Incarnation and self-offering of the incarnate Son, the one whose saving power is now seen to be active in the calling of the Christian church, His Kingdom. But from the New Testament, Christ is seen to have been retroactively at work in the faith of the saints of ancient Israel and Judah, and of the pre-Christ Gentiles who together formed the faithful remnant 'chosen by grace' during the Old Testament. For Christ, appearing in 'the fullness of time,' is the fulcrum of the eternal Covenant of Redemption, and so He is the Redeemer of the elect in every epoch, the same yesterday, today, and forever. Dr. Renihan has further enlivened and enriched his account by numerous historical allusions and quotations mainly from his beloved English Particular Baptists of the seventeenth century. Such a book, so carefully written, requires an equally careful reading. The book will richly repay its readers who take their time to weigh the author's words."

> **Paul Helm**
> Emeritus Professor of the History and Philosophy of Religion, King's College, London

"In recent years the gospel church's discussion of these matters has been enriched by the appearance of Reformed Baptist literature, numbers of excellent new books have rolled off the presses, and in this latest book, written by Dr. Samuel Renihan, we find a considerably important contribution to the issue. It is necessary reading, especially for theological students and thoughtful men who are profiting much from the fellowship, preaching and godly lives of our paedo-baptist brothers, both those alive today and those whose ministries over the centuries we have greatly profited from."

Geoff Thomas
Assistant minister in Amyand Park Baptist Chapel, London

The Mystery of Christ, His Covenant, And His Kingdom

By
Samuel Renihan

 Founders Press

Cape Coral, Florida

Published by
Founders Press

P.O. Box 150931 • Cape Coral, FL 33915
Phone (888) 525-1689
Electronic Mail: officeadmin@founders.org
Website: http://www.founders.org

©2019, 2020 Founders Press

Printed in the United States of America

Second Printing 2020

13 ISBN: 978-1-943539-15-4

Cover Design by Peter Voth

For Owen

My firstborn, precious, only one,

I bid you look to God's own Son.

Receive, inherit, and embrace

In Christ the covenant of grace.

The promise is for you, and all

Whose faith is in the gospel call.

Acknowledgments

This book has been forming in my mind for a long time, shaped by the past and present. My classes and classmates at Westminster Seminary California and the Institute of Reformed Baptist Studies were invaluable for developing my understanding of these truths in a community of diverse and, at times, opposing ideas.

Many people have read and replied to parts and pieces of this work in its development over the years, most of all my brother, Micah, and Richard Barcellos.

I also wish to thank the students who attended the classes in which this material developed into written form, in Palmerston North, New Zealand, then in Bakersfield, California, and in Sydney, Australia. The questions and engagement of the students challenged me and encouraged me to improve the material. They listened with patience to ideas still in the process of refinement and helped me greatly. Thank you to Dafydd Hughes, Chad Vegas, and Mike Prodigalidad for those invitations. Mike Prodigalidad also helped to motivate me to submit my work to publishers, a needed prodding from a supportive friend.

Brandon Adams' writing has often intersected with and influenced my own thought on these matters, in various ways, either pushing my work to greater precision or pointing me to sources and ideas that Brandon had studied in his reading, often sources from the paedobaptist tradition.

Pascal Denault's work, cheerfulness, and zeal has also been an encouragement to me.

Rex Semrad and David Charles have supported my efforts and have lifted my spirits on more than one occasion by providing feedback on the manuscript. Knowing that others would express appreciation and profit from this work, giving all glory to God, has been a great encouragement.

My wife, Kimberly, has been excited about this project all along. My copastors at Trinity Reformed Baptist Church gave me time to work on it as I prepared to teach the abovementioned classes.

I am also thankful to my father for referring my work to Jared Longshore, and to Jared for so excitedly and supportively bringing my manuscript all the way to publication.

Contents

Part Three: The Kingdom of Israel

Preface

This book seeks to develop and present the covenant theology of the Bible through a thorough study of the Scriptures. Studying covenant theology is a devotional experience that enriches one's understanding of the unity of God's purposes, enhances preaching from any text, informs one's understanding of the church, assures God's people of the security of their salvation, and much more. But above all, studying the covenant theology of the Bible magnifies the majesty of the triune God's plan of redemption.

The plan and outline of this book is broken up into four parts, each with their own subdivisions. The first part deals with methodology, system, and hermeneutics. The second, third, and fourth parts move through the Bible in chronological order, covering three kingdoms and their respective covenants.

As a Particular Baptist theologian, Nehemiah Coxe, said in his work on covenant theology,

> I will only add this: that on the whole, my aim has been to speak the truth in love and to take my notions from the Scriptures, not grafting any preconceived opinions of my own onto them. Where the evidence of truth appears, let it not be refused because it is offered in a mean dress and presented under the disadvantage of a rude and unpolished style. But consider instead the reason of what is said and with the noble Bereans search the Scriptures to see whether these things be so or not. And the Lord give you understanding in all things.[1]

---

[1] Nehemiah Coxe, *A Discourse of the Covenants That God made with Men before the Law. Wherein, The Covenant of Circumcision is more largely handled, and the Invalidity of the Plea for Paedobaptism taken from thence discovered* (London: John Darby, 1681), vi-vii.

Part One

Methodology and Hermeneutics

1

Biblical Theology and Systematic Theology in Covenant Theology

Introduction

Covenant theology is not an easy subject to study. It is even more difficult to teach or write about it because covenant theology seeks to understand and explain the united purpose of God in all history past, present, and future. This is no small task.

The Apostle Paul tells us that the riches of God's wisdom, knowledge, judgments, and ways are unsearchably and inscrutably deep (Romans 11:33). And when confronted by the thought of swimming in such a sea of infinity, or even of leading others by the hand through it, our reaction ought to be humble silence broken only by the very doxology Paul proclaimed when confronted by the same: "For from him and through him and to him are all things. To him be glory forever. Amen" (Romans 11:36).

As students of covenant theology, therefore, we must be both humble and diligent. We must be humble enough not to pry and peer into what is not ours to know. Yet we must be diligent in studying that which God has made known for our good and His own glory. This study of the covenants is offered with the sincere desire and intent of testing and limiting all that is asserted by that certain, sufficient, and infallible rule of faith, the Word of God. And in an effort to be as faithful as possible in this purpose, this covenant theology begins by discussing methodology. A subject of such size requires appropriate preparation, tools, and methods.

> Prepare your work outside; get everything ready for yourself in the field,
> and after that build your house (Proverbs 24:27).

Part of this preparation is being aware of key methodological challenges inherent to covenant theology. In particular, we will discuss the challenge of the relationship of biblical theology and systematic theology as it pertains to the study of covenant theology.

In his excellent volume on theology proper, James Dolezal notes that "Biblical theology, with its unique focus on historical development and progress, is not best suited for the study of theology proper."[1] Because God is pure act, effecting creation but unaffected by creation, a method based on progressive developing history is not the appropriate approach for that area of study. Dolezal rightly opts for a contemplative approach to the doctrine of God. However, the covenant theologian is faced with a somewhat more methodologically complex task. Covenant theology specifically addresses the historical development and outworking of God's redemptive plan while simultaneously systematizing the elements into a soteriology, a practical ecclesiology, a sacramentology, and more. All treatments of covenant theology, therefore, must walk the balanced path of a system that pays proper attention to the development of history. To proceed responsibly, this challenge must be considered in at least four ways.

1. Scope and Simplicity

The first challenge to a proper balance between biblical theology and systematic theology in covenant theology is that of scope and simplicity. Covenant theology covers, by necessity, the entirety of the Scriptures, beginning with Adam and creation and ending with Christ and the consummation. Covenant theology discusses, by definition, the forest and the trees, the macro and micro perspectives of the Scriptures. And not only does covenant theology bring to light the large and small details of the progress of redemption, but it also interprets and explains their theological significance and systematic implications.[2]

---

[1] James Dolezal, *All That Is in God* (Grand Rapids, MI: Reformation Heritage Books, 2017), xv.

[2] There is one feature that I am intentionally passing over in this study of the movement of redemptive history and the biblical and systematic theology that summarize it. That is the Sabbath. And my reason for doing so is simply that it has been done in far greater quality and quantity than I can provide by Richard Barcellos in *Getting the Garden Right: Adam's Work and God's Rest in Light of Christ* (Cape Coral, FL: Founders Press, 2017). The Sabbath precedes and transcends Israel and its covenants and finds an abiding and obligatory expression in the first day of the week after the resurrection of Christ.

The scope of covenant theology makes it a subject that defies simplification and generalization. A map that names only the continents, or only countries, will not help the traveler on the ground. So also, a covenant theology that does not draw the small interconnecting lines that unify the larger sections is deficient and unreliable. The author or teacher of covenant theology may strive for a simple and clear style, but there is a quantity of material to be taught that no quality of eloquence can, or should, reduce.

The necessary result of the scope of the subject is that a theological system deriving from covenant theology must be built from the ground up, giving full and due weight to the trees that constitute the forest. A map of a forest should go no farther than the trees themselves. So also, the scope of covenant theology should caution us against facile reductions or generalizations. Whatever is concluded must be built on supporting premises, and the supporting premises must be studied as completely and thoroughly as possible.

2. Creation, Covenant, and Consequences

The second challenge to a proper balance between biblical theology and systematic theology is the fundamental distinction between creation and covenant. That which God created and made, and the ordinary course and progress of the same, can be said to be natural. That which God does beyond nature is supernatural. Covenants fall into the latter category. They are not a part of the natural created order.

By virtue of being a creature, man owes complete obedience to God. By virtue of being Creator, God is owed man's complete obedience. In this natural Creator-creature relationship, God does not owe a reward to man for his obedience. The only due response from God to man is the approval of justice. "You have done what was asked of you." But man's obedience does not merit or earn anything as a reward. Jesus taught His disciples that masters do not owe servants a reward for doing that which they are already obligated to do. And so, the servants are to say, "We are unworthy servants; we have only done what was our duty" (Luke 17:10). The servant cannot hold out his hand for a reward as though he has placed the master in his debt.

Paul taught this to the Athenians.

24 The God who made the world and everything in it, being Lord of heaven and earth, does not live in temples made by man, 25 nor is he served by human hands, as though he needed anything, since he himself gives to all mankind life and breath and everything (Acts 17:24–25).

Elihu taught this to Job.

> 5 Look at the heavens, and see; and behold the clouds, which are higher than you. 6 If you have sinned, what do you accomplish against him? And if your transgressions are multiplied, what do you do to him? 7 If you are righteous, what do you give to him? Or what does he receive from your hand? 8 Your wickedness concerns a man like yourself, and your righteousness a son of man (Job 35:5–8).

And God reinforced the same.

> Who has first given to me, that I should repay him? Whatever is under the whole heaven is mine (Job 41:11).

As God is not worsened by man's unrighteousness, so God is not improved by man's righteousness. Nor does He receive through man's service something that He lacked so as to necessitate a reciprocation from God to man. As Nehemiah Coxe said, "None can oblige God, or make him their Debtor, unless he condescend to oblige himself by Covenant or Promise."[3]

The Westminster Confession, Savoy Declaration, and Second London Baptist Confession affirm this.

> The distance between God and the Creature is so great, that although reasonable Creatures do owe obedience unto him as their Creator, yet they never could have attained the reward of Life, but by some voluntary condescension on God's part, which he hath been pleased to express, by way of covenant (2LCF 7.1).[4]

Covenants, therefore, are not natural arrangements.[5] Covenants involve the distribution of benefits, either freely promised or conditioned on some action, that otherwise would not be available to the creature, such as confirmed eternal life, the land of Canaan, kingship over Israel, or salvation in the blood of Christ. Covenants include obligations beyond those naturally required, such as the commands regarding the trees in Eden, the command of circumcision, or the command of baptism. Covenants are arrangements provided by God beyond the natural Creator-creature relationship.

---

[3] Coxe, *A Discourse of the Covenants*, 6. "Such a priviledg, and nearness to God, as is included in Covenant-Interest, cannot immediately result from the relation which they have to God as Creatures…for the Lord owes not unto Man the Good promised in any Covenant he makes with them, antecedently."

[4] 2LCF is following SD, which slightly modified WCF 7.1.

[5] For an excellent discussion of this, see Richard C. Barcellos, *The Covenant of Works* (Palmdale, CA: RBAP, 2016), 36–46.

Because covenants are not natural arrangements, the specific nature and details of any given covenant are no more and no less than what God makes them to be. Their details cannot be discovered, determined, or defined apart from God's sovereign institution because they do not exist apart from God's sovereign institution. They are not natural. The parties of the covenant and their respective commitments are limited to that which God has instituted.

The distinction between creation and covenant aligns, systematically speaking, with two other distinctions. The first is the distinction between natural law and positive law. The second is the related distinction between natural religion, and instituted religion.

Natural law refers to the universal moral law of God impressed on the mind of man. Positive law refers to indifferent things prescribed or proscribed for a particular period, place, and people. In Romans 2:14–15, Paul teaches that there is an equivalent morality between Jews and Gentiles, an equivalence that connects an innate or natural knowledge of the moral law with the outward writing down of that law in the Ten Commandments at Sinai.

> 14 For when Gentiles, who do not have the law, by nature do what the law requires, they are a law to themselves, even though they do not have the law. 15 They show that the work of the law is written on their hearts.

Thus there is a natural law, a natural knowledge of what is right and wrong, though sinners suppress, pervert, and reject that knowledge.

In addition to these universal and abiding laws, the Scriptures speak of other laws that rose and fell with specific covenants. These are positive laws. For example, Hebrews 9:10 speaks of "regulations for the body imposed until the time of reformation." They were laws added for a time, designed to be removed. Circumcision was once binding, and now it is not. Paul says in 1 Corinthians 7:19, "For neither circumcision counts for anything nor uncircumcision, but keeping the commandments of God." It is interesting that Paul calls a command nothing, then tells us to keep God's commands. That is because circumcision is not a moral or natural duty, and having been abrogated, it is nothing. These kinds of laws are positive laws. As they were added, so they can be subtracted.

Positive laws are a part of the New Testament as well. Consider Philippians 4:8–9,

> 8 Finally, brothers, whatever is true, whatever is honorable, whatever is just, whatever is pure, whatever is lovely, whatever is commendable, if there is any excellence, if there is anything worthy of praise, think about

these things. 9 What you have learned and received and heard and seen in me—practice these things, and the God of peace will be with you.

In verse 8, Paul directs the Philippians to those things that are inherently or naturally true, honorable, and just. They would be so for Jew or Gentile, believer or unbeliever. And then he goes on in verse 9 to refer to those things which have been instituted for their church life.

The point to be grasped is that man has natural obligations to God, but God is free to add additional commands. Those additional commands are no more and no less than what God has made them. And man's obligation is to obey them exactly.

Very much related to this is the distinction between natural religion (or natural worship) and instituted religion (or instituted worship). Many modern Christians know and believe this distinction, but under the name of the Regulative Principle of Worship. Natural religion is the worship that man owes to God by virtue of the Creator-creature relationship. This is a part of natural law. All mankind knows that they must worship God. But the way in which God is to be worshipped, i.e., instituted worship, is regulated by God's commands. As William Ames put it,

> The parts of religion are two; natural worship, and voluntary or instituted worship…Instituted worship is the means ordained by the Will of God, to exercise and further natural worship…This worship [depends] upon the most free institution of God…No worship of this kind is lawful, unless it hath God for the Author, and ordainer of it…There is opposed unto this instituted worship, as unlawful, that will-worship which is devised by men.[6]

Heinrich Bullinger likewise distinguished between the law of nature which is "an instruction of the conscience, and as it were a certain direction placed by God Himself, in the minds and hearts of men, to teach them what they have to do, and what to eschew"[7] and ecclesiastical laws which are "taken out of the holy scriptures, and not invented or brought to light by the wit of man."[8]

The regulative principle of worship, built on this foundation, sums up the truth that we are not to add to or subtract from God's instituted wor-

---

[6] William Ames, *The Marrow of Sacred Divinity* (London: Edward Griffin, 1642), 249, 307–315.

[7] Heinrich Bullinger, *Fiftie Godlie and Learned Sermons, Divided Into Five Decades, Containing The chiefe and principall points of Christian Religion, written in three seuerall Tomes or Sections* (trans. H. I.; London: Ralph Newberie, 1587), 100. (2:1).

[8] Bullinger, *Decades*, 108.

ship, because the way in which He is to be worshipped derives only from God's revelation on the matter. We are not free to draw inferences in this arena.

Consider Cain and Abel, for whom the sacrifice of one was regarded but not the other's. If God requires the firstfruits of the flock, that does not mean, by inference, that the firstfruits of the field are likewise acceptable. Positive laws and instituted religion are not natural, though they presuppose natural obligations of obedience and worship. And therefore, positive laws are to be understood and obeyed exactly as they are instituted. As a Particular Baptist, Edward Hutchinson, said, "You dare not offer strange fire to the Lord, which he hath not commanded, nor profane an Ordinance; you know that Baptism (being a part of instituted worship, not found in nature's garden) has of itself no virtue, but what it receives from the institutor."[9]

The all-important connection of these truths for the relationship between biblical theology and systematic theology in covenant theology is that because covenants are not natural arrangements, "not found in nature's garden," there are certain senses in which they are not the proper subjects of consequential, or inferential, arguments. And thus, one must be careful not to over-systematize or draw connections and proportions from that which is what it is only by virtue of sovereign institution. To put it another way, necessary consequences don't work for covenants because there is no necessity in covenants. Covenants are not natural. They are not a part of the created order.

Necessary consequences are conclusions that must be true, by necessity.[10] The conclusion is necessarily derived from necessary premises. For example, the Scriptures tell us that there is one God who alone is the sub-

---

[9] Edward Hutchinson, *A Treatise Concerning the Covenant and Baptism Dialogue-wise, between a Baptist & a Poedo-Baptist, Wherein is shewed, That Believers only are the Spirituall Seed of Abraham; Fully discovering The Fallacy of the Argument drawn from the Birth Priviledge* (London: Francis Smith, 1676), v of an unpaginated preface.

[10] A Particular Baptist, Thomas Delaune said A necessary consequence is that which proves the matter concluded certainly to be. Yea, *certe ita esse, nec aliter se habere posse* [It is so certain, that it could not be otherwise]. There must be *tam necessaris nexus, & indissolubilis dependentia* [So necessary a connection and indissoluble dependence], such an infallible dependence between the *subject* and *predicate*, that the *conclusion* must be *universally* and *perpetually* true. And every necessary consequence demonstrates *a priori*; For *Demonstratio est ex prioribus, notioribus, & causis* [The demonstration is composed of things prior, things better known, and the causes of the thing]. Thomas Delaune, *Truth Defended, Or a Triple Answer to the late Triumvirates Opposition in their Three Pamphlets* (London: n.p., 1677), 2.

ject of our worship and service. The Scriptures also ascribe divine activity and human worship to the Father, to the Son, and to the Holy Spirit. So, we conclude by necessity that there is one God in three persons, the holy Trinity.

But there is no natural necessity in covenants. Covenants in themselves are not necessary, neither are their parties, precepts, and promises. And thus, what one covenant is has no necessary connection to what another covenants is. This clarifies the connection of the distinction between creation and covenant to the distinctions between natural law and positive law, as well as natural religion and instituted religion. As it would be illegitimate to tell everyone in the world that they must buy red cars, because that is not a part of natural law, and as it would be illegitimate to tell believers to worship God through Mary, because that is not a part of instituted worship, so it would be illegitimate to determine the nature of any given covenant, and any part of it, apart from God's institution of that covenant. On a map, the shape and size of one country is no indication of the same in another country. And to draw up a map where one country becomes the pattern for others, when there is no natural connection, will yield a false and useless map.

A Particular Baptist, Henry Lawrence, expressed this truth,

> But in instituted ordinances, the reason of which lies in nothing else, but a particular will of the institutor, it is bold and unsafe to institute above what is written in the new covenant, at least in any essential thing, concerning either the parts of the ordinance, the manner of administration, and the subject of them...
>
> The sum is, that it is unsafe arguing from one institution to another, because the inferences and consequences cannot be drawn from our reason, as not falling under the judicature of common light, or spiritual reason in the general, but of a particular distinct & independent will in Christ, from whence, not from the reason of the thing they draw all their virtue and efficacy, the reason that makes it good to us, being only the impression of his will upon it; but especially this will take place in ordinances of differing covenants, for the ordinances of each covenant are fitted to the meridian of that covenant.[11]

Too many times, systematic conclusions are included in covenant theologies without an actual necessity in the conclusion. For example, circumcision was given to Abraham as a seal (Romans 4:11). Putting aside for now the full meaning of this text in its context, some conclude that

---

[11] Henry Lawrence, *Of Baptisme* (Rotterdam: n.p., 1646), 179–86. Spelling updated.

therefore all covenants have seals and apply the term to baptism, not as an illustration to explain baptism, but as a part of their theological system to be received and believed. Some have noted that blood is spilled in connection with a covenant and conclude therefore that apart from a blood-ritual there is no covenant. Some have noted that families are included in covenants and have concluded therefore that families are a necessary feature of all covenants.

Each of these conclusions may be true. The point is simply that they are not *necessarily* true because the features of one covenant cannot be used to determine the features of another covenant. There is no natural necessity, inference, or proportion between things instituted, things positive, things supernatural, things covenantal. And systems built on inferences derived from covenants, which are neither natural nor necessary, will therefore contain unnecessary, and likely illegitimate, consequences. As Nehemiah Coxe said, because covenants are instituted by God and do not arise from any natural state, "our Knowledge and Understanding of them, must wholly depend upon Divine Revelation...seeing the nature of them is such as transcends common Principles of Reason or natural Light."[12]

This distinction between creation and covenant, with its methodological implications for consequences, does not deny the analogy of faith. The limitation of the details of one covenant to the institution of the covenant is not the same as the limitation of the details of one covenant to one passage of Scripture. The Word of God may speak of one covenant in many places, and they are all to be consulted and considered as constituting the final word on the matter.

Nor does this distinction teach a hyper-biblicism that refuses to see a covenant without the presence of the word. Quite to the contrary, if covenants are not natural, and if God provides precepts and promises to a party, coupled with threats, then it is this very distinction between creation and covenant that tells us that something special, something beyond nature, is happening. And to identify a covenant in such a case is the necessary consequence of the Word of God, meaning that it is the Word of God.

Neither do these methodological considerations indicate that we are disallowed from developing a systematic vocabulary of covenant theology. Rather, these considerations help us to realize that one's system must not violate the limitations and boundaries of the nature of covenants by connecting that which is not connected, by drawing inferences and proportions where there is no natural necessity.

---

[12] Coxe, *A Discourse of the Covenants*, 13.

3. The Law and the Gospel

Covenant theology must pay attention to biblical theology's progress and specifics, and then build a system that reflects this. In so doing, the Scriptures teach that there is a fundamental continuity that runs through the discontinuity of a progressive story. One way in which classical covenant theology in the Reformed tradition has expressed this balance between that which stays the same and that which changes is through the distinction between the law and the gospel, considered two ways.

The first of those ways is the distinction between the law and the gospel, *substantially* or *doctrinally*. These names are used because this distinction teaches that the law and the gospel are two opposite paths of righteousness. They are opposite in kind (substance). They are opposite teachings (doctrines). This distinction reflects the biblical instruction of many passages, such as Romans 11:6, Ephesians 2:8, and Galatians 3:2. The distinction between the law and the gospel as opposite paths of righteousness was at the heart of the Reformation itself, as theologians began to see the error of Rome's conflation of faith and works.[13] We can see this beginning with Martin Luther who said,

> The law and the Gospel are two contrary doctrines…For Moses with his law is a severe exactor, requiring of us that we should work and that we should give…Contrariwise, the Gospel gives freely and requires of us nothing else but to hold out our hands and to take that which is offered. Now, to exact and to give, to take and to offer are clean contrary and cannot stand together.[14]

The law and the gospel are two opposite paths to a righteous standing before God: a perfect record of personal obedience, or a perfect record of imputed obedience. This substantial distinction between the law and the gospel is the foundational bedrock and common denominator of Reformed covenant theology. If rejected, the heart of the "protest" against Rome is rejected.

In addition to this substantial contrast, the Reformers also spoke of the law and the gospel in a *historical* sense. They spoke of the law and the gospel as two historical time periods, the Old and New Testaments. The

[13] "The doctrine of Faith that justifies without works, ought to be retained unmingled, and uncorrupt in the Church, because…it is most catholic, and altogether unreproveable." Heinrich Bullinger, *Common places of Christian Religion* (trans. Iohn Stockwood London: Tho. East and H. Middleton, 1572), 559. (4:1).

[14] Martin Luther, *A Commentarie of M. Doctor Martin Lvther Vpon The Epistle of S. Paul to the Galathians* (London: Thomas Vautroullier, 1575), fol. 97. Language updated.

Old Testament is called the law in a broad sense due to the prominence and dominance of the law of Moses before the coming of Christ. And the New Testament is called the gospel in a broad sense due to the clarity afforded by the incarnation, Christ's earthly ministry, and the subsequent writings of the New Testament. So, it is common to speak of "the time of the law" and "the time of the gospel." These are simply two historical phases of one united redemptive history. John Calvin defended the legitimacy of both distinctions,

> And hereby also is their error [proven wrong], which do never otherwise compare the law with the gospel, but as they compare the merits of works with the free imputation of righteousness. Although indeed this comparison of contraries be not to be rejected....But the gospel did not succeed in place of the whole law, that it should bring any diverse mean of salvation, but rather to confirm and prove to be of force, what so ever the law had promised, and to join the body to the shadows.[15]

Calvin not only affirms these two distinctions but explains them. He argues that the law and the gospel are indeed substantial opposites relating to righteousness, but that they were both present in the times of the law and the gospel. In other words, condemnation in Adam and salvation by grace through faith in Christ run uninterruptedly throughout a progressive history.[16]

This is the teaching of Hebrews 11 that affirms that there were many believers in the Old Testament who believed in the same promises as New Testament believers, though the promises that they believed were revealed in more shadowy forms. The inheritance and eternal destiny of those Old Testament saints is the same as those of the New Testament. So, though there was a progressive history of revelation, there was a fundamental unchanging continuity of salvific benefits. The law and the gospel as opposite substances or doctrines run throughout the law and the gospel as successive time periods.

Covenant theology must give due attention to the continuity of salvation throughout history, as well as the progressive revelation of God in

---

[15] John Calvin, *The Institvtion of Christian Religion* (London: Reinolde Wolfe and Richard Harrison, 1561), fol. 68r. II. 9. 4. Spelling updated.

[16] In Calvin's context, this counteracted two extremes. It counteracted the Roman Catholic teaching that the gospel was a new law, a more gracious demand that we are able to fulfill. To the contrary, the law and the gospel are mutually exclusive opposites. They are of opposite kinds, i.e., substances. Likewise, these distinctions counteracted the extreme of some Anabaptists who denied salvation in the Old Testament. Each of these two cases conflates the substantial and historical distinction. Reformed theology upheld their balance.

the same. One way in which this balance has not been maintained in the past is by covenant theologies that equate the Abrahamic, Mosaic, and Davidic covenants with the new covenant, or covenant of grace, based on the continuity of salvation throughout them and their contribution to the progressive revelation of Christ and his mission. The problem is that in such a system, a progression of covenants becomes one covenant, and the system therefore controls, reduces, and flattens out the progressive nature of the biblical material from which it is derived. That which stays the same has wrongly reinterpreted that which changes.

In covenant theology, where covenants are not a part of the created order, the system of covenant theology is especially and necessarily dependent on, and determined by, the biblical data. And the covenant theologian, or student of covenant theology, must maintain the proper balance between the law and the gospel, substantially and historically. Salvation is indeed by grace alone through faith alone in Christ alone, as it has been ever since its announcement in Genesis 3:15. But the relation of each subsequent covenant to this promise must be considered individually, and any system raised from these details must account for the ongoing progress of history.

4. History and Mystery

Closely connected to the foregoing consideration of the law and the gospel as doctrinal opposites and successive time periods is the acknowledgement of the relation between history and mystery. Paul states in several places that salvation for a people from all nations through the death and resurrection of the Messiah of Israel is the full and final plan of God for the entire world, and that this was made known prior to the advent of Christ. To use Paul's phrase, this was the "mystery of Christ" (Ephesians 3:4; Colossians 4:3). And, by virtue of being a mystery, this cosmic plan was not known in fullness prior to the death, resurrection, ascension of Christ and the subsequent pouring out of the Spirit at Pentecost.

A mystery, as expressed by Paul, is not something intentionally hidden so as not to be found or understood, but rather something revealed partially, something made known incompletely. Mystery is not a means of concealing but revealing. Mystery is a mode of revelation, a way of communicating.[17] And Paul rejoiced in the privilege of explaining the mystery.

[17] On the concept of mystery, and an analysis of all of its uses in the Bible, see the masterful treatment of G.K. Beale and Benjamin L. Gladd, *Hidden But Now Revealed: A Biblical Theology of Mystery* (Downers Grove, Il: InterVarsity Press, 2014). On page 20, they define mystery as "the revelation of God's partially hidden wisdom, particularly as it concerns events occurring in the 'latter days.'"

Interpreting mystery presupposes that the interpreter is unpacking and explaining in greater fullness some antecedent revelation. This is what Paul did by making the word of God "fully known" (Colossians 1:25). It was his great pleasure and privilege to unveil and explain the master plan of God, the union of a new mankind in the new, and last, Adam awaiting the inheritance and enjoyment of a new creation for all eternity, through a new covenant.

Paul says in Colossians 1:25–27 that the "Mystery" is *Christ in the Colossians* ("Christ in you") and that this mystery was hidden for "ages and generations." The mystery is the inclusion of the Gentiles in the consummation of all things effected by the Jewish Messiah. In Ephesians 3:4–12, Paul tells the Ephesians that the "Mystery of Christ" was "not made known…in other generations as it has now been revealed." This "plan" and "eternal purpose" was "hidden for ages." Paul speaks similarly in Romans 16:25–26, where he calls the preaching of Jesus Christ the "revelation of the mystery that was kept secret for long ages" and has now been announced to the world. This was the plan from the beginning, Paul argues in Ephesians 1:9–10, the "mystery of his will."[18]

This mystery was not clearly perceived, and in most cases it was misunderstood by the very recipients of its revelation.[19] Even after Christ's resurrection, the disciples (n.b., plural) asked Jesus about the restoration of the kingdom to the Jews (Acts 1:6). Even after Pentecost, Peter needed the vision of the clean and unclean animals (Acts 10) to teach him to forget the Jewish lines of social division. The Jerusalem council shows that there were still issues among Christians regarding these matters. The books of Romans, Galatians, Ephesians, and Colossians are especially concerned with explaining what the true gospel is, and how it naturally flows from the Old Testament, *in light of questions from both Jews and Gentiles.*

The Jews struggled to understand how the blessing for the nations through the Jewish Messiah was *not* being Jewish, but rather being some-

---

[18] Paul makes a fascinating statement in 1 Corinthians 2:7–8, that this mystery was so unknown that the rulers of this age would not have crucified Christ had they known it. If Satan knew that this was the means by which his head would be crushed under the heel of the Son, he would not have possessed Judas and precipitated the capture and crucifixion of Christ. "7 But we impart a secret and hidden wisdom of God, which God decreed before the ages for our glory. 8 None of the rulers of this age understood this, for if they had, they would not have crucified the Lord of glory."

[19] Beale and Gladd begin their discussion of mystery by noting the Jewish confusion and disbelief of Jesus' mission and message. Cf. Beale and Gladd, *Hidden But Now Revealed*, 17–19.

thing distinctively not Jewish from their perspective.[20] The Gentiles struggled to understand how they were connected to the Jewish Messiah but not to ethnic Jews, especially in light of the fact that the vast majority of the Jews and their teachers vehemently rejected this specific element of the Christian message. The Gentiles were particularly susceptible to the argument that aligning with the Jewish Messiah meant submitting to the Jewish laws. The general question from both sides is "How is a resurrected Jewish Messiah who gathers a people from all the world, irrespective of Jewish descent or obedience to Jewish laws, the natural fulfillment of the Jewish Scriptures and religion?" Paul delighted in answering this question and prayed for wisdom to know how best to do it (Colossians 4:3–4).

The "Mystery of Christ" as used in the New Testament to explain the relation of the Old and New Testaments is of paramount importance to covenant theology and demands much greater attention in covenantal literature than it has received. If, according to Paul, the "Mystery of Christ" is that which was hidden and is now revealed, any covenant theology that does not address this in fullness is by definition deficient and does not follow the biblical pattern of explaining God's plan for the fullness of time. It is the legend to the map of redemptive history.

Our Lord Jesus Christ Himself declared that the Old Testament speaks of Him (Luke 24:25–27). Paul reasoned about Jesus from the Old Testament (Acts 28:23). Realizing that the Messiah's mission is made known via mystery long before His advent, one's biblical theology and systematic theology must be balanced in light of the manner in which the Bible itself explains the relation between history and mystery. Christ is present throughout all Scripture, and all saints in all ages have derived their salvation through Him alone. But Christ was present as a mystery.

Without jumping into a full consideration of the mystery of Christ at this time, the purpose of mentioning it here is that a covenant theology's treatment of the Old Testament *must* preserve the presence of Christ *as a mystery*. And one's covenantal system must not so flatten out the progress of redemptive history that it effectively, even if unintentionally, unveils the mystery before its actual unveiling.

In a very real way, a proper covenant theology that is sensitive to history and mystery should confuse, though not confound, a pre-Pentecost disciple. Christ and His covenant were made known through mystery, a partial revelation fully unveiled and explained from Pentecost onward.

---

[20] Paul, of course, argues that the most Jewish thing possible is to believe in Christ, because Abraham did, and Jewish identity is nothing other than descent from Abraham (Romans 4:1–3).

Conclusion

These four methodological considerations are necessary foundations for the relationship of biblical theology and systematic theology in covenant theology. The scope of the subject cautions us against simplistic treatments. The distinction of covenants from creation qualifies the role of consequences in covenant theology. The law and the gospel considered substantially and historically remind us that there is a fundamental continuity amidst the discontinuity. And the nature of the revelation of the plan of God in Christ as a mystery requires us to resist unveiling Christ and His covenant before history itself does.

But, in addition to arriving at a proper methodology, there is a reaction much more fundamental that these considerations ought to provoke within us. When one considers the mystery of Christ and the confusion that surrounded it during Jesus' ministry, the apostles' ministry, and ever since, we ought to return to where we began—humble silence and praise. If Paul called God's purposes unsearchable, if Paul asked for prayer that he might have wisdom concerning how to explain God's plan, and if Peter acknowledged that some of the things that Paul wrote were difficult to understand, then it seems like folly even to contemplate writing on the subject.

When one considers the grand scope of covenant theology, the precision of its distinctions, and the balance of its continuity and discontinuity, the teacher, writer, and student of covenant theology should pause and hesitate long before continuing. Each one of us should pray earnestly and humbly for the Spirit's help to have the wisdom necessary to understand the depth of the riches of God's eternal purposes.[21]

Who can sail such a vast sea and not go off course? Who can climb such a tall mountain and never slip? Who can explore such a deep forest and not forget some of its paths? Who can know the mind of God and explain the mystery of His will, the mystery of Christ? Whatever success the believer has, it is only by God's assisting grace illuminating and enabling such a one to sail straight, climb high, and learn the limits of the forest. The one who takes this knowledge and draws a map for others can make no

---

[21] In light of the humility that covenant theology ought to instill in its students, the way in which believers have turned it into a battlefield is unacceptable. When the revelation and explanation of the mystery of Christ becomes a source of aggression and division between brethren, a diligent self-examination and repentance is in order for all parties involved. The mystery of Christ and His covenant is not a weapon of war, means of mischief, or source of schism. It is the gospel for the nations. It is union with God and communion with all His children in one Lord, one Spirit, one baptism, one covenant.

boast and gain no glory because if they succeed, they are only highlighting the majestic glory of God's wise purposes.

> 33 Oh, the depth of the riches and wisdom and knowledge of God! How unsearchable are his judgments and how inscrutable his ways! 34 "For who has known the mind of the Lord, or who has been his counselor?" 35 "Or who has given a gift to him that he might be repaid?" 36 For from him and through him and to him are all things. To him be glory forever. Amen (Romans 11:33–36).

2

Typology

Introduction

Typology is one of the most important pieces of biblical interpretation in general, as well as the mystery of Christ and covenant theology in particular.[1] Gentry and Wellum note that "It is difficult to think of biblical types and patterns that are not associated with the biblical covenants. In other words, to reflect upon typological structures and their development is simultaneously to unpack the biblical covenants across redemptive-history."[2]

1. What is Typology?

Though typology often appears in theological literature, there are distinct differences in the way that authors use typology, whether today, or in the past. Definitions of typology are often similar, or the same, but the application of typological principles differs in important ways.

Greg Beale offers a helpful definition of typology.

The study of analogical correspondence among revealed truths about persons, events, institutions, and other things within the historical framework of God's special revelation, which, from a retrospective view, are of a prophetic na-

---

[1] To avoid confusion, we will use the word "typical" in relation to a type, "antitypical" in relation to an antitype, and "typological" in relation to types and antitypes considered together.

[2] Peter J. Gentry and Stephen J. Wellum, *Kingdom through Covenant: A Biblical-Theological Understanding of the Covenants* (Wheaton, IL: Crossway, 2012), 107.

27

ture and are escalated in their meaning. According to this definition, the
essential characteristics of a type are (1) analogical correspondence, (2)
historicity, (3) a pointing-forwardness, (4) escalation, (5) retrospection.[3]

Other authors have said similar things. Going back in the history of interpretation, Leonhard Goppelt said that "Each typology includes typological
correspondence and heightening."[4] Going further back, Patrick Fairbairn
said that "There are two things which… are held to enter into the constitution of a type. It is held, first, that in the character, action, or institution
which is denominated the *type*, there must be a resemblance… to it under
the Gospel; and secondly, that it must not be *any* character, action, or institution… but such only as had their ordination of God, and were designed
by Him."[5] Henry Lawrence, a Particular Baptist, argued similarly that,

> Now what ever was a type in that wherein it was a type, whether persons
> or ordinances, &c. of all such things as types, it may be affirmed. First
> that they are inferiour to their antitypes, that is, to the thing figured, or
> shewed by them. Secondly that they are not true in themselves, being a
> shadow of things to come, but in the body or truth, which they figure
> or type out. Thirdly that when the antitype, or truth is fulfilled, or per-
> formed, the type ceaseth.[6]

Other examples could be added to these, but a basic agreement is
found in that a typological relationship is seen in *divinely ordained analogy
and escalation.*[7] This means that the New Testament contains the fulfillment of previous patterns in a greater and final way.[8] Conversely, the Old

---

[3] G. K. Beale, *Handbook on the New Testament Use of the Old Testament* (Grand
Rapids, MI: Baker Academic, 2012), 14. See also James M. Hamilton Jr., "The
Typology of David's Rise to Power: Messianic Patterns in the Book of Samuel,"
SBJT 16.2 (2012): 4–25. Hamilton identifies correspondence and escalation as
the most basic elements of a typological relationship.

[4] Leonhard Goppelt, *Typos: The Typological Interpretation of the Old Testament
in the New* (Grand Rapids, MI: Eerdmans, 1982), 202.

[5] Patrick Fairbairn, *The Typology of Scripture* (Grand Rapids, MI: Zondervan,
1965), 46.

[6] Lawrence, *Of Baptism*, 238–240.

[7] Analogy may be called resemblance or correspondence, and escalation may
be called heightening. The idea is the same in each expression.

[8] The idea of historical fulfillment is important so as not to reduce typology
to mere analogy. Typology is built on analogy. Analogy says, "this is *like* (and un-
like) that." Typology takes that analogy and says, "this will also *terminate* in that."
So while the type and antitype are distinct, they have a historical fulfillment that
closely unites them. For example, the Old Covenant will terminate in the New

Testament establishes patterns that find their fulfillment in the New Testament. Beale explains how this functions:

> OT passages contain thick descriptive meanings that are unraveled layer after layer by subsequent stages of canonical revelation. This means that OT passages can be understood more deeply in light of the developing revelation of later parts of the OT and especially of the NT. The OT authors had a true understanding of what they wrote but not an exhaustive understanding. This means that a NT text's contextual understanding of an OT text will involve some essential identity of meaning between the two, but often the meaning is expanded and unfolded, growing out of the earlier meaning.[9]

This is why, as Nehemiah Coxe and other Particular Baptists said, "the best Interpreter of the Old Testament, is the holy Spirit speaking to us in the New."[10]

The mystery of Christ confirms and necessitates this principle. That which was partially and obscurely revealed before Christ is clearly unveiled in the apostle's teaching in the New Testament. All who desire to understand the unity of God's plan must therefore follow their method.[11] Beale states boldly that "The use of the OT in the NT is the key to the theological relation of the Testaments."[12] If a typological hermeneutic is "the key to the theological relation of the Testaments," if it is the method of interpretation practiced by the apostles, and if it properly handles the mystery of Christ, *as a mystery*, then we are not only allowed to use it, *we are required to use it.*

Covenant because the Old Covenant will terminate in Jesus Christ, the yea and amen of all God's promises.

[9] Beale, *Handbook*, 27.

[10] Coxe, *A Discourse of the Covenants*, 3. Here he followed in the footsteps of his father and William Kiffin and Hanserd Knollys who had asserted the same in Benjamin Coxe, William Kiffin, and Hanserd Knollys, *A Declaration Concerning The Publike Dispute Which Should have been in the Publike Meeting-House of Alderman-Bury, the 3d of this instant Moneth of December; Concerning Infants-Baptisme. Together with some of the Arguments which should have been propounded and urged by some of those that are falsly called Anabaptists, which should then have been disputed* (London: n.p., 1645), 14.

[11] Beale says, "Moisés Silva is likely correct in stating, 'If we refuse to pattern our exegesis after that of the apostles, we are in practice denying the authoritative character of their scriptural interpretation—and to do so is to strike at the very heart of the Christian faith.'" Beale, *Handbook*, 26.

[12] Beale, *Handbook*, 26.

The work of typology, then, is not limited to recognizing and assigning typological relationships only where the biblical terminology for such concepts is explicitly stated. On the contrary, "The suggestion is plausible that typological interpretation is normative and that we may seek for more OT types than the NT actually states for us."[13] Fairbairn agrees:

> For it is carefully to be noted, that the scriptural designations of rudiments and shadows, which we have shown to be the same as typical when properly understood, are applied to the entire mass of ancient ordinances in their prospective reference to Gospel realities. And yet, while New Testament Scripture speaks thus of the whole, it deals very sparingly in particular examples... That we are both warranted and bound to give them a Christian interpretation, is manifest from the general character that is ascribed to them. And the fact that so much of what was given to Moses as "a testimony (or evidence) of those things which were to be spoken after" in Christ, remains without any particular explanation in Scripture, sufficiently justifies us in expecting that there may also be much that is typical, though not expressly declared to be such.[14]

Although we may not enjoy the hermeneutical precision of the apostles, we are right in using their method.[15]

Using typology to identify types where the biblical language of types is not explicitly employed is not arbitrary. Typology is divinely ordained. Fairbairn again is helpful:

> For, as Bishop Marsh has justly remarked, "to constitute one thing the type of another, some thing more is wanted than mere resemblance. The former must not only resemble the latter, but must have been designed to resemble the latter. It must have been so designed in its original institution. It must have been *designed* as something preparatory to the latter. The type as well as the antitype must have been preordained; and they must have been preordained as constituent parts of the same general scheme of Divine Providence.[16]

---

[13] Beale, *Handbook*, 25.

[14] Fairbairn, *The Typology of Scripture*, 60–61.

[15] See Hamilton, "The Typology of David's Rise to Power," 9. Hamilton says, "The fact that we are not inspired, as the biblical authors were, simply means that we will lack the epistemological certainty enjoyed by the apostles." He later quotes Beale to say that "all interpretive conclusions 'are a matter of degrees of possibility and probability,' and this will be true of the typological interpretations put forward as we use the method today."

[16] Fairbairn, *The Typology of Scripture*, 46.

We are not free to practice arbitrary interpretation nor to be fanciful in our conclusions. Scripture must interpret Scripture to demonstrate what ultimately enjoys the status of a typological relationship.

The best ground and government of typological interpretation, in addition to the method of the apostles and the *analogia fidei*, is the Christ-centered movement of the Canon. Francis Foulkes states this well:

> All the action of God in the Old Testament history foreshadows his unique action and revelation in Christ. We may say that a type is an event, a series of circumstances, or an aspect of the life of an individual or of the nation, which finds a parallel and a deeper realization in the incarnate life of our Lord, in his provision for the needs of men, or in his judgments and future reign. A type thus presents a pattern of the dealings of God with men that is followed in the antitype, when, in the coming of Jesus Christ and the setting up of his kingdom, those dealings of God are repeated, though with a fullness and finality that they did not exhibit before.[17]

All of Scripture, and thus all redemptive history, is driving towards the arrival of the promised Seed of the woman. Typology provides a rich context not only for when Christ arrives, but also for the sake of the elect throughout the ages who were awaiting Him. Typology without Christ at its center is concerned with something other than the mystery of Christ, His covenant, and His kingdom. And it is therefore, by definition, not typology.

2. The Relation between a Type and its Antitype

These principles are helpful in developing our understanding of a typological hermeneutic, but they are incomplete. As stated, many definitions of typology share these principles, but the application of typology yields disparate conclusions. To clarify and overcome these differences, the study of typology as a system must include a closer examination of the relationship between a type and its antitype.

a. Types reveal something greater, and other, than themselves.

A cursory definition of typology as correspondence and escalation may give the impression that typology is simply a shift from one end of a scale to another. It paints types and antitypes as two ends of a spectrum. The

---

[17] Francis Foulkes, "The Acts of God," in *The Right Doctrine from the Wrong Texts?* (ed. G.K. Beale; Grand Rapids, MI: Baker, 1994), 366–367.

type is dark, grey, and as we move up the scale or cross the spectrum, the type becomes colorful and vibrant until it reaches the point of being the antitype. However, that is not the full and true nature of typology as presented by the Scriptures. The Bible contrasts types and antitypes as two different things. Its language is that of shadows and substances, pictures and realities. The escalation of typology is not merely quantitative, but qualitative. Types are pictures of antitypes. Antitypes are other and greater than the types.

For example, in John 6:32–33, 58 Jesus calls Himself the "true bread" and connects the bread in the wilderness to himself.

> 32 Truly, truly, I say to you, it was not Moses who gave you the bread from heaven, but my Father gives you the true bread from heaven. 33 For the bread of God is he who comes down from heaven and gives life to the world.... 58 This is the bread that came down from heaven, not like the bread the fathers ate, and died. Whoever feeds on this bread will live forever.

The bread was not a lesser version of Jesus. But it pointed to Him.

Paul says in 1 Corinthians 10:4, "and all drank the same spiritual drink. For they drank from the spiritual Rock that followed them, and the Rock was Christ." Old Testament believers drank from the Rock which was Christ. The rock and its water were not Jesus Christ. But they portrayed the Christ.

Referring to the Jewish Mosaic laws, Paul says in Colossians 2:17, "These are a shadow of the things to come, but the substance belongs to Christ." The Jewish Mosaic laws looked forward to Christ and His kingdom, but they were not, in themselves, Christ and His kingdom.

The writer to the Hebrews makes these arguments repeatedly. Referring to the Israelite tabernacle and temple, he says in Hebrews 8:5, "They serve a copy and shadow of the heavenly things. For when Moses was about to erect the tent, he was instructed by God, saying, 'See that you make everything according to the pattern that was shown you on the mountain.'"

And in Hebrews 9:23–24, "23 Thus it was necessary for the copies of the heavenly things to be purified with these rites, but the heavenly things themselves with better sacrifices than these. 24 For Christ has entered, not into holy places made with hands, which are copies of the true things, but into heaven itself, now to appear in the presence of God on our behalf."

And in Hebrews 10:1, "For since the law has but a shadow of the good things to come instead of the true form of these realities."

All of these examples show that types are substantially distinct from their antitypes. Antitypes are other and greater than their types. The blood of goats and bulls is not the blood of Christ, but it foreshadows and portrays Christ. The blood of goats and bulls did not forgive sins, but it made forgiveness of sins in Christ known.

The biblical language of shadows and substances is pivotal. The shadow of a thing is not the thing that cast it. Your shadow is not you. But shadows communicate information such as approximate physical features. Shadows don't show faces. So also, types are shadows that give true information about something other and greater than themselves. The biblical language of pictures and realities makes the same point. Some restaurants have menus with pictures of their food in them. You can't eat the food in the picture, but you can order food based on the information the picture provides.

b. Types function on two levels.

Typology functions on two levels. Types may be temporary and preparatory for antitypes, but it is necessary to appreciate their own meaning and purpose in their own context. This is the first level of typology, and it serves as the basis for the revelation of something greater and other than the type, i.e., the antitype. Types have a meaning in an immediate and provisional context while at the same time they point to a greater and other meaning in a final and Messianic context. For example, the writer to the Hebrews states that the blood of goats and bulls cannot take away sin. And yet that blood did take away sin. This is the clearest example of typology's function on two levels.

The blood of goats and bulls took away sins only on the level of the purification of the flesh. But it could not purify the conscience. Animal blood was a way to satisfy the demands of the Mosaic covenant in order to remain in Canaan. But it could never satisfy the demands of the covenant of works in order to escape Hell. The beauty of typology is that at the same time, this entire system was designed to teach the Israelites about substitutionary atonement and remission of sins through blood.

This is typology functioning on two levels. On an earthly level, animal sacrifices had a real function and purpose and meaning. And that meaning was substantially distinct from its antitypical meaning. The blood of goats and bulls is not the blood of Christ, and their forgiveness was not the forgiveness that Christ's blood affords. Nevertheless, they made Christ's forgiveness known.

This is a vital point of typology. And it is the case in every example of typology. All typology functions on two levels. For instance, the lifting up of the serpent in the wilderness, the provision of the wilderness manna, or the tabernacle and temple sacrifices, each had an initial and provisional meaning in their own original context. At the same time, they all point to a secondary referent and meaning in a Messianic kingdom context.

A clear understanding of two-level typology is foundational because it invests the Old Testament with the information needed for salvation in all post-fall history. Two-level typology does not divest the Old Covenant of its spiritual and religious significance; rather it invests it with *all* of its spiritual and religious significance. Once again, the connection of typology to the mystery of Christ is important. Christ in the Old Testament *as a mystery* is the mode of His revelation, and typology the medium.

The types of the Old Testament were instruments designed by God to reveal Christ and His kingdom in a sufficient, but not exhaustive, way. Scripture tells us that Abraham and other saints like him knew that there was a land greater than Canaan. Yet this did not remove the importance, reality, and meaning of Canaan and its blessings for the people of Israel. It was possible to participate in the kingdom of Israel in all of its rich typology without ever apprehending the pedagogical and revelatory function which those types served. Sadly, this was the life lived by most Israelites.[18]

It may be objected that even in the New Testament we see two levels at work. Believers experience blessings now but look forward to greater blessings later. This is not typology. New Testament ordinances do not signify something other than what they presently symbolize. Old Testament types said "I signify *this*, but I reveal *that*." "This" is one thing; "that" is another. For example, redemption from Egypt is one thing; redemption from the curse of sin and death is another. The New Testament deals in down payments of realities that believers will experience in greater fullness later.

c. Types terminate in their antitypes.

If types are not their antitypes, it naturally follows that when the antitype arrives, the type is discarded. "The Substance being come, the shadow flies away."[19] This is the argument of the author to the Hebrews. A return to animal blood is a denial that Jesus' blood has any meaning. To prefer the shadow over the substance, is to say that the substance has not arrived. To prefer animal sacrifices is to say that Jesus has not come in the flesh and is not the Christ.

If you see the shadow of a friend around a corner, you will not speak to their shadow. When they turn the corner, you will speak with the friend. So also, after you order your food at a restaurant, you don't need the menu anymore.

[18] Cf. Hebrews 4:2 "For good news came to us just as to them, but the message they heard did not benefit them, because they were not united by faith with those who listened."

[19] Hercules Collins, *The Sandy Foundation of Infant Baptism Shaken* (London: n.p., 1695), 8.

When one goes on a trip, it is common to consult and study a map before embarking on one's journey. Perhaps before visiting a city, one will become familiar with the layout and features of the city. The map is informing that person of what to expect and what they will see. However, the map is not the city. It is simply a map. And the experience of the sights of the city itself will far surpass any cartographic enjoyment. We are going to see along the way, that the Old Testament types and shadows pointed to Christ and communicated many truths about Him, but they were not Christ.

d. Types are positive and negative.

Types reveal antitypes that are greater and other than themselves. They do this in different ways—sometimes positively, other times negatively.[20] In some cases, the emphasis of a type is on its failures and deficiencies. The yearly sacrifices of animals were a "reminder" of the Israelites' lasting guilt (Heb 10:3) and yet they gave hope for a lasting remission of sins. The deficiencies of types were designed to glorify and emphasize the perfections of the antitype. David's life, with its triumphs and failures, paints a positive picture at times and a very negative picture at other times.

As a whole, the typical character of the Old Testament will always pale in comparison to its antitypical fulfillment because that fulfillment is found in Jesus Christ, His kingdom, and His covenant. This is summed up and illustrated in Jeremiah's categorical designation of the typical Old Covenant as negative in that the New Covenant will *not be like* the Old Covenant (Jeremiah 31:31–32). And the writer to the Hebrews 10:1 says that same in a sweeping fashion. "The law has but a shadow of the good things to come instead of the true form of these realities."

In summary, types reveal that which is greater and other than themselves. They have a purpose and meaning in their own contexts, and when their fulfillment arrives, they are removed. Interpreting the relationship between the Old and New Testaments in this way is the apostolic hermeneutic, it is a Christ-centered hermeneutic, and it is a necessary hermeneutic.

---

[20] Cf. Dennis Johnson, *Him We Proclaim: Preaching Christ From All The Scriptures* (Phillipsburg, NJ: P&R, 2007), 202, "There is continuity between type and antitype because Old Testament redemptive events, persons, and institutions truly reveal some aspect of God's new-creation reversal of sin and its woeful consequences, a process…that reaches its climax only in Christ and his work. There is also discontinuity because every Old Testament type is marred by human sin or impaired by creaturely limitation."

3. The Application of Typological Principles

Applying the principles of typology is worked out in the rest of this book. But the ways in which differences in the application of typology lead to differences in theological systems can be seen in the diversity of covenant theology in the seventeenth century.

The unity of Reformed covenant theology was founded on the law-gospel distinction expressed in the Covenants of Works and Grace. Condemnation in Adam and salvation in Christ were a source of unity. Salvation through the gospel was available from the fall onward. John Owen acknowledged this unity by saying, "All who contend about these things, the *Socinians* only excepted, do grant that the Covenant of Grace considered *absolutely*, that is, the Promise of Grace in and by Jesus Christ, was the only way and means of Salvation unto the Church, from the first entrance of sin."[21]

Where Owen and others diverged from each other was on the relationship of the Old Covenant to salvation. Reformed theologians commonly assigned a typical character to the Mosaic covenant, recognizing that its symbols and shadows pointed to Christ. But the question arose as to whether their typical character made them distinct from the blessings to which they pointed. If there were a difference in substance between the type and antitype, one would have to acknowledge a difference in substance between the Old and New Covenants. If the difference were merely one of degree or quantity rather than quality, one could retain the teaching that the old and new covenants were simply two phases of the same covenant.

Anthony Burgess argued that the difference was one of degree only, using a variety of illustrations to describe the typical character of the Mosaic Covenant. Yet, for Burgess, "All of these images seek to communicate the nature of progressive development from immature to mature or from inferior to superior, from less to more; these images do not describe a difference in substance."[22]

Owen raised this issue and disagreed. "Here then ariseth a difference of no small importance, namely, whether these are indeed *two distinct Cov-*

---

[21] John Owen, *A Continuation of the Exposition of the Epistle of Paul the Apostle to the Hebrews* (London: Nathaniel Ponder, 1680), 227.

[22] Stephen J. Casselli, *Divine Rule Maintained: Anthony Burgess, Covenant Theology, and the Place of the Law in Reformed Scholasticism* (Grand Rapids, MI: Reformation Heritage Books, 2016), 108. Cf. Burgess, *Vindiciae Legis: Or, A Vindication of the Morall Law and the Covenants, From the Errours of Papists, Arminians, Socinians, and more especially, Antinomians. In XXIX. Lectures, preached at Laurence-Jury, London* (London: James Young, 1647), 252–256.

enants, as to the essence and substance of them, or only different ways of the dispensation and administration of the same Covenant."[23] Owen acknowledged that "The judgment of most *Reformed Divines* is…they are not to be said to be under *another Covenant*, but only a *different administration* of it."[24] Yet Owen, and others such as John Cameron and the Particular Baptists, disagreed on the basis of typology.

Owen appealed to "The relation of Type and Antitype" to describe the relationship between the Old and New Covenants. Owen affirmed that types were not antitypes in lesser forms. They had a "different nature." Specifically, "All the *Levitical* Services and Ordinances were in themselves carnal, and had carnal ends assigned unto them, and had only an obscure representation of things spiritual and eternal."[25] Owen called Israel a "Typical Church State, with a great number of Religious Laws and Ordinances, in themselves *carnal* and *weak*, but mystically significant of spiritual and heavenly things."[26] Thus, "The Old Covenant was *typical, shadowy* and *removeable*, Heb. 10.1. The New Covenant is *substantial* and *permanent*, as containing *the Body which is Christ*."[27]

Through typology, the Old Covenant portrayed salvation in Jesus Christ, but it did not offer salvation in and of itself. Owen distinguished between being saved "under" the Old Covenant, and "by vertue" of the Old Covenant. He affirmed the former and denied the latter. "If *Reconciliation and Salvation by Christ* were to be obtained not only *under the Old Covenant*, but *by vertue thereof*, then it must be the same for substance with the New. But this is not so; for no Reconciliation with God, nor Salvation could be obtained by vertue of the Old Covenant, or the Administration of it."[28] Owen was simply acknowledging the argument of Hebrews that animal blood could not forgive sins. The Old Covenant could not purify the conscience or perfect its members.

Owen's two-tiered typology was shared by the Particular Baptists who had been using it for decades.[29] For example, in 1642 Andrew Ritor argued that circumcision was "both a Covenant and yet also but a signe of another

[23] Owen, *A Continuation of the Exposition*, 224, 226. For this view, Owen referred the reader to Calvin, Vermigli, and Bucanus.

[24] Owen, *A Continuation of the Exposition*, 225.

[25] Owen, *A Continuation of the Exposition*, 375.

[26] Owen, *Exercitations Concerning the Name, Original, Nature, Use, and Continuance of a Day of Sacred Rest* (London: R.W., 1671), 230.

[27] Owen, *A Continuation of the Exposition*, 241.

[28] Owen, *A Continuation of the Exposition*, 228.

[29] On the typology and covenant theology of the Particular Baptists, see Samuel D. Renihan, *From Shadow to Substance: The Federal Theology of the English Particular Baptists (1642–1704)* (Oxford: Regent's Park College, 2018).

Covenant (to wit) of that everlasting Covenant made with *Abraham*, and all his spirituall seed… which is only to be enjoyed by faith."[30] A decade later, Thomas Patient said, "For [Israel's] sacrifices for sin, typed out Christ, but they were not Christ, and their typical remissions…can be understood to be no other but typical."[31] Abraham Cheare and Robert Steed asserted that the Old Covenant was "a covenant ministering or serving to [a] doctrine above or beyond it self."[32] Nehemiah Coxe said that "Circumcision did not only oblige to the keeping of the Law… but did also (as subservient to the Promise) point at the *Messiah*… that thro' Faith in his Name such a Righteousness [that circumcision required] might be obtained."[33]

For Owen and the Particular Baptists, salvation was available in the Old Testament through the promises of the Covenant of Grace which were made known through typology.[34] Nevertheless, the types were not the antitypes. "The substance of what God intended in all his worship was not contained nor comprised in the services of those priests. There were some lines and shadows, to represent the body, but the body itself was not there. There was something above them and beyond them, which they reached not unto."[35] Thus the Old Covenant and the New, though closely connected through typology, were not the same thing. They were not one in substance. And their differences could not be reduced to external administrational changes.[36]

Both the Baptists and the paedobaptists affirmed that the Old Testament is full of typology and described the Old Covenant as such. But for

---

[30] Andrew Ritor, *The Second Part of the Vanity & Childishnes of Infants Baptisme* (London: n.p., 1642), 24.

[31] Thomas Patient, *The Doctrine of Baptism, And the Distinction of the Covenants* (London: Henry Hills, 1654), 125.

[32] Abraham Cheare and Robert Steed, *A Plain Discovery Of The Unrighteous Judge and False Accuser* (London: Henry Mortlock, 1658), 13.

[33] Coxe, *A Discourse of the Covenants*, 171.

[34] *"The New Covenant as recollecting into one all the Promises of Grace given from the foundation of the World, accomplished in the actual exhibition of Christ, and confirmed in his death, and by the Sacrifice of his blood, thereby becoming the sole Rule of new spiritual Ordinances of Worship suited thereunto, was the great Object of the Faith of the Saints of the Old Testament, and is the great foundation of all our present mercies."* Owen, *A Continuation of the Exposition*, 252.

[35] Owen, *A Continuation of the Exposition*, 204.

[36] The ordinances of the old covenant belonged to *"another Covenant"* that was "superadded unto the Promises." It functioned as "the immediate Rule of the Obedience and Worship of the Church. And according unto their observance of this *superadded Covenant*, they were esteemed to have kept or broken Covenant with God. This was the *Old Covenant in Sinai.*" Owen, *A Continuation of the Exposition*, 252.

some, typology was not about something other and greater; it was about two phases of the same thing. So, circumcision and baptism are two outward forms of the same thing. Passover and the Lord's Supper are two outward forms of the same thing. Israel and the church are two outward forms of the same thing. They are, as David Dickson said, only as different as the way a man dresses in his youth and in his maturity.

The Particular Baptists' distinctive was that they applied these principles not just to Moses, like Owen and Cameron, but also to Abraham. And they argued, therefore, that in the Abrahamic Covenant, the Covenant of Grace is revealed and made known by the earthly promises, and more, but remains distinct from it. The writer to the Hebrews tells us Abraham knew there was a country greater than Canaan, a city whose builder and founder is God. Because the Abrahamic Covenant was not, in itself, the Covenant of Grace, it could not be used as the pattern for membership in the New Covenant, nor could circumcision be the pattern for baptism. The type revealed, but was distinct from, the antitype.

Conclusion

Small differences in the application of typology often lead to greater distances than one might suspect. The tips of the branches on one side of a tree may be quite far apart from the tips of the branches on the other side of the same tree. And this is illustrated in the heritage of Reformed covenant theology. Proper principles, as well as proper application of the same, are of extreme importance.

3

Covenant and Kingdom

Introduction

Establishing fundamental definitions of important terms and concepts is a necessary part of developing a methodological toolkit. Two simple questions lie ahead: what is a covenant, and what does a covenant do?

1. What is a Covenant?

a. The definition of a covenant

A covenant בְּרִית in Hebrew, διαθήκη in Greek is a guaranteed commitment.[1] Two parties make commitments to one another. Their commitments are often summed up in "I will, you will" statements.[2] Different covenants have different kinds of commitments, and the varying kinds of commitments in these covenants result in different kinds of covenants.

---

[1] A covenant is a "divinely sanctioned commitment." Meredith G. Kline, *Kingdom Prologue: Genesis Foundations for a Covenantal Worldview* (Overland Park, KS: Two Ages Press, 2000), 2. "Thus a *běrît* is a relationship involving an oath-bound commitment." Gentry and Wellum, *Kingdom through Covenant*, 132. For a lexical analysis of every instance of *běrît* in the Old Testament, see Gentry and Wellum, *Kingdom through Covenant*, 717–778.

[2] Classic treatments of covenant theology often reduced covenants to *stipulation*, what God proposes/imposes, and *restipulation*, man's response to God. English has its own words for this pattern— "swear" and "answer". To answer is to swear back. So then, a covenant's foundation is swearing and answering.

A commitment, in and of itself, however, is not a covenant. Sanctions or threats must be put into place to guarantee the fulfillments of the parties' commitments. This adds a degree of legality and formality that a generic commitment would not carry. We will discuss sanctions below.

Because God is one of the contracting parties in the covenants under consideration, and because covenants are not a natural feature of the Creator-creature relationship, all covenants are the result of God's own free initiative to carry out His purposes and to do good to mankind.[3] Covenants are not "take it or leave it" options. God imposes His covenants on man and determines the commitments.

Yet this language of non-negotiability and imposition should not prevent us from seeing covenants as a gracious and kind condescension. Every covenant provides blessings and benefits for man that would otherwise be unavailable by nature. Covenants advance man's communion with and enjoyment of God beyond nature. Nehemiah Coxe expressed these nuances when he defined a covenant between God and men as "A declaration of [God's] sovereign pleasure concerning the benefits he will bestow on [man], the communion they will have with him, and the way and means by which this will be enjoyed by them."[4]

b. Covenant sanctions

Covenant sanctions are threats that enforce and ensure the fulfillment of the covenantal commitments. They ensure that all commitments will

---

[3] Coxe comments, "The immediate and direct end therefore, of God's entering into covenant with man at any time (so far as concerns man himself) is *the advancing and bettering of his state*; God did never make a covenant with man, wherein his goodness to him was not abundantly manifest; yea such is his infinite bounty, that he has proposed no lower end to his covenant-transactions with men, than to bring them into a blessed state in the eternal fruition of himself." Coxe, *A Discourse of the Covenants*, 7. Spelling updated. Cf. Burgess, *Vindiciae Legis*, 127–128. Burgess considers "[W]hy God will deale with man in a covenant way, rather than in a mere absolute supreme way," and answers, "*That God might hereby sweeten and indeare himself to us*. For, whereas he might require all obedience from us, and annihilate us at last, or at least not vouchsafe heaven and everlasting happinesse; to shew how good and loving he is, he will reward that most bountifully, which is otherwise due to him: for God did not make man, because he needed him, but that there might be objects to whom he would communicate his love." Elsewhere, Burgess notes that due to the "inequality of the Covenanters," God's covenanting with Adam was "[A] mercifull condescension on Gods part, to promise such things to us." Emphasis original.

[4] Coxe, *A Discourse of the Covenants*, 6. Spelling updated.

be fulfilled, whether promises to grant something or promises to perform something. Those who make promises must fulfill their promises. Those who pledge obedience must be obedient.

In Ancient Near Eastern covenants, sanctions were often imposed, symbolically, by cutting animals in pieces and walking through their divided parts. The corpses presented a vivid image of the consequences of infidelity. The idea of such ceremonies was to formalize the commitments into a covenant by protecting the commitments with threats. There are many biblical passages that describe a similar process of imposing sanctions, as well as the reality of their threats.

For example, Jeremiah 34:18–20,

> 18 And the men who transgressed my covenant and did not keep the terms of the covenant that they made before me, I will make them like the calf that they cut in two and passed between its parts— 19 the officials of Judah, the officials of Jerusalem, the eunuchs, the priests, and all the people of the land who passed between the parts of the calf. 20 And I will give them into the hand of their enemies and into the hand of those who seek their lives. Their dead bodies shall be food for the birds of the air and the beasts of the earth.

Some of the inhabitants of the land made a covenant to free their Jewish slaves. And the way they made the covenant was to pass between the parts of animals cut in two. That was an oath with a curse. And God is saying that He's going to pour out the curse that they themselves swore to bear if they did not fulfill their commitment. God speaks in similar terms in Psalm 50:5. "Gather to me my faithful ones, who made a covenant with me by sacrifice!"

An important example of sanctions solemnizing commitments into a covenant is found in 1 Samuel 20:12–16.

> 12 And Jonathan said to David, 'The LORD, the God of Israel, be witness! When I have sounded out my father, about this time tomorrow, or the third day, behold, if he is well disposed toward David, shall I not then send and disclose it to you? 13 But should it please my father to do you harm, the LORD do so to Jonathan and more also if I do not disclose it to you and send you away, that you may go in safety. May the LORD be with you, as he has been with my father. 14 If I am still alive, show me the steadfast love of the LORD, that I may not die; 15 and do not cut off your steadfast love from my house forever, when the LORD cuts off every one of the enemies of David from the face of the earth.' 16 And Jonathan made a covenant with the house of David, saying, 'May the LORD take vengeance on David's enemies.'

1 Samuel 20:16 is a summary statement of the covenant. Jonathan's commitment is to promote and protect David as the successor to the throne. To solemnize his commitment, Jonathan called the Lord to curse him if he does not fulfill his word, "the LORD do so to Jonathan and more also if…." No blood ritual was performed, but a self-directed threat was just as present. And verse 16 calls the oath-bound commitment a covenant.

The same process took place in Genesis 15:9–10, 17 where God commanded Abraham to cut an assortment of animals in half and to place their halves on opposite sides of each other. As God passed through those halves in theophany, He took the death-oath upon Himself.[5]

The sum of these passages is that though covenants were inaugurated in various ways, sanctions are a standard feature among them. One more passage that explains the necessity of sanctions for making covenants is Hebrews 9:16–17 which reads as follows in the ESV,

> 16 For where a will is involved, the death of the one who made it must be established. 17 For a will takes effect only at death, since it is not in force as long as the one who made it is alive.[6]

This is not an adequate translation. A more accurate translation would be,

> 16 For where there is a covenant, the death of the covenanter must be pledged. 17 For a covenant is ratified by corpses, since it would have no power while the covenanter lives.[7]

Key words like "διαθήκη," "φέρεσθαι," and "νεκροῖς" greatly affect the interpretation. When the Old Testament speaks of a covenant (διαθήκη),

---

[5] Kline comments, "To pass through the way between the rows of severed carcasses is to walk through the valley of the shadow of death…Such was the malediction that the Lord conditionally invoked upon himself." Kline, *Kingdom Prologue*, 296.

[6] The Greek text reads as follows, "Ὅπου γὰρ διαθήκη, θάνατον ἀνάγκη φέρεσθαι τοῦ διαθεμένου· διαθήκη γὰρ ἐπὶ νεκροῖς βεβαία, ἐπεὶ μήποτε ἰσχύει ὅτε ζῇ ὁ διαθέμενος."

[7] For a detailed justification of this translation and interpretation, see John J. Hughes, "Hebrews IX 15ff. And Galatians III 15ff. A Study in Covenant Practice and Procedure," in *Novum Testamentm*, Vol. XXI, no. 1 January (1979): 27–96. Hughes translates this passage as "Where there is a covenant, it is necessary to represent (introduce) the death of the ratifier. For a covenant is made legally secure on the basis of (over) the dead (animals). Since it is never valid while the ratifier lives." Hughes, "Hebrews IX," 46. Cf. also J.V. Fesko, *Last Things First* (Scotland, UK: Christian Focus Publications, 2007), 160–161.

and when covenants are made, they are covenants struck between living parties. They are not wills to be activated at the time of death. Thus, when the writer to the Hebrews parallels the New Covenant with a covenant from Israel's history, it would be quite foreign to biblical language and the history of biblical covenants for the concept of a last will and testament to appear suddenly. Rather, it is natural in the context of the Bible's use of covenant as a whole, the context of Jeremiah 31, the context of Hebrews as a whole, and the context of Hebrews 9 to take this for a covenant, not a testament.

The next exegetical question deals with what the covenanter must do. The text says that "the death of the covenanter must be ____." The Greek verb is φέρεσθαι and the ESV renders it as "to be established," treating φέρεσθαι as bringing something forward as evidence.[8] But φέρεσθαι also needs to be read in light of the larger context of Hebrews and connected with a similar word, προσφέρω, used many times in Hebrews to refer to priestly offerings.[9]

In the context of making a covenant, the covenanter is not sacrificed (προσφέρω), but we are told that the death of the covenanter must be "brought forward as evidence" or "pledged" (φέρεσθαι). The idea is that to make a covenant, one must swear an oath that guarantees participation and fulfillment of the covenantal commitments. In this sense, the idea of "bringing forward as evidence" remains true, but it is not the actual death of the covenanter, but the potential death of the covenanter that is brought forward as evidence in a covenantal transaction. This aligns with διαθήκη being used in the Old Testament to describe covenants between living parties, not dead ones. The translation therefore should be, "For where there is a covenant, the death of the covenanter must be pledged."

The next question concerns the prepositional phrase "ἐπὶ νεκροῖς," translated "at death" in the ESV. The prepositional phrase "ἐπὶ νεκροῖς" should not be translated "at death." The Greek word νεκρός does not refer to the event of dying; it refers to the state of death.[10] Throughout Hebrews, νεκρός refers to dead bodies and the state of being dead physically or spiritually.[11] In the preceding verse, the word for the event of dying, "θάνατος," was used to say that the event of death must be pledged by the one cov-

---

[8] In BDAG, 1052, definition 8: "To demonstrate the reality of something, establish." This verse is the only example given of the definition.

[9] Cf. Hebrews 5:1, 3, 7; 8:3, 4; 9:7, 9, 14, 25, 28; 10:1–2, 8, 11, 12; 11:4, 17; 12:7.

[10] Hughes comments that while it may be possible that ἐπὶ νεκροῖς could mean "at death" idiomatically, he finds "no evidence to support this translation." Hughes, "Hebrews IX," 44.

[11] Cf. Hebrews 6:1–2; 9:14; 11:19, 35; 13:20.

enanting. However, here we are dealing with a different word which does not refer to the event of dying but the state of being dead.

Furthermore, νεκροῖς is a plural noun (dead things, not a dead thing). If that is taken into account, the ESV translation ought to read "at deaths," which makes no sense relative to a last will and testament. O. Palmer Robertson, pointing out that the word "covenant" is singular but the word "bodies" is plural, commented, "Only one body is required for the activation of a last will and testament. But a multiple of dead bodies is immediately associated with the inauguration of a covenantal relationship."[12] Robertson is exactly right, and in light of these arguments we should read this phrase as "by corpses" or "over corpses."

The Greek of Psalm 50:5 reinforces this translation.

συναγάγετε αὐτῷ τοὺς ὁσίους αὐτοῦ τοὺς διατιθεμένους τὴν διαθήκην αὐτοῦ ἐπὶ θυσίαις.

Gather to me my faithful ones, who made a *covenant* with me *by sacrifice*!

This verse states that covenants (n.b., διαθήκη) are made by sacrifice (ἐπὶ θυσίαις). The writer to the Hebrews affirms the same. "For a covenant (διαθήκη) is ratified by corpses (ἐπὶ νεκροῖς)."

With these considerations in mind, we can complete the translation of Hebrews 9:16–17 by comparing βεβαία, "formally established, ratified, or valid" with ἰσχύει, "to be in force," or "to be strong." Why are covenants ratified (βεβαία) by corpses and the ritual presentation of the covenanter's death? And what does this have to do with the covenant being in force (ἰσχύει) while the covenanter lives? The writer states that a covenant must be ratified by corpses *so that* the covenant will *not* be in force while the covenanter lives. Though this is somewhat difficult for English speakers to follow, the reverse adds clarity: "since it would have no power if the covenanter does not die."

The threat of the covenanter's death ensures that the benefits of the covenant cannot be enjoyed while simultaneously violating its terms. Were that the case, the covenant would have no force, no power, and its legal ratification would be meaningless. Robertson translated this last section as "for [a covenant] is not strong [valid] while the covenant-maker lives."[13]

The death of the covenanter must be pledged so that the covenant's commitments will be fulfilled. If there is no threat, and if the covenanter can violate the covenant and live, the covenant has no strength, no power,

---

[12] O. Palmer Robertson, *The Christ of the Covenants* (Phillipsburg, NJ: P&R, 1980), 142.

[13] Robertson, *The Christ of the Covenants*, 143.

no validity. In my local supermarket, no one parks in the disabled parking stalls without a disabled parking placard, yet everyone parks in the "Clean-air Vehicle" stalls regardless of the kind of vehicle they drive. The difference is that there are signs with fines in the disabled parking stalls, but not the clean-air stalls. No sanctions, no covenant.

As the biblical data shows, the precise form of the covenant-making ceremony may vary, but they all include sanctions that guarantee the fulfillment of the covenantal commitments. If imprecatory oaths are not sworn, the covenant has no force because there are no sanctions to enforce it. In the same way that a parent who warns their child but will not discipline their child has no power in their parenting, so also a covenant that threatens death but will not destroy the covenanter has no power. In summary, a commitment is solemnized and formalized as a covenant when sanctions are put in place, guaranteeing the participation of the parties and the fulfillment of their commitments.

c. The matter and form of a covenant

Covenants are built out of commitments and oaths that protect those commitments. Distinguishing these two pieces can be expressed helpfully by the categories of matter and form. The commitments are the material basis of the covenant. The sanctions grant it formal completion.

The *matter* of a covenant is the commitments of the two parties. The *form* of a covenant is reached when both parties officially ratify the terms, i.e. *matter*, involved. By way of illustration, a marriage license is a legal document and can be said to be the *matter* of the marriage covenant before the civil magistrate, but until the bride and groom have sworn their marital oaths and signed the marriage license, the marriage has not yet been *formally* concluded or ratified. We could also consider a confession of faith on its own or as it is used by an association or denomination as the document by which the participants will operate. The confession is the *matter* of associational unity, but the *form* of an association is not realized until the parties involved agree to this document as the basis, i.e. *matter*, of their unity.

This distinction helps to highlight differences between varying covenants in Scripture. To begin with an illustration, if you make a ring out of metal, you are shaping a specific kind of *matter* into a specific *form*. If you form a ring from silver, you will have a silver ring. But if you form a ring from gold, your work will yield a gold ring. In each case you have made a ring, but the rings are made from different materials, silver and gold. Analogously, covenants established on different foundations, i.e. *matter*, will produce different *forms*.

Covenantal commitments are based on precepts and promises. Based on the balance of precepts and promises in a given covenant, and based on how the sanctions relate to those precepts and promises, we begin to see different kinds of covenants. A covenant that suspends the enjoyment of its blessings on obedience to precepts is of a different character than a covenant that freely distributes its blessings. A covenant based materially on a commitment of obedience to a command is a covenant of works. A covenant based materially on a commitment of promise is a covenant of grace.

In a covenant of works, you must earn the reward. You get out what you put in. You reap what you sow. Obey and be blessed; disobey and be cursed. The idea of merit or earning, though, is relative in the sense that God dictates the terms of what the obedience rendered will be as well as what the blessing rewarded will be. Apart from God making rewards available through covenantal obedience, the creature could never claim recompense from God because the creature can never place the Creator in its debt. And therefore, if God says "Do this and receive that" then such is the agreement.[14] God is free to dictate the conditions and the rewards as He sees fit according to His own wisdom and justice. And once God has established a work-reward relationship, the blessing can be claimed according to justice. In a covenant of works, your obedience rightly earns the blessing.

Sanctions formalize a covenant of works. A law, or command, considered on its own as the matter of the covenant, is simply a precept that dictates what must be done. But when a reward has been attached to obeying a law, and once sanctions are put in place, the covenant reaches its formal realization because there is a mechanism actively enforcing and legally obligating the covenant partner's participation.

In contradistinction to a covenant based on law is a covenant based on promise, i.e., a covenant of grace. In a covenant of grace, enjoyment of the blessings depends purely on what blessings God chooses to promise. Consequently, the category covenant of *grace* has been used by theologians because the blessings of the covenant are granted *freely*, apart from the

---

[14] John Norton used covenantal merit to explain the extent and intent of the atonement. He said, "The Obedience of Christ is meritorious, not absolutely in it self, but by virtue of the Covenant of God, accepting his obedience as meritorious: *i.e.* as that, whereunto remission and salvation should be due according to Order of justice. The Obedience of Christ was of sufficient value in it self, because he was God, to redeem all mankind: but it could not be a price, *i.e.* a ransom, further then as God was pleased to accept." John Norton, *The Orthodox Evangelist* (London: John Macock, 1654), 223.

works of the covenant partner.[15] This contradistinction is asserted plainly in Romans 11:6.

> But if it is by grace, it is no longer on the basis of works; otherwise grace would no longer be grace.

Paul says the same in Romans 4:4–5.

> 4 Now to the one who works, his wages are not counted as a gift but as his due. 5 And to the one who does not work but believes in him who justifies the ungodly, his faith is counted as righteousness.

And he says in Galatians 3:18, "If the inheritance comes by the law, it no longer comes by promise."

In a covenant of grace, the blessings are external to the covenant partner and are imputed to him apart from merit or works. One does not need to *earn* the blessings of the covenant, but rather one simply *receives* the blessings of the covenant.

As a law alone is not a covenant, so also a promise on its own is not a covenant. A promise is simply a declaration to give something to someone. But what makes a promise a covenant in the formal sense is when the party promising to bestow blessings is also the party who claims responsibility and liability for any failure. Sanctions guarantee that the one promising will indeed make good on the promise. And that solemnizes a promise as a covenant.

Again, we must be cautious to say that these two legal foundations, law and promise, do not exclude the presence of laws or promises in the one or the other in an absolute sense. Their mutual exclusivity has reference only to the *basis* for enjoyment of blessings. So, in a covenant of works, when *obedience* has been rendered, blessings *promised* are enjoyed. Conversely, in a covenant of grace, after *promises* have been *received*, *laws* are introduced. In the first case, the promise must be earned while in the second case the law delivered does not subvert the promise already given. This difference has been summarized often as Edward Fisher did in his *Marrow of Modern Divinity* by contrasting "Do this and live" with "Live and do this."[16]

---

[15] Robert Purnell, a Particular Baptist, expressed this precise contrast between the Covenant of Grace and the Covenant of Works when he said "for grace is not grace, if it be not every way free, Rom. 11.6. and if by grace, then it is no more of works, otherwise grace is no more grace." Robert Purnell, *A Little Cabinet Richly Stored* (London: R. W., 1657), 30–31.

[16] Edward Fisher, The Marrow of Modern Divinity (London: R. Leybourn, 1646), 154.

Accordingly, as a law or promise is imposed by God upon man each one requires a different response on man's part. Nehemiah Coxe expresses this well:

> Yet this restipulation[17] (and consequently, the way and manner of obtaining covenant blessings, as well as the right by which we claim them) necessarily varies according to the different nature and terms of those covenants that God at any time makes with men. If the covenant be of works, the restipulation must be by doing the things required in it, even by fulfilling its condition in a perfect obedience to its law. Suitably, the reward is of debt according the terms of such a covenant. (Do not understand it of debt absolutely but of debt by compact.)[18] But if it be a covenant of free and sovereign grace, the restipulation required is a humble receiving or hearty believing of those gratuitous promises on which the covenant is established. Accordingly, the reward or covenant blessing is immediately and eminently of grace.[19]

The distinction between these two kinds of covenants is laid out in the following table.

Matter:	Restipulation:	Sanction:	Form:
Law →	Obedience →	Covenant partner →	Covenant of Works
Promise →	Reception →	Covenant imposer →	Covenant of Grace

While we can distinguish between the way in which covenant parties respond to laws and promises and the covenants that arise from such a distinction, not all covenants between God and man follow this rigid binary. In the context of obtaining perfect righteousness, the Scriptures are clear that grace and works, law and promise, are absolute opposites. However, not all covenants between God and man have perfect righteousness in view. The covenants God made with Israel offer blessings on the basis of both promise and obedience. That Abraham's descendants would multiply

---

[17] Restipulation refers to man's response to God's proposition of terms in the covenant. God stipulates. Man restipulates.

[18] Coxe is referring to what we have stated earlier, that the reward is due according to the terms of the covenant, not by a supposed value in man's works.

[19] Coxe, *A Discourse of the Covenants*, 9. Spelling updated.

and inherit Canaan was a free promise protected by sanctions (Genesis 15). But whether individuals, families, and tribes would enjoy that inheritance depended on their obedience, a commitment that was likewise sanctioned (Genesis 17:14; Exodus 24:7–8; Deuteronomy 27–28).

The matter (commitments) and form (sanctions) of a covenant are two separate and necessary things. Man's response to God's covenants varies according to the matter of the covenant. If the covenant is based on *law*, the covenant partner will pledge *obedience* to the law. If the covenant is based on *promise*, the covenant partner will receive the *promise*. But until sanctions guarantee the participation of both sides according to the terms of the covenant, and until man has given the appropriate response, the covenant is not formally completed.

d. Federal headship

An essential feature of federal theology is that of federal headship. God transacts covenants with a *federal head*.[20] Nehemiah Coxe stated this.

> This is also worthy to be noted by us: that when God has made covenants, in which either mankind in general or some select number of men in particular have been involved, it has pleased him first to transact with some public person, head, or representative for all others that should be involved in them.[21]

This is the case in Adam, Noah, Abraham, David, and Christ. It is only in the Mosaic covenant where we find a federal head lacking, but this is resolved by the Davidic covenant which provides a federal head for the Mosaic covenant.[22] We will discuss this in a later chapter.

Each covenant determines the extent of its federal headship. God covenants with the federal head on behalf of a specific group of people.

[20] Based on the Latin word, fœdus, "federal" simply means covenantal. A "federal" government should be a government by representation.

[21] Coxe, *A Discourse of the Covenants*, 11–12. Spelling updated. Cf. also Peter Golding, *Covenant Theology* (Scotland, UK: Mentor, 2008), 190. "The solidarity of one person representing a group, involving the whole group in the consequences of his action and receiving promises that apply to the whole group as well as to himself, 'is a familiar facet of covenantal thought,' usually instanced in the case of family and national groups."

[22] The Mosaic covenant also illustrates the difference between a federal head and a mediator. A mediator comes between two parties. A federal head is one of the parties in and of himself. Moses was a mediator, but not a federal head. The beauty and majesty of Christ is that He is not only our Mediator, but also our federal head. Indeed, He is both parties, God and man.

Federal headship is therefore *immediate*. All those whom the federal head represents are connected to the federal head directly, no matter how far removed by time or genealogical descent. Their right to the covenant and its blessings or curses flows exclusively and directly through and from the federal head.

Covenantal membership, therefore, is determined and defined exclusively by federal headship. To determine one's membership in a given covenant, the question that one must ask is "Do I belong to the federal head? Did the federal head covenant on my behalf?" Those of Adam belong to his covenant. Those of Noah belong to his covenant. Those of Abraham belong to his covenant. Those of David belong to his covenant. Those of Christ belong to his covenant.

The Scriptures assert the immediate nature of federal headship in several ways. First, the children of the apostate generation in the Sinai wilderness were not divested of their covenant interest by their parents' disobedience and apostasy. As *Abraham's offspring* they had a right to Canaan, independent of their parents. Coxe again makes this point. He says,

> The right of the remotest generation was as much derived from Abraham and the covenant made with him, as was that of his immediate seed, and did not at all depend on the faithfulness of their immediate parents. Thus, the immediate seed of those Israelites that fell in the wilderness under the displeasure of God were made to inherit the land of Canaan by virtue of this covenant with Abraham. They never could have enjoyed it by virtue of their immediate parent's steadfastness in the covenant.[23]

Second, Scripture's language in Hebrews 7:9–10 tells us that Levi tithed to Melchizedek while in Abraham's loins. Levi, a descendent of Abraham removed by several generations, tithed to Melchizedek. How is this possible? It is possible because Abraham's actions, as federal head of his descendants, counted for Levi. Levi was considered Abraham's offspring *directly* or *immediately*.

Third, the Jews in the time of our Lord's earthly ministry claimed Abrahamic paternity, not only as their self-conscious identity, but also as their right to the blessings of the coming kingdom. This claim was rejected by Christ in Matthew 3:9, not because they were not the offspring of Abraham, but because that was not a valid claim to membership in the

---

[23] Coxe, *A Discourse of the Covenants*, 61. To avoid confusion, we must note that Coxe is using the term "immediate" in contrast to "remote," whereas we are using the term "immediate" in contrast to "mediate." His point, however, is our point, namely that the number of generations separating Abraham and his offspring had no prohibitive effect on their connection to him as their federal head.

kingdom of God. They were indeed Abraham's offspring and had an immediate federal relation to Abraham, thus granting them the right to the kingdom of Israel, but they failed to see that a new federal head and a new covenant had been provided in Christ Jesus through which the right to the kingdom of God was obtained. The children of Abraham's body needed to be the children of his faith in order to inherit this kingdom.

Fourth, Paul argues in Romans 5 that just as *one* man's sin brought the curse on *all* those whom he represented, so also *another* man's obedience brought blessing upon *all* those whom he represented. This is not true only in the covenant of works and the covenant of grace. It is the nature of federal headship in any covenant.[24]

Federal headship is vital to a proper understanding of covenant theology. One of its applications is that it reforms the idea that God always covenants with families.[25] Because God always covenants through a federal head, covenantal membership depends directly and solely on the federal headship God establishes. And the result is that when investigating one's own place in a given covenant, the determining factor is whether you belong to the federal head.

Are parents uninvolved in this process? They are involved when a federal head is appointed to represent his natural posterity. In such cases, parental lineage is the efficient cause of a child entering a covenant, but the material cause would be the rights of their federal head and the formal

---

[24] Charles Hodge, while discussing immediate imputation, comments, "This representative principle pervades the whole Scriptures. The imputation of Adam's sin to his posterity is not an isolated fact. It is only an illustration of a general principle which characterizes the dispensation of God from the beginning of the world." Charles Hodge, *Systematic Theology* (Peabody, MA: Hendrickson, 2008), II:198.

[25] Cf. Kline, *Kingdom Prologue*, 195–197. Kline says, "We thus learn that from the very beginning of redemptive history the constituency of the holy congregation of God's people in its historical existence and continuance followed along family lines....This is a constant principle of covenant polity, even in the administration of the church under the new covenant." When asking whether the Covenant of Grace was made with Adam and his seed, John Barret answered, "This is the perpetual way and manner of Gods Covenant, to include and reckon the *Children with their parents.* Thus the Covenant of Grace was made with *Adam,* and his Seed, such as were to Descend from him, till such time as any of them Degenerated *into the seed of the Serpent,* and by their willful Apostacy from God, and his Ways, they did *cut off themselves, and theirs* from the Covenant." John Barret, *God's Love to Man, and Man's Duty towards God: Manifested in several Discourses on the Covenants of Works and Grace. Wherein divers Propositions are laid down, and sundry Cases resolved* (London: Jonathan Robinson, 1678), 304.

cause would be the covenant arrangement. The parents may bring about a covenantal member, but they do not bring about covenantal membership.

This remains true irrespective of how many generations follow the federal head. As long as the covenant made with that federal head remains valid so do the promises to the offspring. And the offspring have a direct and immediate relation to the federal head. But each covenant has a different federal head, thus each covenant determines whom the federal head represents. Federal headship and families are not at odds, necessarily. But their proper relationship must be understood. Covenant membership is ultimately derived directly and immediately from federal headship.

Having discussed the definition of a covenant, having explained covenant sanctions, having distinguished between the matter and form of a covenant, and having delineated the nature of federal headship, we now turn to addressing the relation of covenants to kingdoms in greater detail.

2. What is a Covenant's Function?

In this section we will tie together various strands of thought in a simple way. So then, what is a covenant's function? What do covenants do?

God's covenants delegate dominion. God has supreme dominion over all; all creation is His kingdom.[26]

> 1 The earth is the LORD's and the fullness thereof, the world and those who dwell therein, 2 for he has founded it upon the seas and established it upon the rivers (Psalm 24:1–2).

> 13 The LORD looks down from heaven; he sees all the children of man; 14 from where he sits enthroned he looks out on all the inhabitants of the earth, 15 he who fashions the hearts of them all and observes all their deeds (Psalm 33:13–15).

> 34 His dominion is an everlasting dominion, and his kingdom endures from generation to generation; 35 all the inhabitants of the earth are accounted as nothing, and he does according to his will among the host of heaven and among the inhabitants of the earth; and none can stay his hand or say to him, "What have you done?" (Daniel 4:34–35).

[26] O. Palmer Robertson comments, "It is not only the rise and fall of nations that is determined by God's sovereign will. Even the hairs of every human head are numbered by the Almighty. His kingdom is over all, and it shall not fall." O. Palmer Robertson, *The Israel of God* (Phillipsburg, NJ: P&R, 2000), 113.

In addition to His universal kingship over creation, God has used covenants to establish particular kingdoms on earth, all of which belong to him, are accountable to Him, and depend upon Him.[27]

Covenants function as the legal basis upon which God interacts with man in a given kingdom. Covenants establish the boundaries of a kingdom, appoint federal heads, grant promises, impose laws, define the offspring of the federal head, and specify all other pertinent and necessary details of how God will exercise His dominion through the federal head and his offspring. By way of covenant, every party involved in a kingdom can know how to act and what to expect. Kingdoms manifest themselves in visible forms through the terms of their covenants. The kingdom is the covenant realized, implemented, or actualized.

This sounds rather abstract at first. But throughout biblical history, from past to present, God has established kingdoms through covenant. This work will discuss three kingdoms, each established and governed by its own distinct covenants: *the kingdom of creation, the kingdom of Israel, and the kingdom of Christ.* They can be visualized and remembered easily in the following table.

The Kingdom of Creation	The Kingdom of Israel	The Kingdom of Christ
Covenant of Work	Abrahamic Covenant	Covenant of Redemption
Noahic Covenant	Mosaic Covenant	Covenant of Grace
	Davidic Covenant	

Each of these kingdoms depends on the king or figurehead to whom God covenants the kingdom to which they are entitled. So, the kingdom of creation depends on Adam and later on Noah, the kingdom of Israel depends on Abraham, Moses, and the line of David, and the kingdom of Christ depends on Jesus Christ.

---

[27] "There is a close connection between divine covenant and divine kingdom. Viewed as commitment transactions with their rituals, documents, and stipulated terms and procedures, covenants function as administrative instruments of God's kingly rule." Kline, *Kingdom Prologue*, 4.

These kingdoms will be treated individually in later portions of this work, but they are not separated, independent, or unrelated projects that have their own parallel destinations. Ultimately, they *all* terminate in *one* kingdom of God under one king, Jesus Christ. Tracing God's actions and dealings with mankind in these kingdoms and covenants ultimately traces the unveiling of the mystery of the covenant and kingdom of Christ in whom *all things* in heaven and on earth are brought to consummation (Ephesians 1:9–10).[28]

Conclusion

In summary, a covenant is a divinely sanctioned commitment defining the relationship between God and another party. And a covenant functions as the God-ordained legal basis upon which a kingdom is founded and by which a kingdom is governed. With this foundation laid and settled, we will begin our exposition of the mystery of Christ in the kingdoms and covenants of Scripture, beginning with the kingdom of creation and the covenant of works.

---

[28] "Taking the kingdom of God as our central, organizing theme, we inevitably find ourselves fully involved with the subject of the divine covenants of Scripture; for to follow the course of the kingdom is to trace the series of covenants by which the Lord administers his kingdom." Kline, *Kingdom Prologue*, 1.

Part Two

The Kingdom of Creation

God is King over all creation. Thus, all creation is His kingdom, the realm of His rule, the domain of His dominion. "For from him and through him and to him are all things. To him be glory forever. Amen" (Romans 11:36). Out of the infinite abundance of God's goodness, God has delegated dominion to man through covenant. This section is entitled "The Kingdom of Creation" because the scope of the dominion delegated by the ensuing covenants extends to the whole world, beginning with the covenant of works.

4

The Covenant of Works

Introduction

The biblical doctrine of the Covenant of Works depends on the distinction between that which was natural to Adam at creation, and that which was granted beyond nature. The Covenant of Works falls into the latter category. Opponents of the Covenant of Works sometimes cite the lack of the term "covenant" as evidence against a covenantal arrangement between God and Adam.[1] However, when the biblical data of God's dealings with Adam beyond his condition as a creature are considered, the Covenant of Works shines forth brightly.

1. Man's Created Condition

Creation, distinct from the Creator, is good. God declared it to be good seven times in Genesis 1, summing this up in a declaration of exceeding goodness in Genesis 1:31. Being a part of creation, man as body and soul created in the image of God was good. The natural and inherent goodness and blessedness of man sets the stage for that which God promised to man beyond what was his by nature.

---

[1] This objection commits the word-concept fallacy. Just because the word associated with a given concept is absent, it does not follow that the concept is absent. Gentry and Wellum rightly argue that "The absence of the word for 'covenant'…is no argument at all against the notion that a divine-human covenant is established at creation, if exegesis can demonstrate that the idea is there." Gentry and Wellum, *Kingdom through Covenant*, 178.

By nature, Adam the creature was obligated to obey God the Creator in all things. By nature, however, God was not obligated to reward Adam's obedience with anything other than the approval of justice which acknowledges that a work has been performed according to its command. Though there was an infinite disparity between the Creator and the creature in terms of rights and responsibilities, the complementary accounts of the creation of man reveal that God placed before Adam the possibility of attaining something beyond his created condition.

Genesis 1 and 2 offer complementary perspectives that explain this. Genesis 1 has a universal macroscopic perspective, describing the creation of all things with man as God's image-bearer placed at the summit of the creation account at the end of the sixth day. The all-inclusive categories of creatures are reiterated as being under man's dominion. Adam is to have dominion "over all the earth" (v. 26) and he is also commissioned to "fill the earth and subdue it" (v. 28). Genesis 1, therefore, designates the created world as a realm over which Adam is to exercise dominion. This is laid out before him as something which he must accomplish and bring to pass. He must fill the earth. He must subdue it. Meanwhile, God sits enthroned in eternal rest, having laid out a work-rest pattern for Adam to follow.

The universal kingdom task must begin somewhere. And God chose Eden to be that place. Genesis 2 shifts to a local microscopic perspective and in a complementary way explains the conditions under which Adam will achieve the task of his universal mandate. Genesis 1 sets the stage for the scope of the Covenant of Works, but Genesis 2 provides the details.[2]

2. Man's Covenantal Condition

A covenant is a commitment with divine sanctions. God placed Adam under commitments beyond his created obligations and added sanctions to guarantee Adam's participation. God also committed to provide a reward for Adam's obedience, a reward unavailable apart from God's free provision. This sanctioned commitment is the Covenant of Works. Tracing God's dealings with Adam beyond his created state demonstrates this.

a. God placed Adam in the garden of Eden

Genesis 1 presents a scene of heaven and earth. Genesis 2 carefully localizes the perspective of the narrative in Genesis 2:8, stating that within

---

[2] See Barcellos, *The Covenant of Works*, 72–75. Barcellos comments, "The shift from creation at large to the creation of man then to man's Edenic vocation instills covenantal implications with what follows."

the completed cosmos "the LORD God planted a garden in Eden, in the east, and there he put the man whom he had formed."

Eden was not man's initial and natural location. Adam was formed, then Eden was prepared, then Adam was placed in Eden. The description of Eden tells us the purpose for which Adam was placed there. The garden contained the tree of life and the tree of the knowledge of good and evil (Genesis 2:9). And Adam was placed in this garden, "to work it and keep it" (Genesis 2:15).

The biblical description of Eden makes it a temple of God's special presence. There are numerous features of the text of Genesis 2 that mark this out for the reader, such as its eastern designation, its mountaintop location, its rivers, its trees, its precious stones, and its metals as indicators of its temple character.[3] These features do not seem especially significant on their own. But when compared with the way that later Scriptures employ the same imagery, one finds that later temples are described in language that evokes the imagery of Eden. Eden was a prototypical temple template from which later Scriptures draw their imagery and language.[4]

For example, Eden is described as an elevated or mountaintop location because it is said that water flowed out from it, and, as common knowledge understands, water flows downhill. Elsewhere in scripture, God's presence is often manifested on mountain tops. God met with Moses on Mt. Sinai, the temple was constructed on the hilltop of Jerusalem, and we are said to belong to Mt. Zion as citizens of Jerusalem above (Hebrews 12:22).

The presence of precious stones is prospective of the aesthetic beauty and excellence required in the construction of the tabernacle and temple, and of Aaron's breastplate, as well as aligning perfectly with the repeated mention of rare gemstones in the descriptions of heaven in John's Revelation.

The trees are prospective of the Menorah placed within the tabernacle and temple which were made to resemble almond trees with branches and blossoms (Exodus 25:31–39). Furthermore, the tree of life is specifically named in John's description of heaven in Revelation 22.

Additional proof is found in that throughout the history of redemption, God refuses to allow sin in His holy sanctuaries. After the fall, Adam

[3] Cf. Fesko, *Last Things First*, 57–67.

[4] When describing God's presence in the tabernacle, the Solomonic temple, the heavenly sanctuary, and other places of divine presence, the same language and features are mentioned and used. Gentry and Wellum provide a similar list, adding that God's decrees are made known in the garden and that God "walks to and fro" there as He is described doing in the tabernacle elsewhere in the Bible. Gentry and Wellum, *Kingdom through Covenant*, 211–213.

was banished from Eden. The tabernacle, the temple, and even the holy land of Israel itself were to be kept pure from sin (with a threat of expulsion for noncompliance). And as the individual believer is to act purely because he is a temple of the Holy Spirit, so also the church must guard the boundaries of its membership from unrepentant and unbelieving individuals. God's holy spaces are to be protected and preserved according to God's holy laws.

These factors indicate that God made Eden to be a temple sanctuary in which His presence would be manifested. And He placed Adam there to work and keep it. As will be discussed shortly, Adam's work demonstrates the temple character of Eden more than anything.

By placing Adam in the garden of Eden as a worker, God granted to Adam a particular realm to rule, a sphere of sovereignty. God placed Adam as king over Eden. God's rule would be established within this sphere through Adam. Eden was Adam's kingdom, and he was its king.

b. God appointed Adam federal head over his natural offspring

Adam was a federal head by God's appointment. In Romans 5:19, Paul describes the connection of "one man" to "the many," speaking of how Adam's "one trespass" brought condemnation on those whom he represented. In 1 Corinthians 15:22 we read that "in Adam all die." Verses 47–49 elaborate on this principle. Paul says, "47 The first man was from the earth, a man of dust; the second man is from heaven. 48 As was the man of dust, so also are those who are of the dust, and as is the man of heaven, so also are those who are of heaven. 49 Just as we have borne the image of the man of dust, we shall also bear the image of the man of heaven." As goes the king, so goes the kingdom.

Adam's federal headship is evident in Genesis 1 and 2 from the fact that *he* is to fill the earth with his offspring. This may seem to be an overstatement because in Genesis 1:28 God gave a broad commission to both Adam and Eve. The imperatives related to filling the earth are in the plural form. Adam and Eve are to fill the earth with their seed. But the universal scope of Genesis 1 must be connected with its local recapitulation in Genesis 2 where Adam was created, placed in the garden, and charged with its royal, priestly, and prophetic care, *prior* to the creation of Eve.

Eve's creation serves the purpose of *helping* Adam to perform his tasks and to fulfill his commission. So, although the command to fill the earth is delivered to them both, it runs through Adam first. Though Eve was closely involved in Adam's work, she was a helper, suited for assisting Adam.

Beyond his created condition, Adam was placed in a sanctuary and constituted a federal head over his natural offspring. All mankind, our

Lord excepted by virgin birth, were thus represented in Adam. In the words of Hercules Collins, a Particular Baptist, "A publick Head, so Adam stood, as Christ is of his Spouse; And what he did, as our chief Head, We did it gain or lose."[5]

c. God obligated Adam to a law of obedience

By nature, Adam owed absolute obedience to God. Beyond the law of nature written on Adam's heart, God gave Adam a positive law of obedience, prescribing some actions while proscribing others. These were positive laws, commands arising not from natural deduction or relation but simply from God's revealed will. Through these commands, Adam did not accrue more obligation to obey his Creator, but more obligations. When the law of nature and this specific command are combined, that is the Covenant of Works.[6] And the fact that obedience constitutes the foundational principle governing the obtaining and enjoying of blessings in the covenant is the reason why this covenant is called the Covenant of *Works*. Adam's obedience to God's law was the determining factor of the outcome.

Placed in the garden sanctuary of Eden, a temple of God's presence, Adam was commanded to guard and keep the garden (Genesis 2:15). This temple-task must be understood in priestly terms, not only because those who work in temples are priests, but because the words translated "work" and "keep" in the ESV translation of Genesis 2:15 are the same words (in italics below) God used in Numbers 3:6–10 to describe the Levites' priestly duties in guarding the tabernacle.

> 6 Bring the tribe of Levi near, and set them before Aaron the priest, that they may minister to him. 7 They shall *keep guard* over him and over the whole congregation before the tent of meeting, as they *minister* at the tabernacle. 8 They shall guard all the furnishings of the tent of meeting, and keep guard over the people of Israel as they minister at the taber-

---

[5] Hercules Collins, *The Marrow of Gospel History* (London: n.p., 1696), 10.

[6] This is why it is important to distinguish the Covenant of Works from the moral law. The Covenant of Works is founded on the moral law but includes positive commands related to the garden of Eden and the trees. If we simplistically equate the moral law with the covenant of works, then the moral law *is* a Covenant of Works and cannot possibly function in any other way. The 2nd London Confession of Faith avoids this mistake by pointing out in 19.6 that while the same moral law applies to believers, it is *not [given] as a covenant of works*. A law is one thing. A covenant founded on law is another. The moral law was certainly a *natural* foundation of the Covenant of Works, but the positive laws God gave to Adam constitute the *covenantal* commitment.

nacle. 9 And you shall give the Levites to Aaron and his sons; they are
wholly given to him from among the people of Israel. 10 And you shall
appoint Aaron and his sons, and they shall guard their priesthood. But if
any outsider comes near, he shall be put to death.

Adam's role was precisely the same.[7] No unclean thing shall enter the
sanctuary of the Lord. *"If any outsider comes near, he shall be put to death."*
Adam's law of obedience was to serve and protect the temple of God. As
goes the priest, so go the people.

Protecting God's sanctuary means guarding whatever commands God
has issued regarding the ordering of His sanctuary. The general command
to guard the sanctuary is made specific in the next two verses, Genesis
2:16–17.

> 16 And the LORD God commanded the man, saying, 'You may surely eat
> of every tree of the garden, 17 but of the tree of the knowledge of good
> and evil you shall not eat, for in the day that you eat of it you shall surely
> die.

The guarding and purity-keeping of the sanctuary is measured by obedience to these commands.[8]

[7] Gentry and Wellum comment that in comparison to Genesis 2:15 "The
only other passages in the Torah where the same two verbs occur together are
Numbers 3:7–8; 8:26; 18:5–6, which describe the duties of the Levites in guarding and ministering in the sanctuary." Gentry and Wellum, *Kingdom through Covenant*, 212. Cf. also, Fesko, *Last Things First*, 71.

[8] "It pleased the sovereign Majesty of Heaven to add to this eternal law a
positive precept in which he charged man not to eat of the fruit of one tree in the
midst of the garden of Eden. This tree was called the tree of the knowledge of
good and evil (Genesis 2:16, 17; 3:3). The eating of this fruit was not a thing evil
in itself but was made so by divine prohibition. So it was necessary that the will of
God concerning this should be expressly signified and declared to man. Otherwise
by the light of nature he would have been no more directed to abstain from the
fruit of this tree than of any other in the garden; indeed, he would not have been
under any bond of duty to it. But the command being once given out, this positive
law had its foundations surely laid in the law of nature." Coxe, *A Discourse of the
Covenants*, 19. Spelling updated. Cf. also, Francis Turretin, *Institutes of Elenctic
Theology*, 3 vols. (Phillipsburg, NJ: P&R, 1994), I:579. "God selected this tree [of
the knowledge of good and evil] then, to explore (*exploandum*) the obedience of
Adam. Thus arose the special law given to him concerning not tasting its fruit: "of
every tree of the garden thou mayest freely eat: but of the tree of the knowledge of
good and evil, thou shall not eat of it: for in the day that thou eatest thereof thou
shalt surely die" (Gen. 2:16, 17). This is called 'a positive law' because it did not
bind man from the nature of the thing (which was in itself indifferent), but from
the mere will of God."

The fact that God gave these directions directly to Adam imbues his priestly commission with an equally prophetic character. In scripture, receiving the word of the Lord directly constituted one a prophet. As Moses the prophet received the Levitical commands and relayed them to the Levitical priests (Numbers 3:5–6), so God declared His decrees in a personal way to Adam, giving him the most fundamental qualification of prophetic commission. Adam was both priest and prophet of Eden.

Prophets are required not simply to receive the pure word of God, but also to relay it in its purity and to rebuke all gainsayers. As a prophet, Adam must ensure that he fulfills his priestly duties according to the prophetic word and that no threat to God's pure word is admitted or unconfronted in Eden.

Immediately after the priestly commission was delivered to Adam, Eve was created as Adam's helper. And Adam and Eve were given the universal commands of multiplication and dominion. This sequence highlights two related aspects of Adam's commission.

First, Adam's role was kingly. Adam was to bring creation to consummation, being fruitful and filling the earth with a holy and God-honoring seed. He was to imitate God as a kingdom builder and attain the rest that awaited completion of such a work. The local reach of Eden was to extend to the universal reach of all creation. Adam was commanded to rule the world, king of a covenanted kingdom.

Second, Adam's universal rule would be determined by his local rule. Adam's conditions of obedience focused the universal to the local in Eden, and, more specifically, into whether Adam would guard the purity of the garden's sanctity by upholding God's command not to eat of the tree of the knowledge of good and evil.

To summarize, the laws of the Covenant of Works were partly derived from Adam's natural constitution and the moral law to which he was bound, but more specifically from positive laws imposed by God. These laws bound Adam positively to serve and guard in the garden, and negatively not to eat from the tree of the knowledge of good and evil. Adam as priest, prophet and king of Eden was to begin his universal dominion in a specific realm, under a specific law of obedience. Adam must guard the divine sanctuary by upholding the word of God. And to test his obedient protection of the garden, he was prohibited from eating from the tree of the knowledge of good and evil.

d. God promised eternal life to Adam

The most prominent feature of the garden was its two trees, the tree of life, and the tree of the knowledge of good and evil. Each tree played an important role in the Covenant of Works made with Adam.

Adam's obedience was not simply for the sake of obedience. After all, a law is just a law, not a covenant. But a law that functions as a means of establishing a sanctioned commitment between two parties, *that* is a covenant. Adam's obedience functioned within a covenantal arrangement that suspended promises on his obedience, i.e., he was in a covenant of works. The goal set before Adam was signified to him by the tree of life.

If Adam obeyed his Creator, the tree of life stood before him as a pledge of life eternal. Geerhardus Vos said, "The tree was associated with the higher, the unchangeable, the eternal life to be secured by obedience throughout his probation."[9] Confirmed eternal life and immutable perfect communion with God were not a part of Adam's natural constitution. He was sinless and upright, but he was able to sin. "Sin is lawlessness" (1 John 3:4), meaning that sin is a violation of God's law. Adam was capable of violating God's law, and that is what he did.

The tree of life was a covenantal symbol of what was promised to Adam upon completion of his errand—confirmed eternal life and communion with God in His presence. This is established in Scripture by John's use of the tree of life in heaven in Revelation 2:7, promising its benefits to the one who conquers, i.e. the one who perseveres, trusting in Christ. It also appears in John's description of the consummation in Revelation 22 where God dwells with His people, and is equated with eternal life in that consummation. Further confirmation of this is the fact that man's expulsion from the garden is specifically connected to a barring from the tree of life which offers eternal life (Genesis 3:22–24).

> 24 "Now, lest he reach out his hand and take also of *the tree of life* and eat, *and live forever*—" 23 therefore the LORD God sent him out from the garden of Eden to work the ground from which he was taken. 24 He drove out the man, and at the east of the garden of Eden he placed the cherubim and a flaming sword that turned every way *to guard the way to the tree of life.*

The later uses of the tree of life in the Bible are built upon the earliest use, the garden of Eden.

Paul's comparison of Adam and Christ in Romans 5, mentioned above, indicates that had Adam been the obedient one, the result of his obedience would have been, in a way, the same as Christ's obedience—the invincible righteousness of those whom he represented. Christ's successful mission of obedience was not the paradigm for Adam's role. Adam was the paradigm for Christ. Paul's point is that where Adam failed, Christ prevailed.

[9] Geerhardus Vos, *Biblical Theology* (Banner of Truth: Carlisle, PA: 2007), 28.

Similarly, in Romans 3:23, Paul speaks of a glory of which Adam fell short because of sin. There was a glory which he did not possess by nature, a glory to which he could have attained had he been obedient in this covenant.[10] Jesus Christ entered into that glory and is bringing "many sons" there (Hebrews 2:10).

Because eternal life in a consummated and consecrated cosmos is in view in this covenant, there was not the least amount of mercy afforded for Adam. He must obey perfectly, personally, and perpetually. This is clear not only by what it took for Christ to earn eternal life for His people, but also by the fact that the first breach of the covenant brought its curses to bear upon Adam and his posterity.

The pattern of God's Sabbath rest also adds a dimension of futurity to the Covenant of Works. Adam is covenanted a kingdom awaiting his work and rest, just as God created His own kingdom and then rested. Genesis 1 sets the stage for the scope of this prospect. As the image-bearer of God, Adam was called to bring creation to consummation. And that consummation would be a kingdom of perfect and immutable righteousness. God covenanted entrance into this consummation kingdom through a covenant of works based on Adam's obedience.

The attachment of the promise of the reward of life to Adam's obedience establishes the identity of this covenant. Adam's obedience would not have been meritorious for any reward at all, not to mention the "reward of life", were it not for an arrangement established by God to arrange it.[11] The only reason that Adam's obedience to the positive laws would be meritorious for eternal life, was because God condescended to make it so according

---

[10] See Barcellos, *Getting the Garden Right*, 70–74.

[11] Cf. John Flavel, *Planelogia. A Succinct and Seasonable Discourse of the Occasions, Causes, Nature, Rise, Growth, and Remedies of Mental Errors* (London: R. Roberts, 1691), 281. "God might have dealt with us in a supream way of mere Sovereignty and Dominion, commanding what Duties he pleased, and establishing his Commands by what Penalties he had pleased, and never have brought himself under the tye and obligation of a Covenant to his own Creatures: but he chuses to deal familiarly with his People, the way of Covenanting being a familiar way." Thomas Manton, *A Practical Commentary, or an Exposition with Notes on the Epistle of James* (London: J. Macock, 1651), 129. "Some Divines say, That in innocency we could not merit; when the Covenant did seem to hang upon Works, we could, in their sence, *impetrare*, but not *mereri*; obtain by vertue of doing, but not deserve: Merit and desert are improper notions to express the relation between the work of a creature, and the reward of a Creator." Owen, *A Continuation of the Exposition*, 221–222. Cf. also Hugh Binning, *The Common Principles of Christian Religion* (London: R.S., 1666), 238; Patrick Gillespie, *The Ark of the Testament Opened* (London: R.C., 1661), 301.

to covenant.[12] The law makes universal demands, but only within a covenantal arrangement do promises accompany those demands.

Thus, when the Scriptures use the tree of life as a foundational symbol of eternal heavenly life, when the Scriptures speak of a glory Adam failed to attain, when the Scriptures contrast eternity relative to Adam and Christ in Romans 5, and when Adam is banished from eternal life in Genesis 3, we can conclude with ample biblical data that confirmed eternal life in righteousness was set before Adam. And because such a reward could only be obtained in a voluntary condescension from God, this is a covenantal relationship.

If Adam obeyed, the reward would belong to him and to all those whom he represents by justice. He would be fruitful and multiply and extend Eden to the ends of the earth. In other words, creation would reach consummation in which there is no distinction between heaven and earth. All of earth would be as much a place of divine presence and communion as heaven is, and mankind would dwell with God, sinless and blissful.[13] As glorious as that thought is, what followed the law of obedience given to Adam was a specific sanction to guarantee that he would fulfill his commission.

e. God threatened Adam with sanctions

Sanctions formalize covenantal commitments. God clearly threatened Adam with death if he disobeyed the law of the covenant. If Adam violates the commitments of the covenant, he will surely die (Genesis 2:17). There was no affordance of mercy, no allowance for partial fulfillment, and no admittance of failure. If Adam ruptured God's rule, he would surely die. His commission to bring creation to consummation would end in ruin, and the seed he was supposed to bring to glory would fall with him. As goes the king, so goes the kingdom.

As the tree of life was a symbol of the promise of the covenant, so the tree of the knowledge of good and evil was a sacramental symbol of the

---

[12] This is, again, what the English seventeenth-century Reformed confessions affirm in their opening comments on covenant in chapter seven. The reward of life could never have been attained by man apart from God voluntarily condescending to provide some arrangement in which man could attain the reward of life, which he did in covenant. On the background of this language, see Andrew A. Woolsey, *Unity and Continuity in Covenantal Thought* (Grand Rapids, MI: Reformation Heritage Books, 2012), 45–50, 92, 97. Woolsey traces this argumentation through Ussher, Ball, the Westminster Confession, and on into the 19th century.

[13] As only Meredith Kline can put it, the *polis* will become *megapolis*, and then *megapolis* will become *metapolis*. Kline, *Kingdom Prologue*, 96–101.

threat of the covenant. It served as a constant reminder to Adam of the necessity of his obedience and the price of unfaithfulness. Adam must persist in obedience, or he will suffer the consequences of his rebellion.

f. God made a Covenant of Works with Adam

When God's dealings with Adam beyond that which was natural to him are considered, it is clear that God made a covenant of works with Adam. Adam was placed in a defined kingdom, appointed as a federal head, given a law of obedience, promised a reward upon fulfillment, and threatened with a curse. He was in a covenant of works which governed entrance into a consummated cosmos.

Matter:	Restipulation:	Sanction:	Form:
Law →	Obedience →	Covenant partner →	Covenant of Works

Nehemiah Coxe argued that,

> It is evident that God dealt with Adam not only upon Terms of a Law, but in a way of Covenant, and that this Transaction with him was of a Fœderal Nature…altho it be not in Scripture expressly called a Covenant, yet it hath the express Nature of a Covenant, and there is no reason for Nicety about Terms where the thing itself, is sufficiently revealed to us.[14]

Given that all of the features described above advance Adam beyond his created state, it is neither invention nor imposition to assign a name to the way in which God dealt with Adam. Rather, because we are basing our conclusions on the evidence of the Word of God itself, we are safe in giving a name to what was transacted between God and Adam. It was a covenant, the Covenant of Works.

In fact, *any* objection to this foundational biblical doctrine is a serious matter. Undercutting Adam's role as federal head of mankind undercuts the very heart of salvation. Coxe pointed this out and said, "It could only be on the account of such a covenant that Adam's posterity should be involved as they were in his standing or falling. Let the first be denied and the latter is altogether unaccountable."[15] If we deny Adam's place as

[14] Coxe, *A Discourse of the Covenants*, 27–28.
[15] Coxe, *A Discourse of the Covenants*, 28.

a federal head of a covenant that would either vindicate or condemn him according to his works, then we remove the possibility for mankind to fall in him. And if that is the case, we remove the reason for the incarnation of the eternally begotten Son of God. In fact, we remove the reason for God's wrath towards mankind and man's spiritual deadness in sins and trespasses. More than that, we remove the biblical framework within which to understand the category of imputation, so vital to Paul's argument concerning Adam and Christ in Romans 5. If we fail to grasp this foundation, we will be building on sand from the start.

Another area that requires caution is in construing this covenant in any negative or sinister tones. It does threaten death, but it is only ominous because Adam failed and the curse was executed upon him. Let us not forget that God's covenants with man are always designed to do good to man. This covenant is no exception. Coxe states this in an appropriate balance. He says,

> This covenant that God made with Adam and all mankind in him, as to the terms and condition of it (we see) was a covenant of works. With respect to immediate privilege and relationship it was a covenant of friendship. With regard to the promised reward it was a covenant of rich bounty and goodness. But it did not include or intimate the least iota of pardoning mercy. While its law was perfectly observed it raised man within a degree of the blessed angels. But the breach of that law inevitably brought him under that curse which sank him to the society of apostate devils and left him under a misery like theirs.[16]

The Covenant of Works was a supreme blessing and privilege, an opportunity for mankind to dwell in blissful communion with God for all eternity. If we depreciate that truth, we will depreciate the depths of Adam's infidelity. Adam did not fall out of bed and bonk his head. He fell from orbit and was obliterated when he hit the ground.

g. God tested Adam's obedience

The Covenant of Works was not an unbounded endless demand for obedience in the garden. It had an eschatological goal. For that reason, Adam's obedience had to be tested in a definable way, and that took the shape of a probationary test. The tripwire command of the Covenant of Works was the positive law regarding the tree of the knowledge of good and evil. Adam was commissioned to fill the earth, and bring it to consummation,

---

[16] Coxe, *A Discourse of the Covenants*, 29.

but whether that would happen depended on the microcosm of Eden, and this one command in particular.

As Jesus was tempted in the wilderness, so Adam was tempted. He was called to keep God's sanctuary pure, and to uphold God's Word, His commands. Eve was seduced by the Serpent, and Adam heeded the voice of his wife. He did not exercise dominion over the kingdom covenanted to him, he did not obey the law placed over him, and thus the sanctions of the covenant were activated in full against him, and his sin was imputed federally to all of his posterity.

As argued above, Romans 3:23 and Romans 5:17–18 indicate that had Adam obeyed, he would have attained the glory of God and constituted the many righteous. Meredith Kline expressed this probation as follows,

> Under God's covenant with mankind in Adam attainment of the eschatological kingdom and Sabbath rest was governed by a principle of works. Adam, representative of mankind, was commissioned to fulfill the probationary assignment; he must perform the one meritorious act of righteousness. This act was to have the character of a victory in battle. An encounter with Satan was a critical aspect of the probationary crisis for each of the two Adams. To enter into judicial combat against this enemy of God and to vanquish him in the name of God was the covenantal assignment that must be performed by the servant of the Lord as his 'one act of righteousness.' And it was the winning of this victory of righteousness by the one that would be imputed to the many as their act of righteousness and as their claim on the consummated kingdom proffered in the covenant.[17]

Sadly, Adam failed this probation, and mankind died in him. This brings us from man's created condition to man's covenantal condition to man's cursed condition.

3. Man's Cursed Condition

God told Adam that on the day he ate of the fruit of the tree of the knowledge of good and evil, he would surely die. But Adam did not die that day. This might indicate that the curses of the Covenant of Works were not activated against him. That is not the case. They were poured out on Adam in full. Death, in numerous senses, descended upon Adam that day. Death came to all men, and all of man.

---

[17] Kline, *Kingdom Prologue*, 117.

a. Death

As a federal head, Adam was a representative of his natural offspring in the Covenant of Works. Thus, when Adam was cursed the whole of mankind was cursed. Paul says in Romans 5:12 that "Just as sin came into the world through one man, and death through sin, and so death spread to all men because all sinned." One man sinned and brought death upon himself. Through him, all men sinned, and therefore death has come to all men. Collective death is the result of the breaking of the Covenant of Works.

Paul makes the same point in 1 Corinthians 15:21–22. "21 For as by a man came death, by a man has come also the resurrection of the dead. 22 For as in Adam all die." Here is another example of Adam's actions being accounted to mankind. When Adam sinned, I sinned. When a curse of death was pronounced on Adam, a curse of death was pronounced on me. Adam's sin was *imputed* to his offspring. Legally, judicially, our record of righteousness or unrighteousness is Adam's record. His disobedience is credited to mankind, imputed to mankind, and thus all mankind is considered to be in a cursed state in Adam. In Adam, all die. This is collective death.

God told Adam that he would surely die. Death came to all of man, body and soul. Physical death is the first part of this curse. Death did not come on Adam instantly, but surely. There is nothing so certain as death, and nothing so uncertain as life. Disease, affliction, weakness, and ultimately collapse and death await mankind. Paul tells us in 1 Corinthians 15 that because we died in Adam, we bear his image, the image of the man of dust. As we bear the image of the man of dust, so we die and return to the dust. Robert Purnell, a Particular Baptist, expressed our fragile mortality well.

> Lo here is the anatomy of our life; it is a shrub, a leaf, a reed, a rush, a grass, a smoke, a post, a cloud, a wind, a water, a bubble, a vapor, a shadow, a nothing. We no sooner have our being, but we are going to our end; and our strength is as the grass, our beauty as the flower, the grass fades, the flower withers, and so our glory is gone. Life is uncertain, but death is certain; for we are more sure to die than live; for what is more certain than death? And what is so uncertain as life?[18]

In Adam, we are all on a collision course with the grave.

Man is body and soul. The body will die, physically. And in a manner of speaking we are dying. But regarding our immaterial part, our soul or spirit, *man is already dead.*

[18] Robert Purnell, *The Weavers Shuttle Displayed* (London: Giles Calvert, 1652), 13. Spelling updated.

1 And you were dead in the trespasses and sins 2 in which you once walked, following the course of this world, following the prince of the power of the air, the spirit that is now at work in the sons of disobedience— 3 among whom we all once lived in the passions of our flesh, carrying out the desires of the body and the mind, and were by nature children of wrath, like the rest of mankind. (Ephesians 2:1–3)

Conceived in sin, born in Adam, we, like the rest of mankind, are spiritually dead.

Those virtues of human nature once given to man are polluted and corrupted. Our mind, will, and affections, are bent towards sin.[19] Paul tells us in Romans 1, that though man knows that God exists, he suppresses that knowledge in unrighteousness, and exchanges the truth for a lie. Paul also tells us in Ephesians 4:18 that man's mind is darkened. And he tells us in 1 Corinthians 2:14 that the natural man, that is the man born in sin, cannot discern spiritual things.

To put it plainly, fallen man believes lies and rejects the truth. This is not done passively, as though it just happens, though that is true. It is also done actively. Fallen man suppresses the truth, distorts the truth, and disbelieves the truth. Our minds, our understanding, are cursed. This is the new "natural" for mankind. It is our nature in Adam.

Because man is spiritually dead man is unable to choose or do spiritual good. Man has not lost the power of choice. Man remains a free agent. But as a free agent, man's will is not free from his nature. And his nature is inclined to do evil. Thus, man chooses according to what he is, a sinner, and his will is enslaved to sin and unable to choose or do *spiritual* good. In other words, though man is not as sinful as he possibly could be, and although man can do civic good, things which are outwardly good, man cannot do anything that would in any way recover him from a sinful state or please God or satisfy God's law. Scripture teaches us plentifully that man, in his

---

[19] It is helpful to consider the affections as an illustration of the corruption of our nature. The affections are the motions of the mind and will relative to perceived good or evil. In other words, you analyze something as good or evil, and then you respond to it. You love or hate, you're happy or sad, you're merciful or vengeful, etc. You have affections, and as you relate to the world around you, you interpret that world and respond to it. Because the mind is darkened and the will enslaved, man's affections are polluted. Man loves evil and hates good. Man is angered by holiness, pleased with injustice, unmoved to mercy, and pleased by evil. This comports with Paul's description of fallen man in Ephesians 2:3, "we all once lived in the passions of our flesh, carrying out the desires of the body and the mind." All of these horrible effects are the direct result of our participation in the Covenant of Works in Adam our federal head. The curse of the covenant remains active and pertinent to this very day.

spiritually dead state, cannot change himself from that, or choose contrary to his nature (Matthew 7:17–18; Romans 5:6; 8:7–8; Titus 3:3).

The most terrifying part of the curse, however, is eternal death. Scripture teaches that when Christ returns and raises the dead, there will be a final judgment. And the result of that final judgment will be that one group of people is sent to everlasting life and blessedness, but the other group will be sent to everlasting death and suffering. Jesus divides these groups in Matthew 25, saying that those who do not belong to Him "will go away into eternal punishment" while those who do belong to Him will go "into eternal life." Revelation 20 paints the same picture. There, the devil, death itself, and all those whose names are not found in the Lamb's book of life are cast into the lake of fire. And it says "They will be tormented day and night forever and ever."

Eternal death is the opposite of eternal life. The fact that the breach of the Covenant of Works carried such an impact reinforces the previous statement that eternal life would have belonged to Adam by covenant had he been faithful. The two are combined when man is cursed and expelled from the garden, "lest he reach out his hand and take also of the tree of life and eat, and live forever" (Genesis 3:22). Thus, man's cursed condition involves death, in every way, culminating in a permanent and eternal exclusion from beholding and enjoying the glory of God in the face of Jesus Christ.

b. The abrogation of the covenant of works

Adam's breach of the covenant activated its curses, expelled him from the temple of God's presence, and condemned him to death. This means that the covenant remains in force today in that its curse continues to apply to all of Adam's offspring. But, the covenant does not remain in force today in the sense of promising life to those who obey its commands. The Covenant of Works depends on positive laws. It is much more than the moral law. And with no more Eden and no more sacramental trees, there are no more positive commands to obey. Furthermore, the Covenant of Works was made with a federal head, Adam, not his descendants. Therefore, the promise of the Covenant of Works is permanently shut up and abrogated.

Going back down the path of the Covenant of Works after the fall leads not to heaven, but back to Eden, a cursed ruin. The more you try to get in, the more the cherubim will hack you to pieces. It is an impossible path to life not only because of fallen man's own inability to keep its requirements, and not only for fallen man's own demerit, but also from God's active and intentional debarring of any and all who would seek to take such a path.

That being said, the abrogation of the Covenant of Works and its positive precepts in no way affects the abiding authority of the moral law. The moral law preceded and transcends the Covenant of Works. Nehemiah Coxe expressed this well, "The Law of Creation binds when the Covenant of Creation is broken."[20] As the confessions say, it remains as a "rule of life" for all mankind.[21]

The abidance of the moral law independent of the Covenant of Works carries no promise with it because the obligation to obey is a part of the Creator-creature relationship, but a reward is not. A reward may not be due by nature for obedience to the moral law, but a curse for disobedience is. So, there is no hope of eternal life through obedience to the law, whether through the broken Covenant of Works itself or through simple obedience to the moral law of God.

The abrogation of the Covenant of Works' positive laws did not cancel man's obligations to work and multiply. But the curse changed them significantly. First, man's work will never give him anything more than a somewhat longer, and perhaps somewhat easier life under the sun. There is no greater life or deliverance from judgment that man can achieve through cultural work. No effort on man's part can mitigate the severity or inevitability of the curses of the Covenant of Works. Second, the curses pronounced on man and woman directly affect their ability to fulfill these mandates. The woman is cursed with dangerous and painful childbearing. The primary mechanism designed for fruitfulness and multiplication will be difficult and deadly. And Adam will be resisted by the ground he is supposed to subdue. When he tills and toils in the soil, it will not yield easily, nor will it yield consistently. By sweat and work will life be perpetuated. Rather than bringing creation to consummation by successful and skillful excellence in sinless perfection, Adam will struggle just to survive.

Though the Covenant of Works is abrogated as to its promises and positive laws, its moral commands and its curses continue to oblige, exact, require, and condemn.

c. A merciful curse

God did not exact the full rigor of the curse upon Adam and Eve immediately upon their disobedience. This was mercy and kindness on God's part. The full sentence was assuredly promised and applied, but not to its full extent at that very moment.

[20] Coxe, A Discourse of the Covenants, 44.
[21] WCF/SD/2LCF 19.2.

In fact, before man's curse was even announced, God cursed Satan. And God's curse on Satan was a promise of salvation for Adam and Eve. Adam and Eve were hopeless in and of themselves. Eternal life was out of reach; curses were about to be pronounced. But before that happened, God declared that He would act on behalf of mankind.

> I will put enmity between you and the woman, and between your off-spring and her offspring; he shall bruise your head, and you shall bruise his heel (Genesis 3:15).

By obeying Satan, Adam and Eve had transferred their loyalty to Satan as their king. Rather than being the covenant servant-king of God, Adam's allegiance and fealty were aligned with Satan. But whereas Satan desired to be at the top, his curse places him beneath all, at the feet even of man, in the dust, pictured by a snake's low place on earth.

Note that God declared that Eve will have offspring. No curses had yet been pronounced on Adam and Eve which means that hearing this curse on Satan would have told Adam and Eve that all was not lost right then and there. There would be a future. There would be hope. In fact, the amity that Adam had established with Satan would be turned into enmity by God Himself, and Satan's dominion would be destroyed. There is therefore a promise of life in the curse on Satan. And we have reason to believe that Adam and Eve believed this promise of life and deliverance through the promised seed because after this Adam named his wife Eve, the mother of all living.

The fact that Adam and Eve are cursed subsequent to the promise of deliverance changes their curses to chastisement rather than absolute judgment. They come as discipline from a father, not as a death sentence from a judge. Adam and Eve were not immediately freed from the curses of the Covenant of Works, but they were freed from its ultimate curse of eternal death. And their hopes now lay in a descendant, the offspring of the woman.

This promise of a deliverer was not a command of work in Adam or Eve. It was not a new commission for self-deliverance or self-improvement. It was not a command followed by obedience coupled with a threat of death for disobedience. It was a promise that God must make good, a promise to be received and believed. It was the beginnings of the revelation of a new Covenant of Grace established on the infinite goodness and kindness of God, freely delivered to all those who trust and rest in its promises. This was the first dawning light of the mystery of Christ, His covenant, and His kingdom. And the rest of the Scriptures trace this promise as it is carried, expanded, augmented, increased, and unveiled by farther steps from Adam to Christ.

4. The Protological Nature of the Kingdom

The Covenant of Works is protological. Protology is the establishment of foundational symbols, concepts, and constructs that are repeated and reused by God in His Word. The garden of Eden and the Covenant of Works are paradigmatic. As noted above, the temple imagery in the Bible, the symbolism of the tree of life, and more establish the initial stages of a vast progression and development of revelation. There is a movement from protology to eschatology, which is simply another way of describing types and antitypes in typology. Protology refers to the first stage of types, the first patterns used in a developing tapestry of typology.

In Genesis 1–3 a covenant was made with a son of God commissioned to make the entire cosmos a consummated kingdom of God, filled with a perfect and sinless seed in perfect communion with God, building and creating culture to God's glory and with God's blessing. Israel is portrayed as a new son of God in a new paradise with a new covenant for a new kingdom. That kingdom will have a temple, requirements of righteousness, and promises of life. An everlasting covenant was made with the true and eternal Son of God granting life in an eternal kingdom. That kingdom will have a temple, requirements of righteousness, and promises of life.

Conclusion

In conclusion, in the Covenant of Works God delegated dominion over Eden to Adam through covenant, making him a king of that realm. God established Adam's federal headship, His laws of obedience, His promises of reward, and His threats of curse through a Covenant of Works. The Covenant of Works was designed to take creation to consummation. Eden would extend until there is no distinction between the temple of God's presence and the cosmos. Creation would have been filled with a holy and righteous seed, working to the glory of God in a crescendo of progress and praise. The Covenant of Works, therefore, established and governed the kingdom of creation. And because Adam broke the Covenant of Works, all creation remains governed, and thus cursed, by the Covenant of Works. It is the inescapable government and reality of human existence. God, however, promised deliverance from this curse, and what follows is a major step towards that deliverance.

5

The Noahic Covenant

Introduction

The Covenant of Works has all creation in view. So does the Noahic Covenant. It is another covenant through which God governs the kingdom of creation and its members, mankind. As man multiplied, so did man's sinfulness. And God permitted the sinfulness of man to increase to such an extent that it appeared to human eyes that those who served the Lord and believed in His promises would be all but destroyed. It was in that context that God sent the flood as a judgment upon mankind.

1. A New Creation and Commission

Moses, by the inspiration of the Holy Spirit, composed this account of Noah with language that treats it as a new creation account. Echoing Genesis 1, the flood narrative presents the *Ruach*, or wind and the great deep, dry land emerging from the waters, birds again filling the heavens, and man and animals filling the earth. Noah, like Adam, received a commission to be fruitful and fill the earth. All of this is to say that the flood narrative is presented to us as a new creation story.

Despite the similarities, this is not a resetting of the system. In other words, through the Noahic Covenant man does not return to paradise or receive a new one. Man does not return to innocence or obtain a new righteousness. In the narrative of the flood, God said in Genesis 8:21 that "the intention of man's heart is evil from his youth." The flood event saved the lives of Noah and his family, but not their souls. It did not change the heart of man. And the new creation that Noah and his family entered remains cursed by sin. The face of the earth may be less full of wickedness, but the heart of man remains just as full as ever. The realm that Noah and his family are entering is not Eden. It is not paradise. It is not a sacred place of God's presence. It is simply the fallen world.

Not only is the flood narrative presented as an echo of the original creation, but also the commands given to Noah and his offspring echo Eden. Noah received a new commission from God.

> 1 And God blessed Noah and his sons and said to them, "Be fruitful and multiply and fill the earth. 2 The fear of you and the dread of you shall be upon every beast of the earth and upon every bird of the heavens, upon everything that creeps on the ground and all the fish of the sea. Into your hand they are delivered" (Genesis 9:1–2).

In Genesis 1 God told Adam and Eve to be fruitful, to multiply, to fill the earth, to subdue it, and to rule over it. But whereas that commission had a largely positive significance, an idea of building and mastery and usefulness and synergy, this commission brings with it the idea that man will achieve mastery over the animal kingdoms by fear and force, not wisdom and excellence. The same kind of language occurs when Israel is going to enter Canaan. God says that he will put the *fear and dread* of the Israelites upon the Canaanite nations. So also, Noah and mankind are called to build and cultivate and expand and construct and establish human civilization. They are to take advantage, in the best sense of the phrase, of the natural world around them.

This is a cultural mandate as part of a covenant ruling a kingdom. And it applies to all mankind equally. Everyone must take this very seriously. God rules His kingdoms through covenant. We belong to the kingdom of creation, thus we are accountable to this covenant. We are a part of mankind, with whom God made this covenant, and this commission applies to mankind today, as it did in the days of Noah. Federal headship reaches to all generations so long as the covenant remains active.

So then, all mankind is called to raise up and establish structured and successful societies, pursuing cultural achievement and growth. Man is not called to sit in the dirt and mope. We are called to work. Though the ground may sprout thorns and our brows may pour forth sweat, despite resistance and setback, curse and difficulty, God has called all mankind, men and women, to be workers. We are to be fruitful, multiply, fill the earth, and master it.

Yet again, this is very different from Adam's task. Adam and Eve were called to extend Eden, to make the world a temple. Their cultural progress and family multiplication would have yielded a holy and righteous offspring gradually constructing a consummated paradise, a situation where all creation harmoniously serves God and enjoys His blessing and presence. It is not so for Noah and for us. Our cultural achievements, however impressive and enjoyable they may be by God's common grace, are not building the consummated kingdom of God. We are not making the world a temple. And our children are by no means filling the earth with a holy seed. So even as we are faithful to this command, being fruitful and multiplying, building culture, we are not progressing or promoting a holy land or a holy culture or a holy family.

Noah's covenant, therefore, is not a covenant of salvation or eternal life. The success or failure of Noah and mankind in obedience to these commands will neither bring them eternal life, nor will it bring upon them eternal death. Man is already condemned in Adam. And the only escape known at that time was God's promise concerning the offspring of Eve that would crush the serpent's head.

Though this covenant does not offer eternal life of any kind, it nevertheless served and serves the purpose of promoting the fulfillment of that greater promise of salvation. The Noahic Covenant subserves the progress of God's promise of salvation in that its new commission of reproduction and expansion will be a means whereby the seed of Eve can be born. Mankind reached a height of evil that threatened the extinction of the holy line, so the Lord destroyed humanity to preserve His promise of salvation, and now human multiplication can again serve that purpose. This is man's new commission.

2. A Judicial Retribution

God establishes and governs His kingdoms through covenant. In the Noahic Covenant, God renewed the culture-building mandate to Noah and mankind. God also laid down laws about justice. These are universal laws that all societies may and must enforce.

> 5 And for your lifeblood I will require a reckoning: from every beast I will require it and from man. From his fellow man I will require a reckoning for the life of man. 6 Whoever sheds the blood of man, by man shall his blood be shed, for God made man in his own image. 7 And you, be fruitful and multiply, increase greatly on the earth and multiply in it (Genesis 9:5–7).

All mankind, wherever they live, are held to this command. Man's commission is to be fruitful and multiply, as repeated in verse 7. Murder directly opposes and prevents the fulfillment of this commission. Thus, to control mankind's sinful nature and to prevent extreme bloodshed, those who murder are subject to death. This is an establishment of a system of legal and judicial retribution in society. Mankind has power, derived from God Himself through covenant in his kingdom, to punish those who harm society, in this case by murder. A death penalty, justly deserved and prescribed, is an act of God's judgment on the murderer and an act of deliverance for the society in which that murderer committed his crime.

In the Noahic Covenant, human societies therefore have two basic and related jobs: to preserve life, and to preserve the family. Mankind is to be fruitful and multiply. Society, man looking out for man, should promote human fruitfulness and multiplication. And that multiplication takes place in the context of families. As a result, any society or government that corrupts the family or murders the innocent is a government in direct treason and disobedience to the God of the universe. They are abusing the sword entrusted to them by turning it on the innocent, rather than the guilty.

And is there not a more poignant, convicting, and blatantly sinful example of this in our society than the active, government-funded, government-supported, legal status, pursuit, and protection of abortion? Is there anything more contrary to mankind's basic commission to be fruitful and multiply than to murder our own children, and to protect that murder by law? The promotion of abortion and the erosion and destruction of marriage through rampant divorce, homosexual unions, and all kinds of sexual perversion, are high treachery and boldfaced rejection of the most basic duties of all mankind according to the Noahic Covenant ruling the kingdom of creation.

Countries have constitutions or similar founding documents. But there is a more fundamental constitution by which we are all to live, and that is the Noahic Covenant governing the common kingdom of mankind. As a society we must promote, preserve, and protect the life of individuals, and the life of the family. These are our most basic commitments. As a result, we must punish the wicked, we must put to death murderers, and we must seek, with God's help, to exemplify and manifest real loving thriving families in our own homes.

3. A Promised Preservation

Covenants are often reducible to "I will" and "you will" statements. God has laid out man's commitments in the covenant. Now God makes a commitment to man.

8 Then God said to Noah and to his sons with him, 9 "Behold, I establish my covenant with you and your offspring after you, 10 and with every living creature that is with you, the birds, the livestock, and every beast of the earth with you, as many as came out of the ark; it is for every beast of the earth. 11 I establish my covenant with you, that never again shall

all flesh be cut off by the waters of the flood, and never again shall there be a flood to destroy the earth." 12 And God said, "This is the sign of the covenant that I make between me and you and every living creature that is with you, for all future generations: 13 I have set my bow in the cloud, and it shall be a sign of the covenant between me and the earth. 14 When I bring clouds over the earth and the bow is seen in the clouds, 15 I will remember my covenant that is between me and you and every living creature of all flesh. And the waters shall never again become a flood to destroy all flesh. 16 When the bow is in the clouds, I will see it and remember the everlasting covenant between God and every living creature of all flesh that is on the earth." 17 God said to Noah, "This is the sign of the covenant that I have established between me and all flesh that is on the earth" (Genesis 9:8–17).

The Noahic Covenant expands from Noah to his family to all mankind to all the earth to all flesh. In a repetitious manner God makes it clear that this covenant applies to all people. God promises that the great deep will not overtake the world again. Mankind will not be wiped out by flood ever again. And as a sacrament, or visible word, as a sign of the covenant, God designated the rainbow to be a visible promise of this reality.

Seasons, natural processes, and life in general will continue in a stable, predictable, recurring cycle. "While the earth remains, seedtime and harvest, cold and heat, summer and winter, day and night, shall not cease" (Genesis 8:22). This is promised irrespective of man's obedience. This is a covenant with obligations, but its promised blessings will not be removed. God will not flood the earth again. And the rainbow is God's visible promise to the world.

The sun will shine on the righteous and the wicked equally. God promises to preserve creation, not eternally, but never again will a flood destroy earth. And note again that this promise is not conditioned on what God requires of us. Though He may pour out judgment on peoples and nations for their wickedness, the whole of mankind will not suffer for it. God will not destroy the earth by flood, however tumultuous events in one place may be.

The reason and purpose for this promise of preservation is that it creates a stable platform upon which God's plan for salvation can play out. The mystery of Christ will unfold in this theater of preservation. And therefore the people of God can know at all times whether before or after the advent of the promised seed that God will not destroy the earth until He has fulfilled every last promise to His people. This covenant is a comfort, therefore, that however insane life becomes, however much instability we see around us, God's promises will be fulfilled.

4. A Common Cursed Kingdom of Common Grace

Putting all the pieces together in this section on the kingdom of creation and its covenants yields the conclusion that the kingdom of creation is a common cursed kingdom of common grace.

The sphere of Adam's and Noah's covenants is identical. For both, the whole world stands in view. Adam began in Eden, but his commission was to extend Eden to the world, to make the world a temple. More importantly, Adam was a federal head of all mankind. In Adam's fall sinned we all. All of creation is governed by the Covenant of Works. And this is proven by the fact that when Adam broke that covenant, all creation was cursed. Mankind and the ground, all things, were cursed. God established the kingdom of creation by the Covenant of Works, and creation remains under God's judgment and curse through that covenant.

In Noah's case, the flood narrative and the commission given to Noah are presented as a new creation and a new commission. It's echoing, not repeating, Adam in Eden. And as Adam's covenant included all mankind and creation, so also Noah's covenant includes all mankind and creation. The kingdom of creation is governed by two covenants. The Covenant of Works curses mankind. The Noahic Covenant stabilizes that cursed world so that redemptive history can play out and God's promises can be fulfilled.

The Noahic Covenant and the Covenant of Works are not at odds with each other. They simply have different purposes. The Covenant of Works curses and condemns. The Noahic Covenant dictates how to live in that world. Both are active covenants by which God governs mankind and grants authority to mankind. Adam forfeited his authority, but we have seen that in Noah all are called to build culture, to be fruitful and multiply.

This kingdom of creation is the common kingdom in which mankind lives today, and in which all human societies exist. Its curses apply to all mankind, and its promises and blessings apply to all mankind. This kingdom does not offer salvation, or saving grace, but it is pure kindness from God to pour out rain and sunshine on all mankind, commonly, rather than curse and death. Thus, we can speak of this kingdom existing in the realm of common grace. God is preserving the world with everyone in it, and the unbeliever has just as much a right to the promise of common kindness as the believer because we are both citizens of a common cursed kingdom of common grace.

Ecclesiastes describes life in this kingdom as life under the sun. Things don't work right. The system is broken. Hard work doesn't always pay off. Sometimes laziness pays off. But everyone dies. Everyone is cursed, and everyone lives through the difficulties of success and failure, unpredictable to mankind. Our obligation, as the preacher concludes, is simply to fear

God, to acknowledge the King of our common covenant kingdom, and to keep His commandments. We can do no more than trust and obey.

Conclusion

So then, kingdom and covenant give us a clear and concrete way not just of describing the world in convenient terms, but of defining the world biblically. We live in the kingdom of creation, a common cursed kingdom of common grace, established and governed by the Covenant of Works and the Noahic Covenant. This kingdom is destined for destruction in the Covenant of Works, like the City of Destruction in Bunyan's *The Pilgrim's Progress*. But it is also promised preservation in the Noahic Covenant for the sake of the fulfillment of all of God's promises, and all mankind benefits from that kindness and common grace.

Part Three

The Kingdom of Israel

The Covenant of Works and the Noahic Covenant establish and govern the kingdom of creation. Both covenants have the same realm in view, they both include commands for the people of that realm, and they provide certain blessings for the people in that realm. The Covenant of Works condemns and curses mankind, but the Noahic Covenant preserves mankind for the sake of the fulfillment of God's promises.

Within the stabilized stage of creation, thanks to the Noahic Covenant, God established a new realm, a new kingdom, covenanted to a special people through a federal head. That kingdom is the kingdom of Israel. From Genesis 12 onward, the entirety of the Old Testament Scriptures has this kingdom in view, and therefore it is in this kingdom that we see the progressive typological revelation of the mystery of Christ.

This in turn makes the kingdom of Israel a subservient kingdom, and its covenants subservient covenants. In other words, they serve the purposes of preparing the world for the unveiling of the mystery of Christ, His covenant, and His kingdom. They provide the preparatory foundation out of which and upon which the eternal plan of God will be realized. The kingdom of Israel is the matrix of the kingdom of Christ; the covenants of Israel are the matrix of the covenant of Christ; Israel is the true and real mother of the Christ.

6

The Abrahamic Covenant

Introduction

Up to this point in our study the nation of Israel did not exist. Its progenitors existed, but there was no formal or official recognition of the nation that we know as Israel. Nor was there one particular people recognized as the people of God. Neither was there one particular place recognized as the land of such a people. The Israelite kingdom was established by covenants through which God delegated dominion over Canaan to Abraham and his descendants. This began with the Abrahamic Covenant.

1. The Initiation of the Covenant

The beginnings of the covenant God made with Abraham[1] are found in Genesis 12:1–7. Subsequent portions of Scripture elaborate on and expand on this foundation.

> 1 Now the LORD said to Abram, 'Go from your country and your kindred and your father's house to the land that I will show you. 2 And *I will make of you a great nation,* and I will bless you and make your name great, so that you will be a blessing. 3 I will bless those who bless you, and him who dishonors you I will curse, and *in you all the families of the earth shall be blessed.'* 4 So Abram went, as the LORD had told him.... When they came to the land of Canaan, 6 Abram passed through the land to

---

[1] Though Abraham does not receive this name until Genesis 17, it is easier to use the same name throughout.

the place at Shechem, to the oak of Moreh. At that time the Canaanites were in the land. 7 Then the LORD appeared to Abram and said, '*To your offspring I will give this land.*'

There are three things to note in the initiation of Abraham's covenant.

a. The federal head

God always transacts His covenants through federal heads. One person stands for the whole. In the Covenant of Works, God covenanted with mankind through Adam, so also with Noah in the Noahic Covenant. And in this case, God made a covenant with Abraham as a federal head over his natural posterity. Genesis 12:2, 3, 7 make this clear. God tells Abraham that he will become the father of a great nation and that *his* descendants will inherit Canaan. Abraham is the federal head of this covenant. God said, '*To your offspring* I will give this land.' Participation in these promises depends on whether you are encompassed by the federal headship of Abraham. The blessings and curses of the covenant flow through the federal head. As goes the king, so goes the kingdom.

b. The inheritance of Canaan

God promised to Abraham in verse seven that he and his descendants would inherit the land of Canaan. It would belong to them by right. This is not just the beginning of a covenant; this is the beginning of a kingdom granted through a covenant. This is the beginning of the kingdom of Israel. A realm has now been set aside for a people belonging to a federal head. Before this, there was no Israel. There was no land that peculiarly belonged to a people in covenant God. This covenant constituted Abraham and his descendants a kingdom-people by promising them the land of Canaan.

c. The blessing for the nations

The Israelite kingdom and its covenants are preparatory and subservient to God's final purposes (Ephesians 1:10; 3:8–12). They carry and expand the revelation of God's plan of salvation precisely because of the foundational promise that a universal blessing will flow through Abraham's descendants to the world who now have a specific location on the global map. In Abraham's family, whose inheritance is Canaan, will all the nations of the earth be blessed. The mystery of Christ will unfold in this place among this people. Israel is the matrix of the mystery of Christ.

This promise must be treated carefully, and its full explanation must be deferred until later. But note for now that though God covenanted the birth of the Messiah to Abraham, this is first a promise of connection by birth, a connection according to the flesh. In other words, this covenant provides a descendant who will bless. But it does not provide a relationship to that descendant beyond a common genealogy. The descendant will provide the blessing, and enjoyment of that blessing will depend on one's relationship to the descendant, not to Abraham.

In the beginnings of God's covenantal dealings with Abraham, God established a nation. But from the beginning, this promise of universal blessing from one nation involved a transnational mindset. The blessing that was to come from their midst, genealogically, was meant for all nations. As a result, the nation of Israel should never have prided itself in its national identity in any way that would eclipse or subvert the transnational teleology of its existence. The nation is established by covenant in order to bring about a blessing for all nations. As we will see later, the purpose of the people is to bring forth the messiah. The Old Covenant is to give birth to the New Covenant. The kingdom of Israel is to give birth to the kingdom of Christ.

2. The Confirmation of the Covenant

The covenant initiated in Genesis 12 through promises is confirmed in Genesis 15. This is a confirmation of the covenant because it includes an official covenant-making ceremony. A promise is just a promise, as a command is just a command, but sanctions formalize and finalize a covenant.

1 After these things the word of the LORD came to Abram in a vision: "Fear not, Abram, I am your shield; your reward shall be very great." 2 But Abram said, "O Lord GOD, what will you give me, for I continue childless, and the heir of my house is Eliezer of Damascus?" 3 And Abram said, "Behold, you have given me no offspring, and a member of my household will be my heir." 4 And behold, the word of the LORD came to him: "This man shall not be your heir; your very own son shall be your heir." 5 And he brought him outside and said, *"Look toward heaven, and number the stars, if you are able to number them." Then he said to him, "So shall your offspring be."* 6 And he believed the LORD, and he counted it to him as righteousness. 7 And he said to him, "I am the LORD who brought you out from Ur of the Chaldeans to give you this land to possess." 8 But he said, *"O Lord GOD, how am I to know that I shall possess it?"* 9 He said to him, "Bring me a heifer three years old, a female goat three years old, a ram three years old, a turtledove, and a young pigeon." 10 And he brought him all these, cut them in half, and laid each half over against

the other. But he did not cut the birds in half. 11 And when birds of prey came down on the carcasses, Abram drove them away. 12 As the sun was going down, a deep sleep fell on Abram. And behold, dreadful and great darkness fell upon him. 13 Then the LORD said to Abram, "Know for certain that your offspring will be sojourners in a land that is not theirs and will be servants there, and they will be afflicted for four hundred years. 14 But I will bring judgment on the nation that they serve, and afterward they shall come out with great possessions. 15 As for you, you shall go to your fathers in peace; you shall be buried in a good old age. 16 And *they shall come back here in the fourth generation,* for the iniquity of the Amorites is not yet complete." 17 When the sun had gone down and it was dark, behold, a smoking fire pot and a flaming torch passed between these pieces. 18 *On that day the LORD made a covenant with Abram, saying, "To your offspring I give this land,* from the river of Egypt to the great river, the river Euphrates, 19 the land of the Kenites, the Kenizzites, the Kadmonites, 20 the Hittites, the Perizzites, the Rephaim, 21 the Amorites, the Canaanites, the Girgashites and the Jebusites."

In verses 5 and 7 God promised to make Abraham's descendants as numerous as the sand on the sea and to place them in the land of Canaan. This repeats the promises in Genesis 12, but now places them in an official covenant making ceremony. What was initiated in Genesis 12 is confirmed in Genesis 15. Genesis 15:18 provides the biblical summary of the covenant. "On that day the LORD made a covenant with Abraham, saying, 'To your offspring I give this land.'" These are the promises of the Abrahamic Covenant.

God's promises prompted a childless Abraham to ask for a confirmation beyond a bare promise. "8 But he said, 'O Lord GOD, how am I to know that I shall possess it?'" At this point, sanctions are added to confirm the covenant.

Sanctions guarantee the fulfillment of covenantal commitments. Abraham asked for confirmation from God regarding the promise of the multiplication of his descendants and their settling in Canaan, and *God swore an oath to Abram that these promises would indeed be fulfilled.* He commanded Abraham to split several animals and put their carcasses in two rows. Then God put Abraham into a deep sleep, and gave him a vision where a smoking fire pot and a flaming torch passed through the animal pieces. Having reviewed the biblical data on sanctions previously, the significance of the fire pot and torch passing through the animal parts is clear. God is making an oath saying, "May the same be done to Me and more also if I fail to keep My promise." God sanctioned His commitment to Abraham, making it a covenant. God will multiply Abraham's offspring, and He will give them the land of Canaan. Genesis 12 and 15 constitute a complete covenant by definition, but the Abrahamic covenant was not yet complete. Genesis 17 expands the commitments of the covenant.

3. The Expansion of the Covenant

It is important to note the continuity of promises between Genesis 12, 15, and 17. Genesis 15:18 summed up the covenant as a covenant to give the land to Abraham's offspring, as it had likewise been described in Genesis 12:7. The scope of Genesis 17 is identical and deals directly with Abraham's offspring receiving and living in the land. The promises of multiplied descendants and their territorial inheritance in Canaan are repeated in Genesis 17:4–8. Genesis 17 is an *expansion* of the covenant because God expanded and enlarged it through a promise of royalty, and a demand for loyalty.

In Genesis 17:6 God said, "I will make you exceedingly fruitful, and I will make you into nations, and kings shall come from you." Not only will Abraham's descendants be multiplied into nations, and not only will they live in Canaan, but they will be governed by their own ruling kings. This promise is repeated to Sarah in verse 16. "I will bless her, and moreover, I will give you a son by her. I will bless her, and she shall become nations; kings of peoples shall come from her." It is also repeated to Jacob in Genesis 35:11. "I am God Almighty: be fruitful and multiply. A nation and a company of nations shall come from you, and kings shall come from your own body."

In Jacob's sons Israel began to branch into nations and tribes. The promise of royalty and kingship was narrowed to one tribe in particular in Genesis 49:8–10.

> 8 Judah, your brothers shall praise you; your hand shall be on the neck of your enemies; your father's sons shall bow down before you. 9 Judah is a lion's cub; from the prey, my son, you have gone up. He stooped down; he crouched as a lion and as a lioness; who dares rouse him? 10 The scepter shall not depart from Judah, nor the ruler's staff from between his feet, until tribute comes to him; and to him shall be the obedience of the peoples.

This is an expansion and development of the kingdom of Israel, promised to Abraham in general, specified to Judah in particular. The kingdom is established and governed by the covenant.

God's demand for loyalty in Abraham's offspring is of utmost importance.

> And God said to Abraham, "As for you, you shall keep my covenant, you and your offspring after you throughout their generations" (Genesis 17:9).

The verb "to keep" is the same verb used in Genesis 2:15 when God placed Adam in the garden to work and keep it. In other words, this is a demand for strict obedience from Abraham and his descendants. The way in which they will keep the covenant is the circumcision of all males on the eighth day after their birth. Circumcision will be the sign of the covenant, making the covenant "in [their] flesh" "throughout [their] generations."

A sanction was put in place to guarantee the fulfillment of this commitment. Failure to keep the demand of the covenant will result in disinheritance.

> Any uncircumcised male who is not circumcised in the flesh of his foreskin shall be cut off from his people; he has broken my covenant (Genesis 17:14).

Ongoing participation in the blessings of Abraham's covenant depended on obedience to a positive law. Circumcision was not a moral issue. It was a positive law that could be, and was, removed later in history. A failure to circumcise prior to this command was in no way a form of disobedience to God, by anyone. But circumcision was added to the covenant as a positive law, deriving its obligation and the details of its administration purely from the divine authority of God.

The primary purpose of circumcision was to mark the boundaries of the people of this covenant. The offspring of Abraham and inheritors of his covenant are not just those who dwell in Canaan, but those who bear the sign of his covenant in their flesh. The blessing for the nations will come from the people who belong to the covenant of circumcision.

Abraham's offspring, circumcised according to God's command, had a legal covenantal right to Canaan. But their inheritance could be annulled by breaking the law of circumcision. Disobedience forfeited the rights to the blessings of the covenant. Circumcision thus signified not only the special promises that God made to Abraham and his descendants, but it also served as a sign of curse sanctions for Abraham and his descendants. Just as God passed through the bisected animals as a self-directed threat, so also God placed Abraham and his descendants under threat. If they did not obey, they would be cut off from the people just as their flesh had been cut off. Genesis 17:14 uses the language of cutting off very specifically and intentionally. The one who does not cut off his foreskin will be cut off from the covenant. Circumcision was thus a promise of blessings and a threat of curses at the same time.

The children of Abraham were a marvelously blessed people. Sadly, throughout their life as a nation Israel became overinflated with pride. They often divided the world into the "circumcised" and "uncircumcised." The uncircumcised are always spoken of in derogatory terms as those who were unclean, not chosen, not special, to be excluded, to be avoided, to be conquered, to be mocked. The Israelites turned circumcision into a badge of pride. They were always eager to appeal to God's special favor and promises. But they were very rarely eager to recognize the transnational purpose of their own existence, or to give two seconds of thought to the threatened curses in circumcision.

It is important to notice how Genesis 12, 15, and 17 build on each other. Some have strongly contrasted Genesis 15 and Genesis 17 because Genesis 15 seems to be unilateral and guaranteed while Genesis 17 seems to be bilateral and conditional. But all of these elements of the Abrahamic Covenant go together. God promised Abraham that He would multiply his descendants into nations with kings that would dwell in Canaan after a time of slavery, and that from these numerous descendants an offspring would be born who would mediate blessing to the world. As for Abraham and his descendants, they must keep God's commands, particularly circumcision, or else they forfeit participation in the promised blessings.

The apparent tension between God's guaranteed promises and the threats of expulsion from the kingdom for disobedience is resolved in that although the promises were nationally guaranteed, they were not individually guaranteed.[2] God kept His promises. Abraham's descendants did multiply. They did inherit Canaan. The promised seed was born. But not every Israelite enjoyed the full benefits of God's blessings. They did not fulfill their commitments. The promises were nationally guaranteed, but not individually guaranteed. The wilderness generation and Moses are good examples of this. The wilderness generation did not enter Canaan because of their disbelief at their first arrival. Moses did not enter the promised land because he disobeyed God's command about speaking to the rock and struck it instead. Yet God fulfilled His promises corporately and nationally to Israel though individuals cut themselves off from the covenant through unfaithfulness. The Bible itself declares that God discharged His duties and fulfilled His obligations completely.

---

[2] Anonymous, *Truth Vindicated in Several Branches* (London: n.p., 1695), 279–280. Speaking of the Abrahamic Covenant (which included the Mosaic), "This Covenant is partly absolute, and partly conditional, that some of *Abraham's* Seed should possess the Land of *Canaan*, that was absolute…but their continuance in it, and their Posterity in the enjoyment of it, did hang all on Conditions of their Obedience, *Deut.* 28:1–2."

The Abrahamic Covenant includes sanctioned commitments for both God and the offspring of Abraham. Both sides must keep their commitments, and sanctions guarantee their participation. But, from man's perspective, the principle that governs enjoyment of the blessings of the covenant is obedience to a positive command. God will not fail to fulfill His promises, but the Israelites must not fail to persevere. Consequently, this covenant can be classified as a covenant based on works, or obedience. God kept all of His promises and fulfilled all of His commitments. The covenant was realized in full. But all lack of enjoyment and fulfillment stemmed from the unfaithfulness of the covenant people to their covenant God.

4. The Realization of the Covenant

The Scriptures carefully record God's fulfillment of His promises. God gave the land of Canaan to Abraham's descendants.

> 43 Thus the LORD gave to Israel all the land that he swore to give to their fathers. And they took possession of it, and they settled there. 44 And the LORD gave them rest on every side just as he had sworn to their fathers. Not one of all their enemies had withstood them, for the LORD had given all their enemies into their hands. 45 Not one word of all the good promises that the LORD had made to the house of Israel had failed; all came to pass (Joshua 21:43–45).

> 7 You are the LORD, the God who chose Abram and brought him out of Ur of the Chaldeans and gave him the name Abraham. 8 You found his heart faithful before you, and made with him the covenant to give to his offspring the land of the Canaanite, the Hittite, the Amorite, the Perizzite, the Jebusite, and the Girgashite. And you have kept your promise, for you are righteous (Nehemiah 9:7–8).

God multiplied Abraham's descendants.

> Judah and Israel were as many as the sand by the sea. They ate and drank and were happy (1 Kings 4:20).

> Therefore from one man, and him as good as dead, were born descendants as many as the stars of heaven and as many as the innumerable grains of sand by the seashore (Hebrews 11:12).

God brought forth the promised seed from Abraham's descendants. Mary and Zechariah declare this.

54 He has helped his servant Israel, in remembrance of his mercy, 55 as he spoke to our fathers, to Abraham and to his offspring forever (Luke 1:54–55).

68 Blessed be the Lord God of Israel, for he has visited and redeemed his people… 72 to show the mercy promised to our fathers and to remember his holy covenant, 73 the oath that he swore to our father Abraham, to grant us 74 that we, being delivered from the hand of our enemies, might serve him without fear, 75 in holiness and righteousness before him all our days (Luke 1:68, 72–75).

God was faithful to all His promises to Abraham. The Abrahamic Covenant was fully realized according to God's Word.

5. The Foundation of the Old Covenant

Genesis 12–17 establishes a foundation for redemptive history until the advent of Christ. The laws and promises of these chapters constitute Israel as a kingdom. The Abrahamic Covenant created their identity and defined them. The Israelites' entire lives were spent with these promises as their identifying features. As the kingdom of creation began with the Covenant of Works and was developed and expanded in the Noahic Covenant, so also the Abrahamic Covenant is merely the first among other covenants that will be added to this one in governing the kingdom of Israel.

Through this covenant, the kingdom realm, Canaan, is marked out. The kingdom people, Abraham's descendants, are marked out. And the Israelites from this point onward looked back to Abraham and his covenant for their identity and privileges. This is evident in the way that the Israelites themselves speak of themselves and this covenant. Many passages of Scripture emphasize Abraham as the federal head of this covenant and Canaan as its primary promise. Consistently, the covenant is described in an earthly sphere.

Isaac said to Jacob in Genesis 28:4, "May he give the blessing of Abraham to you and to your offspring with you, that you may take possession of the land of your sojournings that God gave to Abraham!"

God said to Jacob in Genesis 35:12, "The land that I gave to Abraham and Isaac I will give to you, and I will give the land to your offspring after you."

God said to Moses in Exodus 6:2–4, "2 I am the LORD. 3 I appeared to Abraham, to Isaac, and to Jacob, as God Almighty, but by my name the LORD I did not make myself known to them. 4 I also established *my covenant with them to give them the land of Canaan*, the land in which they lived as sojourners."

Moses said to the Lord in Exodus 32:13, "Remember Abraham, Isaac, and Israel, your servants, to whom you swore by your own self, and said to them, 'I will multiply your offspring as the stars of heaven, and all *this land that I have promised I will give to your offspring*, and they shall inherit it forever.'"

Moses said to the people of Israel in Deuteronomy 1:8, "See, I have set the land before you. Go in and take possession of *the land that the LORD swore to your fathers*, to Abraham, to Isaac, and to Jacob, to give to them and to their offspring after them."

God said to Joshua in Joshua 1:6, "Be strong and courageous, for you shall cause this people to inherit *the land that I swore to their fathers to give them*."

Psalm 105:6–11 is a wonderful example of this.

> 6 O offspring of Abraham, his servant, children of Jacob, his chosen ones! 7 He is the LORD our God; his judgments are in all the earth. 8 He remembers his covenant forever, the word that he commanded, for a thousand generations, 9 the covenant that he made with Abraham, his sworn promise to Isaac, 10 which he confirmed to Jacob as a statute, to Israel as an everlasting covenant, 11 saying, "To you I will give the land of Canaan as your portion for an inheritance."

God said to Jeremiah in Jeremiah 11:2–5,

> 2 Hear the words of this covenant, and speak to the men of Judah and the inhabitants of Jerusalem. 3 You shall say to them, "Thus says the LORD, the God of Israel: Cursed be the man who does not hear the words of this covenant 4 that I commanded your fathers when I brought them out of the land of Egypt, from the iron furnace, saying, Listen to my voice, and do all that I command you. So shall you be my people, and I will be your God, 5 that I may confirm *the oath that I swore to your fathers, to give them a land flowing with milk and honey, as at this day*."

The covenant is consistently summed up as a covenant to give the land to the descendants of Abraham. And later generations, no matter how far, looked to Abraham's federal headship as the foundation of their identity. Paul said in Romans 11:1 "I ask, then, has God rejected *his people*? By no means! For I myself am an Israelite, a descendant of Abraham, a member of the tribe of Benjamin."

Peter said in Acts 3:25–26, "25 You are the *sons* of the prophets and *of the covenant that God made with your fathers, saying to Abraham*, 'And in your offspring shall all the families of the earth be blessed.' 26 God, having raised up his servant, sent him to you first, to bless you by turning every one of you from your wickedness."

Stephen said in Acts 7:2–3, 8, "2 Brothers and fathers, hear me. The God of glory appeared to *our father Abraham* when he was in Mesopotamia, before he lived in Haran, 3 and said to him, 'Go out from your land and from your kindred and go into the land that I will show you.'… 8 And he gave him *the covenant of circumcision*. And so Abraham became the father of Isaac, and circumcised him on the eighth day, and Isaac became the father of Jacob, and Jacob of the twelve patriarchs."

Paul said in 2 Corinthians 11:22, "Are they Hebrews? So am I. Are they Israelites? So am I. Are they *offspring of Abraham*? So am I."

The writer to the Hebrews said in Hebrews 7:5, "And those descendants of Levi who receive the priestly office have a commandment in the law to take tithes from the people, that is, from *their brothers, though these also are descended from Abraham*."

John the Baptist said to the Jews in Luke 3:8–9, "8 Bear fruits in keeping with repentance. And do not begin to say to yourselves, *'We have Abraham as our father.'* For I tell you, God is able from these stones to raise up children for Abraham. 9 Even now the axe is laid to the root of the trees. Every tree therefore that does not bear good fruit is cut down and thrown into the fire."

These passages emphasize and reinforce the fact that the Abrahamic Covenant is first and foremost an earthly covenant of national earthly promises. Whether examining the covenant itself in Genesis 12, 15, and 17, or whether tracing Israel's own self-conscious identity throughout its generations, the consistent theme is that those who descend from Abraham according to the flesh inherit the land of Canaan. This is the foundational identity of Israel through Abraham's covenant.

As a covenantal foundation, we find that in the Scriptures subsequent covenants are made with the same parties (Abraham's offspring) in the same kingdom-realm (Canaan) with the same promises (blessed life in Canaan) with the same precepts (positive laws) and the same penalties (disinheritance). Therefore, what is commonly known as the Old Covenant began with Abraham and ought to be viewed collectively in such a way that the Old Covenant includes the Abrahamic covenant, the Mosaic Covenant, and the Davidic Covenant.[3] This argument is developed in the ensuing chapters, but it simply notes that what the Abrahamic Covenant establishes, the Mosaic and Davidic Covenants connect to and expand.

[3] Referring to the covenant of circumcision, "Yet we say, it was a distinct Covenant, and therefore called the Old Covenant, and the Covenant of grace the new Covenant." Hutchinson, *A Treatise Concerning the Covenant and Baptism*, 93.

a. The Abrahamic Covenant anticipates the Mosaic Covenant

The Abrahamic Covenant anticipates the Mosaic Covenant in that it tells the Israelites that they will be disinherited if they don't keep the covenant. Circumcision is the first among many positive laws and covenantal obligations that determine whether the Israelites enjoy the blessings that God provides. From Genesis 17 onward, they can forfeit their inheritance through disobedience. That is a prominent feature of the Mosaic Covenant, and it's important to see it begin in the Abrahamic Covenant. Nehemiah Coxe stated, "In *this Mode* of transacting [the Abrahamic Covenant], the Lord was pleased to draw the first Lines of that Form of Covenant-Relation, which the natural Seed of *Abraham*, were fully stated in by the *Law of Moses*, which was a *Covenant of Works*, and its Condition or Terms, *Do this and live.*"[4]

The covenant God made with Israel through Moses is a giant expansion of what begins with Abraham in circumcision. As for Abraham and his descendants, they will keep the covenant, or they will be expelled from it. The Mosaic Covenant lays out laws and tells Israel that if they obey it will go well with them in the land. If they disobey, they will be exiled. The Abrahamic Covenant, therefore, anticipates the Mosaic Covenant. The scope of both covenants is identical—life in Canaan, as is the people to whom the covenants apply—the offspring of Abraham. Abraham's covenant establishes the covenantal kingdom foundation. Moses' covenant plays out in it and expands upon it.

The time that passed between the two covenants, just over 400 years, helps to explain the connection and relation between circumcision and the larger list of laws given through Moses. While still a nomadic people, the complete kingdom laws were unnecessary and of no use. While slaves in Egypt, the same was true. But as soon as the Exodus took place and Israel began its march toward the promised land, the full complex of laws was delivered to them. The circumcised must obey these laws in order to enjoy the inheritance. The passage of time between the two covenants, which was promised by God in Genesis 15:13 therefore shows how the Abrahamic Covenant anticipates the Mosaic Covenant above all through circumcision and the threat of disinheritance.

---

[4] Coxe, *A Discourse of the Covenants*, 104. He added, "This Chapter leads us on a great Step towards the *Sinai Covenant*, and the Terms thereof." Coxe, *A Discourse of the Covenants*, 105.

b. The Abrahamic covenant anticipates the Davidic Covenant

The Abrahamic Covenant includes a promise of royalty twice, once to Abraham, once to Sarah. That promise is picked up and carried along at least twice again, once to Jacob, and once to Judah. Abraham and his descendants, which will be a numerous nation in a large land, have been promised kings. This anticipates the Davidic Covenant.

c. The Abrahamic Covenant anticipates the New Covenant

The Abrahamic Covenant anticipates the New Covenant in two ways. First, it promises the New Covenant. Second it typologically pictures or prefigures the New Covenant.

As mentioned above, this covenant promises to provide one who will bless the world. The Scriptures reveal that the blessing for the world is the New Covenant. The benefits of Jesus Christ's salvific life, death, and resurrection are made available to all the world through the New Covenant. So, from its inception, the Abrahamic Covenant is not just anticipating the New Covenant but carrying it within itself. The Old Covenant is pregnant with the New Covenant. It promises the New Covenant because it promises the Mediator of the New Covenant to be born from their midst. The Abrahamic Covenant provides Christ. Christ provides the New Covenant.

Typologically, the Abrahamic Covenant is a picture of something other and greater than itself. Its people, land, and kingship were pictures of a greater, and other, people, land, and kingship. As Meredith Kline said,

> We have found that in the course of biblical revelation two distinct levels of fulfillment, one provisional and prototypal, the other messianic and eternal, are clearly distinguishable in the king promise given to Abraham. What is true of the promise of the king must inevitably be true of the promise of the kingdom, both kingdom-people and kingdom-land.[5]

In other words, the multiplied offspring of Abraham's body in Canaan under their own rulers are types. But as types, they point onward to an antitypical fulfillment on a heavenly level, through a heavenly covenant. The great privilege of Israel, established in the Abrahamic Covenant, is that the one who will effect and bring about that final fulfillment will be one of their own.

The Abrahamic Covenant promises a particular offspring through whom the nations of the world will be blessed. From the beginning, there-

---

[5] Kline, *Kingdom Prologue*, 334.

fore, there is in the Abrahamic Covenant an anticipation of a transnational blessing that includes people beyond the borders of the Abrahamic people (Romans 4:10). The Abrahamic Covenant looks forward to one through whom all nations can be united and blessed, not just one people in one place. The typology of the Abrahamic Covenant and its special relation to Christ according to the flesh make it a covenant of guardianship. The purpose of the Abrahamic Covenant is to bring the New Covenant into existence by bringing its founder, head, and mediator into existence.

There is no covenant prior to Christ that reveals His covenant as directly as the Abrahamic Covenant does. The unilateral and free gift of the earthly typical promises most clearly demonstrates the unilateral and free gift of the heavenly antitypical promises to the elect. And Abraham's belief in the greater reality that those earthly promises pointed to is set forth by Scripture as the paradigmatic model for belief in all history. Abraham is the man of faith, and all those who believe as he did, are his children, not according to the flesh, and not according to his covenant, but according to the Spirit, according to the pattern of his faith, and according to the New Covenant of the offspring of Abraham, Jesus Christ.

Scripture tells us that Abraham and other Old Testament saints understood these things, not completely, but sufficiently. They believed the mystery as revealed by typology. Hebrews 11:9–10 says that "9 By faith he went to live in the land of promise, as in a foreign land, living in tents with Isaac and Jacob, heirs with him of the same promise. 10 For he was looking forward to the city that has foundations, whose designer and builder is God." Abraham knew there was a land greater than Canaan.

But Abraham was not alone. Old Testament saints understood typology. They knew there was a greater reality beyond their earthly inheritance and blessings. And they are therefore one people with believers today. The universal church did not begin with Christ and the apostles. It began with Adam and Eve and included Noah, Abraham, Isaac, Jacob, Moses, David, and so many more Israelites who believed in the promises of the gospel as they were made known through shadows and pictures, through typology. Their experience of salvation was the same as ours, though their knowledge of it was incomplete. They saw and greeted from afar that which they never fully understood. But their inheritance is a heavenly city, a new Jerusalem, and they are our brothers and sisters among the children of God.

Their heavenly inheritance did not come to them through the Abrahamic Covenant, the covenant of circumcision. Their inheritance came through the one promised in the Abrahamic Covenant and His covenant, the New Covenant of grace. The Abrahamic Covenant was designed to push history towards this by marking out the people and place of the Messiah's birth, and it was designed to foreshadow it, positively and negatively, in God's promises and Israel's failures.

The covenant of circumcision is a covenant of guardianship. It is a covenant that constitutes Abraham's descendants the womb of the Messiah. And as Abraham trusted in the Son of his covenant, he became a child of the Son's covenant. As Abraham looked past the earthly blessings to the heavenly ones, and believed in them, all Israel was called to do the same. But they were so pleased with their menus, that they didn't want to eat the food when it arrived.

d. The Abrahamic covenant echoes Eden

Typology develops progressively. What was established protologically in the garden of Eden with Adam is picked up and expanded in the Abrahamic Covenant. The Abrahamic Covenant does not simply anticipate redemptive history; it also echoes redemptive history. In Eden, God created a special place where a particular person was entrusted with a commission that would bring blessing and progress to the world. Abraham was given a new special place where a particular descendant of his will bring blessing to the world. Abraham's descendants must be faithful to God's commands in order to remain in that special land of blessing. Throughout the Old Testament, Israel is treated as a new son of God with a new temple in a new paradise. But like Adam, they were an unfaithful son and they were cursed, disinherited, and expelled.

Conclusion

In successive stages, God made a covenant with Abraham, promising him that his multiplied offspring would inherit Canaan and live there under their own rulers after a period of several hundred years of sojourning and slavery. God will assuredly make this happen. As for Abraham and his descendants, they must keep the covenant by circumcising their males on the eighth day. If they do not keep the covenant, they will be disinherited not as a nation, but as individuals. From among the children of Abraham, one of them will bring a blessing for all the families of the earth, for all the nations.

7

The Mosaic Covenant

Introduction

The source of God's first dealings with Abraham was the infinite goodness and kindness of God. That Abraham and his family should be the womb of world blessing, and that they should be given the opportunity to live in Canaan was not the result of any goodness or worthiness in them, but rather it was the result of the abundant graciousness and lovingkindness of God. Israel had every natural and covenantal reason to serve God and obey Him out of gratitude and thanksgiving. But their enslavement in and Exodus from Egypt provided an even richer context for their obedience.

1. The Context of the Covenant

a. The promise of oppression and affliction

In Genesis 15:13–16 God had made it known to Abraham that prior to receiving the full inheritance of the land of Canaan, four hundred years would pass, a large portion of which would be spent in a foreign land serving foreign masters. That is a considerable span of time. Many churches today use confessions of faith from the sixteenth and seventeenth centuries. Those confessions of faith are around four hundred years old. Much changes in four hundred years.

For an Israelite slave who grew up in Egypt, the stories of their grandfathers were just stories. The only things that they knew were enslavement and the grandeur of ancient Egypt in its economic, military, and religious glory. The names of Jacob, Isaac, and Abraham were just names. It was in this context that the Israelites cried out to the God they barely knew.

23 During those many days the king of Egypt died, and the people of Israel groaned because of their slavery and cried out for help. Their cry for rescue from slavery came up to God. 24 And God heard their groaning, and *God remembered his covenant with Abraham*, with Isaac, and with Jacob. 25 God saw the people of Israel—and God knew (Exodus 2:23–25).

God had promised that Israel's bondage would expire four hundred years from Genesis 15. Exodus 12:40–41 reaffirms this.[1]

40 The time that the people of Israel lived in Egypt was 430 years. 41 At the end of 430 years, on that very day, all the hosts of the LORD went out from the land of Egypt.

Time was up.

b. The promise of liberation and fulfilment

The context of the Mosaic Covenant is first Israel's slavery in Egypt. In addition to that, God promised that He would bring Abraham's descendants into the inheritance of Canaan, a promise not yet fulfilled. So there had to be some kind of deliverance in order for that to take place.

Exodus 3:13–17 initiates this deliverance. God appeared to Moses in the burning bush, telling Moses to go speak to the people on God's behalf. Moses asked God what he should say to the Israelites because their relationship with God was very estranged, and the promises were very old.

13 Then Moses said to God, "If I come to the people of Israel and say to them, 'The God of your fathers has sent me to you,' and they ask me, 'What is his name?' what shall I say to them?" 14 God said to Moses, "I AM WHO I AM." And he said, "Say this to the people of Israel, 'I AM has sent me to you.'" 15 God also said to Moses, "Say this to the people of Israel, 'The LORD, the God of your fathers, *the God of Abraham*, the God of Isaac, and the God of Jacob, has sent me to you.' This is my name forever, and thus I am to be remembered throughout all generations. 16 Go and gather the elders of Israel together and say to them, 'The LORD, the God of your fathers, *the God of Abraham*, of Isaac, and of Jacob, has appeared to

---

[1] 430 years is calculated from Genesis 12. Cf. Owen, *Exercitations on the Epistle to the Hebrews Concerning the Priesthood of Christ...With a Continuation of the Exposition on the Third, Fourth, and Fifth Chapters* (London: John Darby, 1674), 261; Coxe, *A Discourse of the Covenants*, 73–74.

me, saying, 'I have observed you and what has been done to you in Egypt,
17 and I promise that I will bring you up out of the affliction of Egypt to
the land of the Canaanites, the Hittites, the Amorites, the Perizzites, the
Hivites, and the Jebusites, a land flowing with milk and honey.'

God declared Himself to be the God of the Israelites' fathers. He was
now going to fulfill His promises to Abraham. In Exodus 6:1–5 God announced that His deliverance of Israel from Egypt is taking place because
of the Abrahamic Covenant.

> 1 But the LORD said to Moses, "Now you shall see what I will do to
> Pharaoh; for with a strong hand he will send them out, and with a strong
> hand he will drive them out of his land." 2 God spoke to Moses and said
> to him, "I am the LORD. 3 I appeared to Abraham, to Isaac, and to Jacob,
> as God Almighty, but by my name the LORD I did not make myself
> known to them. 4 I also established *my covenant with them to give them the
> land of Canaan,* the land in which they lived as sojourners. 5 Moreover, I
> have heard the groaning of the people of Israel whom the Egyptians hold
> as slaves, and *I have remembered my covenant.*"

The context of the Mosaic Covenant, therefore, is the Abrahamic
Covenant.[2] God had promised to Abraham that all of this would happen.
It came to pass, and God was now going to deliver Israel out of Egypt
according to His Word. God made this known to Israel through Moses,
declaring that the God of their fathers was about to fulfill the covenant
He had sworn to their fathers. They, being the offspring of Abraham, had
a right and title to those promises, no matter how much time had passed
since the giving of the promise. God's deliverance of this generation was
His faithfulness to Abraham, their federal head.

With incredible power, might, and majesty, God redeemed His people
Israel. God overpowered the greatest human power, the Egyptians, and
overpowered the greatest natural power, the great deep, and as Psalm 77:20
says, "You led your people like a flock by the hand of Moses and Aaron."
If Israel's relationship with God was minimal prior to these events, the
Exodus profoundly impacted the Israelite mind. God swept Israel off its
feet as their redeemer, their husband, here to take her home to safety and
blessing and prosperity, ready to shower her with good gifts. The rest of the
Old Testament is full of direct references and allusions to the Exodus as
one of the most foundational events in its history.

---

[2] Cf. Thomas R. Schreiner, *Covenant and God's Purpose for the World* (Wheaton, IL: Crossway, 2017), 59. "Some mistakenly separate [the Mosaic Covenant]
almost altogether from the covenant with Abraham."

This is the context of the Mosaic Covenant. And it is important because the Mosaic Covenant is a development of the same covenantal relationship that God had initiated Abraham and his descendants.[3] The connection to the Abrahamic Covenant is heavy in the narrative, strengthening this bond, a bond that will continue.

2. The Kind of Covenant

The Mosaic Covenant is a development of the Abrahamic Covenant in which God made promises which He would fulfill nationally to Abraham's descendants while they, the descendants, must keep the covenant if they want to enjoy the benefits and blessings promised by God. The same kind of arrangement is established through the Mosaic Covenant. God declares the blessings He intends to pour out on Israel, but for the Israelites to enjoy the blessings, they must keep the covenant, the law.

a. Its laws

The nature and function of the laws of the covenant made through Moses demonstrate the kind of covenant that this is. The Mosaic Covenant revolves primarily, but not exclusively, around the laws which God gave to Israel through Moses. In Exodus 19:3–8 Israel has arrived at Sinai and God began giving the law to Israel through Moses.

> 3 The LORD called to [Moses] out of the mountain, saying, "Thus you shall say to the house of Jacob, and tell the people of Israel: 4 'You yourselves have seen what I did to the Egyptians, and how I bore you on eagles' wings and brought you to myself. 5 Now therefore, *if you will indeed obey my voice and keep my covenant, you shall be my treasured possession among all peoples, for all the earth is mine;* 6 and you shall be to me a kingdom of priests and a holy nation. These are the words that you shall speak to the people of Israel.'" 7 So Moses came and called the elders of the people and set before them all these words that the LORD had commanded him. 8 All the people answered together and said, *"All that the LORD has spoken we will do."* And Moses reported the words of the people to the LORD.

This covenant is based on God's commitment to bless the people of Abraham, and it is based on the people's commitment to obey God's laws.

---

[3] Cf. Fesko, *Last Things First*, 160. "What applies to the inauguration of the Mosaic covenant also applies to the Abrahamic covenant; the former is founded upon the latter (Exod. 2:24)."

The context of the giving of the law is the Exodus, God's powerful and gracious actions to free Israel from Egypt. But added to God's kindness is a demand for loyalty. As for them, they must obey God's voice and keep His covenant, so that they will be His treasured possession. The people respond, "All that the Lord has spoken we will do." Israel must obey the law in order to remain a blessed people. This is an identical arrangement to Genesis 17 where God rehearsed His kindness to Abraham before demanding obedience with a threat of disinheritance. The people with whom this covenant is transacted align identically with those of Genesis 17, the offspring of Abraham according to the flesh.

In the next chapter, God delivers the Ten Commandments to Moses. They begin with a repetition of God's powerful deliverance. "1 And God spoke all these words, saying, 2 'I am the LORD your God, who brought you out of the land of Egypt, out of the house of slavery.'" God's demand for loyalty is based on what He has done for Israel. Nevertheless, Israel must be faithful in order to remain in the blessings of the covenant.

After the law was delivered to Moses, which the people already pledged to keep, Moses came down the mountain to deliver the law to the people. There the people respond again in Exodus 24:3–8. Their response is a confirmation by covenant, placing them under sanction.

> 3 Moses came and told the people all the words of the LORD and all the rules. And all the people answered with one voice and said, *"All the words that the LORD has spoken we will do."* 4 And Moses wrote down all the words of the LORD. He rose early in the morning and built an altar at the foot of the mountain, and twelve pillars, according to the twelve tribes of Israel. 5 And he sent young men of the people of Israel, who offered burnt offerings and sacrificed peace offerings of oxen to the LORD. 6 And Moses took half of the blood and put it in basins, and half of the blood he threw against the altar. 7 Then he took the Book of the Covenant and read it in the hearing of the people. And they said, *"All that the LORD has spoken we will do, and we will be obedient."* 8 And Moses took the blood and threw it on the people and said, "Behold the blood of the covenant that the LORD has made with you in accordance with all these words."

The sprinkling of blood is an oath of loyalty and a vow of accountability. It is the placement of sanctions in the covenantal relationship. "The same be done to us, and more also" is the idea behind it. As they had pledged in Exodus 19, so here they are pledging to be obedient.

Hebrews 9:18–23 tells us that this ritual not only produced sanctions, but also sanctification. The blood was a purification rite, a way of saying "You are my pure and precious people." And this idea combines with sanctions in that one must remain pure according to the covenantal commands or suffer the consequences. Despite their pledge of fidelity, Israel proved itself unfaithful soon after and asked Aaron to make a golden calf. Moses smashed the first set of the Ten Commandments, so God ordered him to make another set.

The way that God spoke of the law in Exodus 34:27–28 (the second giving of the law) is important.

> 27 And the LORD said to Moses, "Write these words, for *in accordance with these words I have made a covenant with you and with Israel.*" 28 So he was there with the LORD forty days and forty nights. He neither ate bread nor drank water. And he wrote on the tablets *the words of the covenant, the Ten Commandments.*"

The words of the covenant are the Ten Commandments. Therefore, the law, both moral and positive, is the foundation of this covenant. Israel swore obedience to the law, the law which God said if Israel kept they would be His treasured possession. This is a covenant based on obedience to the law. It has an oath of obedience and sanctions directed at those who must obey. If Israel obeys the law, they will enjoy the benefits of the covenant.

b. Its promises

The laws of the covenant are a large expansion on the initial command of circumcision in the Abrahamic Covenant. Yet they were fitting for a people about to settle in a land, a people about to establish an actual kingdom. A clan of nomads four hundred years separated from occupying Canaan did not need all of the social regulations imposed by the Mosaic law. Israel's exodus was supposed to funnel directly into the promised land, and it was only their disobedience and unbelief that kept them from it.

The promises of the Mosaic Covenant, therefore, are simply the enjoyment of what had already been declared to Abraham. If Israel keeps the law, then they will enjoy what God will surely provide for them. The command to honor parents is directly connected to long life in the land. And, as noted above, the exodus from Egypt took place in order that God might fulfill His promise to Abraham to bring his descendants into the land. But in order to enjoy the promises of the Abrahamic Covenant, Israel must obey not only the command of circumcision in the Abrahamic Covenant, but also the laws and statutes of the Mosaic Covenant.

This is demonstrated clearly in Jeremiah 11:2–5,

> 2 Hear the words of this covenant, and speak to the men of Judah and the inhabitants of Jerusalem. 3 You shall say to them, "Thus says the LORD,

the God of Israel: *Cursed be the man who does not hear the words of this cov-*
enant 4 *that I commanded your fathers when I brought them out of the land of*
Egypt, from the iron furnace, saying, Listen to my voice, and do all that I
command you. So shall you be my people, and I will be your God, 5 that I
may confirm *the oath that I swore to your fathers, to give them a land flowing*
with milk and honey, as at this day" (cf. Jeremiah 7:3–7).

Because the Abrahamic Covenant and the Mosaic Covenant work
together, as two covenants governing the kingdom of Israel, the corpo-
rate and individual principles intertwine. God will provide the promised
blessings to the people as a nation, corporately. Individually, those who are
unfaithful will be cut off. This is illustrated by at least two cases. When
Aaron and many of the Israelites committed idolatry with the golden calf,
many individual Israelites were killed for their infidelity according to the
covenant. But Moses appealed to God's promise to preserve the nation in
general according to the Abrahamic Covenant as the basis upon which
God must not destroy them entirely (Exodus 32:13). Additionally, a whole
generation of Israelites died in the wilderness for their disobedience and
disbelief, but God made the promises good to the next generation.

The promises of the Mosaic Covenant are nothing more and nothing less than those of the Abrahamic Covenant. If Israel obeys the Mosaic Covenant, they will enjoy the blessings of the Abrahamic Covenant.[4]
God told Israel that if they would heed His voice, then they would be His
treasured possession. If they will not heed His voice, they will not enjoy
the promises given to them through Abraham. The curses of the covenant
make this point most clearly.

c. Its threats

In Israel's covenant making ceremony, blood was spattered on them.
Israel vowed obedience to the law, recognizing that their pledge was sanctioned with a threat of death. The blood of the covenant was sprinkled on
them. Moses made it crystal clear to the Israelites that if they obey, they
will be blessed in the land. If they disobey, they will be cursed and even
exiled.

The threat of curses is pronounced by Moses as Israel approaches entry
into the promised land after the unfaithful generation died in the wilderness. In Deuteronomy God renewed the same covenant made at Sinai
with the second generation. The same promises and the same threats are

[4] Cf. Schreiner, *Covenant and God's Purpose,* 61. "The tie between the two
covenants is evident, for the promises of the covenant with Abraham are secured
as Israel keeps the stipulations of the covenant at Sinai."

directed to the descendants because they remain the offspring of Abraham, the federal head through whom those blessings are inherited.

Though a thorough investigation would require reading the entirety of Deuteronomy, select passages must suffice to demonstrate the function of the sanctions relative to the laws and promises of the covenant.

> 20 "When your son asks you in time to come, 'What is the meaning of the testimonies and the statutes and the rules that the LORD our God has commanded you?' 21 then you shall say to your son... 24 'And *the LORD commanded us to do all these statutes*, to fear the LORD our God, for our good always, *that he might preserve us alive*, as we are this day. 25 *And it will be righteousness for us, if we are careful to do all this commandment* before the LORD our God, as he has commanded us'" (Deuteronomy 6:20, 24–25).

When Israelite children want to know what the covenant means, what the law is, the parents are to tell them that blessings accompany obedience.

> "26 See, I am setting before you today a blessing and a curse: 27 *the blessing, if you obey the commandments of the LORD your God, which I command you today*, 28 *and the curse, if you do not obey the commandments of the LORD your God*, but turn aside from the way that I am commanding you today, to go after other gods that you have not known" (Deuteronomy 11:26–28).

Deuteronomy 27:26 summarily states this principle. "Cursed be anyone who does not confirm the words of this law by doing them. And all the people shall say, 'Amen'"

Interestingly, God told Israel in Deuteronomy 29:22–28 that they would be unfaithful, that they would be cursed, and that they would be exiled. And God told Israel that when the curses are poured out on them, they are to tell their children that their own disobedience was the cause.

> 22 And the next generation, your children who rise up after you, and the foreigner who comes from a far land, will say, when they see the afflictions of that land and the sicknesses with which the LORD has made it sick— 23 the whole land burned out with brimstone and salt, nothing sown and nothing growing, where no plant can sprout, an overthrow like that of Sodom and Gomorrah, Admah, and Zeboiim, which the LORD overthrew in his anger and wrath— 24 all the nations will say, *'Why has the LORD done thus to this land? What caused the heat of this great anger?'* 25 Then people will say, *'It is because they abandoned the covenant of the LORD*, the God of their fathers, which he made with them when he brought them out of the land of Egypt, 26 and went and served other gods and worshiped them, gods whom they had not known and whom he had not allotted to them. 27 *Therefore the anger of the LORD was kindled*

against this land, bringing upon it all the curses written in this book, 28 and
the LORD uprooted them from their land in anger and fury and great
wrath, and cast them into another land, as they are this day.'"[5]

To be unfaithful to the covenant results in disinheritance and curse. That
is how it is set up beforehand, and that is how it ought to be explained in
hindsight. One more passage will bring this to a conclusion, Deuteronomy
30:15–20, a summary of the covenant.

> "15 See, I have set before you today life and good, death and evil. 16 *If
> you obey the commandments of the LORD your God that I command you today,*
> by loving the LORD your God, by walking in his ways, and by keeping
> his commandments and his statutes and his rules, *then you shall live and
> multiply, and the LORD your God will bless you in the land* that you are en-
> tering to take possession of it. 17 *But if your heart turns away, and you will
> not hear,* but are drawn away to worship other gods and serve them, 18 I
> declare to you today, that you shall surely perish. *You shall not live long in
> the land* that you are going over the Jordan to enter and possess. 19 I call
> heaven and earth to witness against you today, that *I have set before you
> life and death, blessing and curse.* Therefore choose life, that you and your
> offspring may live, 20 loving the LORD your God, obeying his voice and
> holding fast to him, for he is your life and length of days, *that you may
> dwell in the land that the LORD swore to your fathers, to Abraham, to Isaac,
> and to Jacob, to give them.*"

Based on the laws, the promises, and the threats of the covenant, the
Mosaic Covenant was a covenant of works for life in the land of Canaan.
The summary states that whether the Israelites enjoy the land sworn to
their fathers depends on whether they keep the commandments. Insofar
as Israel obeys the Mosaic law, they will enjoy the guaranteed blessings of
the Abrahamic Covenant. Insofar as Israel disobeys the Mosaic law, they
will experience the guaranteed curses of the covenant.

[5] (Jeremiah 2:17–22) "17 Have you not brought this upon yourself by forsak-
ing the LORD your God, when he led you in the way? 18 And now what do you
gain by going to Egypt to drink the waters of the Nile? Or what do you gain by
going to Assyria to drink the waters of the Euphrates? 19 Your evil will chastise
you, and your apostasy will reprove you. Know and see that it is evil and bitter
for you to forsake the LORD your God; the fear of me is not in you, declares the
Lord GOD of hosts. 20 For long ago I broke your yoke and burst your bonds; but
you said, 'I will not serve.' Yes, on every high hill and under every green tree you
bowed down like a whore. 21 Yet I planted you a choice vine, wholly of pure seed.
How then have you turned degenerate and become a wild vine? 22 Though you
wash yourself with lye and use much soap, the stain of your guilt is still before me,
declares the Lord GOD."

3. The Kindness of the Covenant

The Mosaic Covenant is a covenant of obedience for life in the land of Canaan. But it is not the original covenant of works made with Adam in the garden of Eden. The Mosaic Covenant echoes Adam's covenant in Eden and revives the Covenant of Works in key ways, but it is not the same covenant. The place is different, the parties are different, the promises are different, and the positive laws are entirely different. The threats, though, are very different.

The threats of the Mosaic Covenant demonstrate one aspect of the kindness of this covenant. In Adam's covenant, he was threatened with immediate and complete condemnation if he disobeyed. It was an all or nothing arrangement dealing with perfect absolute righteousness. In the Mosaic Covenant, God makes demands of obedience and threatens curses based on Israel's performance, but there are many things about the Mosaic Covenant that make it a kinder covenant than Adam's covenant.

a. The absolute dominion of God

God's kindness in the Mosaic Covenant is visible in comparison with His absolute dominion. Covenants derive from God's infinite goodness and kindness. God is sovereign Lord over everything, the maker of all things. Given that fundamental reality, any covenant that God makes with man that provides a reward for a work, a "do this, and I will grant you that" arrangement, is a kind and gracious action on God's part. God was not obligated to deal with Israel in this way, going all the way back to Abraham. For God to place blessed life in Canaan before Israel was a kind and gracious gift from God. It was a blessing. And for God to make it available through civic obedience is likewise gracious. The obedience demanded was an obedience an unbeliever could render.

Covenants create a relationship where man can work for a reward from God. According to God's own appointment, if Israel obeys, they will enjoy life in the land. And they knew, according to the covenant, according to the law, that that's how it worked. And it should have made them thankful and diligent, not entitled and lazy.

The kindness of covenants in light of the Creator-creature distinction is important. But this is heightened when the creature is a sinner. God not only owes sinners no blessings, but He has every right to execute full judgment upon them. So, for God to make a covenant with man after the fall, a covenant of blessings and good promises, is not only kindness in light of His absolute dominion, but also in light of man's fallen and sinful condition as a rebel and enemy of God. The Abrahamic Covenant had not changed the nature of Abraham's children or granted them a new heart, yet God was merciful and kind in providing blessed life in Canaan for them.

b. The promises to Abraham

Sin against grace and light is exceedingly wicked. Israel's idolatry with the golden calf made by Aaron is almost unthinkable in light of the amazing things God had done for Israel. He brought them out of Egypt with riches and safety, parted the Red Sea, defeated the Egyptian armies, and Israel repaid God's grace with this. But this should be contextualized. While it's true that Israel had already been given the Ten Commandments verbally, and they had already sworn to obey them, only a short time had passed in comparison to the length of time Israel spent in Egypt.

Egypt's religion was extremely visible and idol-centered. It was ancient, beautiful, artistic, creative, and tangible. It was powerful. The pyramids, tombs, statues, sphynx, obelisks, and the rest of Egypt's culture continue to bedazzle and impress today. Israel was immersed in the original glory of Egypt for generations. It is no surprise, then, that Israel broke the covenant only days after its pledge to keep the same. You can take Israel out of Egypt. But you can't take Egypt out of Israel. Their infidelity is no less excusable, but it is certainly much more explainable from that perspective.

Israel was unfaithful to God. They committed idolatry. They broke His laws. And according to the covenant, they were liable to punishment. And they were punished. The Levites killed the fornicators, Moses made the people drink the powder of the ground up idol, and a plague was sent on the people. In Exodus 32:13–14 Moses asked God for mercy based on the Abrahamic promises.

> 13 Remember Abraham, Isaac, and Israel, your servants, to whom you swore by your own self, and said to them, 'I will multiply your offspring as the stars of heaven, and all this land that I have promised I will give to your offspring, and they shall inherit it forever.' 14 And the LORD relented from the disaster that he had spoken of bringing on his people.

Moses was saying to God that if Israel were destroyed now, the promises to Abraham would not be fulfilled.[6] This was a means that God used to teach Israel a lesson. It was true throughout Israel's life, that they would not be entirely cut off because God had made promises to them through Abraham, promises that had to be fulfilled or else God would be unfaithful.

---

[6] Numbers 14:1–23 is another excellent example of this when the people refuse to enter the promised land, and Moses pleads with God not to completely disinherit them or else the nations will know that God did not fulfil His Word.

God's faithfulness to Abraham, then, was a kind guarantee of Israel's ongoing status as a blessed nation. And as noted in the section on the Abrahamic Covenant, the Bible accurately records the fulfillment of God's promises to Abraham. God delivered in full, according to His Word.

There is kindness in the Mosaic Covenant in light of God's absolute dominion and God's promises to Abraham. It was not an all-or-nothing arrangement where on the day they broke the covenant they would surely die. God will fulfill His promises, despite Israel's unfaithfulness. And He did fulfill His promises, despite Israel's unfaithfulness.

c. The sacrificial system

Sinners are terribly bad at obeying God's commandments, and terribly good at disobeying them. The Abrahamic Covenant and the Mosaic Covenant did nothing to change the nature of the Israelites. They did not grant them a new heart. They provided no help for compliance with the demands of the covenant. Israel's disobedience and unfaithfulness are unsurprising as a result. But God provided the sacrificial system as a way to forgive their sins.

Leviticus and Numbers appear to be repetitive lists of the details of the positive laws of Israel. However tedious and laborious this may seem at first, it is very important. Without these rules of kindness in the sacrificial system, Israel would have been exiled long before it was. Leviticus 5:14–19 will serve as an example.

> 14 The LORD spoke to Moses, saying, 15 "If anyone commits a breach of faith and sins unintentionally in any of the holy things of the LORD, he shall bring to the LORD as his compensation, a ram without blemish out of the flock, valued in silver shekels, according to the shekel of the sanctuary, for a guilt offering. 16 He shall also make restitution for what he has done amiss in the holy thing and shall add a fifth to it and give it to the priest. *And the priest shall make atonement for him with the ram of the guilt offering, and he shall be forgiven.* 17 If anyone sins, doing any of the things that by the LORD's commandments ought not to be done, though he did not know it, then realizes his guilt, he shall bear his iniquity. 18 He shall bring to the priest a ram without blemish out of the flock, or its equivalent for a guilt offering, and *the priest shall make atonement for him for the mistake that he made unintentionally, and he shall be forgiven.* 19 It is a guilt offering; he has indeed incurred guilt before the LORD."

There were many kinds of offerings. The sin offerings and the guilt offerings, which had the same laws, are the most important. If someone sinned unintentionally, or in some cases intentionally broke the law, they could find forgiveness and atonement through sacrifice. The spilling of the blood of another would pay the penalty that they deserved. This achieved atonement, the reconciliation of two parties so that they are "at one" again. Sacrifices provided reconciliation in the covenantal relationship. The law condemned the guilty, and sacrifices redirected the guilt to the sacrificial victim. This would have been a daily, weekly, monthly, and yearly endeavor, teaching Israel repeatedly of its own sinfulness and of the kindness of God in bringing atonement through sacrifice.

Once a year, the High Priest would offer a sacrifice on behalf of the people to cleanse the entire nation. The details of this sacrifice are important.

> 21 And Aaron shall lay both his hands on the head of the live goat, and confess over it all the iniquities of the people of Israel, and all their transgressions, all their sins. And he shall put them on the head of the goat and send it away into the wilderness by the hand of a man who is in readiness. 22 The goat shall bear all their iniquities on itself to a remote area, and he shall let the goat go free in the wilderness.

> 30 For on this day shall atonement be made for you to cleanse you. You shall be clean before the LORD from all your sins. 31 It is a Sabbath of solemn rest to you, and you shall afflict yourselves; it is a statute forever. 32 And the priest who is anointed and consecrated as priest in his father's place shall make atonement, wearing the holy linen garments. 33 He shall make atonement for the holy sanctuary, and he shall make atonement for the tent of meeting and for the altar, and he shall make atonement for the priests and for all the people of the assembly. 34 And this shall be a statute forever for you, that atonement may be made for the people of Israel once in the year because of all their sins. And Aaron did as the LORD commanded Moses (Leviticus 16:21–22, 30–34).

The priest would represent the entire nation in this event. It wasn't the people atoning for their own sins, but the appointed priest of God's pure and holy temple cleansing the people. Their sins would be taken away, quite literally, before their eyes as the goat was led out to the wilderness. Through this sacrifice, they would know that they were again pure and right with the law.

This is kindness. God never changed His standard of justice. The law never became more lenient, but the sacrifices accounted for Israel's sin and provided a way of atonement. All of this was intended to be a teaching lesson to Israel. The people of Israel were supposed to learn that forgiveness comes through a sacrifice administered by the high priest.

But, the writer to the Hebrews tells us that this forgiveness was not eternal forgiveness. It was earthly forgiveness. It was "purification of the flesh." It was restoration to life in Canaan, which is precisely the level on which the Abrahamic and Mosaic Covenants operate. This means that while there was a positive message in the sacrifices, there was also a reminder of sins and a lack of purification of the conscience. They had outward purity, outward forgiveness, forgiveness in the court of Canaan, but not forgiveness in the court of the conscience, in the court of heaven.

The Mosaic Covenant demonstrates God's kindness and graciousness by providing not only a way for Israel to address and redress their sins against the law, but also to teach them in all of this about true forgiveness to be found in a heavenly sacrifice administered by a heavenly High Priest in a heavenly temple.[7]

The kindness of the covenant is visible in light of God's absolute dominion, in light of the Abrahamic promises, and in light of the sacrificial system. The history of Israel is a public record of God's kindness.

d. The history of Israel

The history of Israel recounts everything stated thus far. Israel disobeyed, as God said they would. God forgave their sins when they rightly worshipped Him and rightly offered sacrifices. God fulfilled all His promises to Abraham and brought about a line of kings. Eventually Israel did not worship God purely but went after other gods. God sent His prophets to warn Israel to return to the law and to obey it and offer pure worship. But when Israel played the harlot and served other gods, God would not regard their offerings. He would not accept their sacrifices. They were impure and unholy. So, God exiled Israel, as He had said that He would. And yet still He was gracious and kind to Israel. This was all predicted beforehand.

25 When you father children and children's children, and have grown old in the land, *if you act corruptly* by making a carved image in the form of anything, and by doing what is evil in the sight of the LORD your God, so as to provoke him to anger, 26 I call heaven and earth to witness against you today, that *you will soon utterly perish from the land* that you are going over the Jordan to possess. You will not live long in it, but will be utterly destroyed. 27 And the LORD will scatter you among the peoples, and you will be left few in number among the nations where the LORD will drive you. 28 And there you will serve gods of wood and stone, the work of human hands, that neither see, nor hear, nor eat, nor smell. 29 *But from there you will seek the LORD your God and you will find him*, if you search after him with all your heart and with all your soul. 30 When you are in

---

[7] A discussion of the typology of the Mosaic Covenant must be deferred until finishing the Davidic Covenant.

tribulation, and all these things come upon you in the latter days, you will return to the LORD your God and obey his voice. 31 For the LORD your God is a merciful God. *He will not leave you or destroy you or forget the covenant with your fathers that he swore to them* (Deuteronomy 4:25–31).

A principle of disobedience leading to curses is clear, but so is the promise that God will not forget the covenant made with the fathers, the Abrahamic Covenant. God would not fully and finally disinherit Israel in exile because there was one promise yet unfulfilled even at the time of the exile. The blessing of the nations, the seed of the woman, had not yet been born. God preserved Israel long enough to bring about the seed, and even then the Son of God ministered to Israel. God was so very kind to Israel, as seen in its history. But Israel was utterly faithless.

Israel tells its own history this way in several places, one of which is found in Nehemiah 9 after the exiles returned with Ezra and were rebuilding Jerusalem. Israel had come home and they were trying to come to grips with what had happened. A few verses are sufficient.

7 You are the LORD, the God who chose Abram and brought him out of Ur of the Chaldeans and gave him the name Abraham. 8 You found his heart faithful before you, and made with him *the covenant to give to his offspring the land* of the Canaanite, the Hittite, the Amorite, the Perizzite, the Jebusite, and the Girgashite. And you have kept your promise, for you are righteous.

13 You came down on Mount Sinai and spoke with them from heaven and gave them right rules and true laws, good statutes and commandments.

29 And you warned them in order to turn them back to your law. Yet they acted presumptuously and did not obey your commandments, but sinned against your rules, which if a person does them, he shall live by them, and they turned a stubborn shoulder and stiffened their neck and would not obey. 30 Many years you bore with them and warned them by your Spirit through your prophets. Yet they would not give ear. Therefore you gave them into the hand of the peoples of the lands. 31 Nevertheless, in your great mercies you did not make an end of them or forsake them, for you are a gracious and merciful God. 32 Now, therefore, our God, the great, the mighty, and the awesome God, who keeps covenant and steadfast love, let not all the hardship seem little to you that has come upon us, upon our kings, our princes, our priests, our prophets, our fathers, and all your people, since the time of the kings of Assyria until this day. 33 *Yet you have been righteous in all that has come upon us, for you have dealt faithfully and we have acted wickedly* (Nehemiah 9:7–8, 13, 29–33).

God's kindness to Israel is professed by Israel itself. God was true to His name from beginning to end. He is the God who keeps covenant and steadfast love. Israel's history proves the point. The Mosaic covenant may have been built on laws and obedience, but God was extremely kind to Israel by making the covenant, by providing the sacrificial system, and by restoring Israel time after time.

4. The Function of the Covenant

A kingdom is a sphere of sovereignty, granted by God. It's delegated dominion. God grants a sphere of authority to someone. And He does this through His covenants. Covenants govern kingdoms. The kingdom of creation was granted to Adam in the Covenant of Works. It is a cursed kingdom due to Adam's sin. The Noahic Covenant governs the same kingdom. Noah's covenant encompasses the whole world and applies to all men. Mankind is to exercise dominion, to be fruitful and multiply, to promote families and prevent murder, etc. But in Noah's covenant, they don't do this to create or extend Eden. It's simply God's common grace preserving mankind for the greater purpose of bringing about His promises of salvation. The Covenant of Works and the Noahic Covenant establish and govern the kingdom of creation.

In the Abrahamic Covenant, God granted a kingdom to Abraham. This was the kingdom of Israel. God gave Abraham a space, Canaan, He gave him laws and promises relating to that space, and He promised a line of kings to rule over Abraham's descendants. The Mosaic Covenant, delivered for its first and second times, was given to Abraham's descendants in the context of impending entrance into their promised inheritance, the Abrahamic kingdom, the kingdom of Israel. The Mosaic covenant is a development, a very large development, of the kingdom of Israel. It functions to rule the kingdom, in its entirety, along with the Abrahamic Covenant.

a. The covenant governs the people

The offspring of Abraham are going to enter the land, and as the people of God, living in his kingdom, there are specific rules by which they are to live. The Mosaic Covenant governs the people.

> 1 And now, O Israel, listen to the statutes and the rules that I am teaching you, and do them, that you may live, and go in and take possession of the land that the LORD, the God of your fathers, is giving you. 2 You shall not add to the word that I command you, nor take from it, that you may keep the commandments of the LORD your God that I command you (Deuteronomy 4:1–2).

Moses told the people that as they go in and live in Canaan they are not to add to or subtract from the law. They are to keep it and obey it because it governs them.

Among the laws by which God governed Israel, there are two basic kinds. Israel was governed by moral laws and by positive laws. As covered previously, moral laws transcend transcription. They are known by nature, though suppressed by fallen nature. God delivered the moral law to Israel, summarized in the Ten Commandments.

In addition to moral laws, God gave positive laws to Israel. Positive laws are added laws, additional laws. These laws are not morally right or wrong in and of themselves. Circumcision, how to build the tabernacle, which animals to sacrifice for which sins, and what foods you can or can't eat are positive laws. They were added by God to Israel's covenantal obligations. Every covenant has its own positive laws that govern the people of that covenant, like the trees in Eden. The Moral law and the positive laws of Israel governed the people. That was their function.

Israel's positive laws are often split up into two groups: the civil law, and the ceremonial law. The civil law is sometimes called the judicial law. It governs the daily lives and affairs of the people. It governs things like how people are to be punished, and for what crimes. It deals with everyday affairs of life. The ceremonial law refers to the priesthood and the sacrificial system and everything that has to do with cleanness or uncleanness. All of this is to say that the Mosaic Covenant, in its moral and positive laws, governs the people of the kingdom of Israel. The Mosaic Covenant controls everything in the kingdom.

b. The covenant governs the priesthood

There are many examples of the law of Moses regulating the priests. It was the Mosaic law that appointed the tribe of Levi to be the priestly tribe. The book of Hebrews contrasts Jesus' priesthood, derived from the Father's appointment, with Aaron's priesthood, derived from a law of bodily descent. The law appointed priests in their weakness, but Jesus is appointed priest forever. The law controlled the priesthood.

Two examples will suffice to demonstrate this. First, Exodus 40:12–16 describes the initial consecration of Aaron and his sons, a pattern not to be contradicted. No other tribe could claim this right. It was "a perpetual priesthood throughout their generations." Second, Leviticus 10:1–2 describes what happened when Aaron's sons, Nadab and Abihu deviated from the law of God concerning priestly work. They were guilty of offering strange fire "which [God] had not commanded them." The priests had no right or authority to do anything beyond what God had commanded them to do. They could not break the law, or they would be punished. The Mosaic law functioned to create the priesthood, to control it, and to correct it, if need be. The covenant established and governed the priesthood, just one part of the whole kingdom.

c. The covenant governs the kingship

Everyone is under God's authority, from the people to the priests to the kings. God's delegated dominion is never handed over as though God relinquishes His sovereignty. The kings of Israel were under the law.

In the Abrahamic Covenant a line of kings was promised for this kingdom, and in the Mosaic Covenant a set of laws was established for them. Deuteronomy 17:14–20 describes this.

> 14 When you come to the land that the LORD your God is giving you, and you possess it and dwell in it and then say, 'I will set a king over me, like all the nations that are around me,' 15 you may indeed set a king over you whom the LORD your God will choose. One from among your brothers you shall set as king over you. You may not put a foreigner over you, who is not your brother. 16 Only he must not acquire many horses for himself or cause the people to return to Egypt in order to acquire many horses, since the LORD has said to you, 'You shall never return that way again.' 17 And he shall not acquire many wives for himself, lest his heart turn away, nor shall he acquire for himself excessive silver and gold. 18 'And when he sits on the throne of his kingdom, *he shall write for himself in a book a copy of this law, approved by the Levitical priests.* 19 *And it shall be with him, and he shall read in it all the days of his life, that he may learn to fear the LORD his God by keeping all the words of this law and these statutes, and doing them,* 20 *that his heart may not be lifted up above his brothers, and that he may not turn aside from the commandment, either to the right hand or to the left, so that he may continue long in his kingdom, he and his children, in Israel.*

The Mosaic Covenant controls or governs the kingship. The king must be from one of their brothers, not a foreigner. And besides not amassing wives or horses like foreign kings, he must write a copy of the law, read it, learn it, and keep it, *so that he and the people will be blessed in Canaan.* The king is to lead the people in keeping the law. This passage will reappear when discussing the Davidic Covenant.

This is a strong contrast between ancient kings and Israel's kings. In other nations, the king creates the law. The king is the law. In Israel, the king is created by the law, and the king must keep the law. God is king in Israel, and His law controls the kingship.

d. The covenant governs the prophets

God establishes and governs His kingdoms through covenants. Israel, as a national political and religious kingdom was regulated from top to bottom by the Mosaic Covenant. God gave them instructions for identifying true prophets in Numbers 12:6. "And he said, 'Hear my words: If there is a prophet among you, I the LORD make myself known to him in a vision; I speak with him in a dream.'" In the context of this passage, Miriam and others grumbled that the Lord only spoke with Moses. God's reply was that the prophets are only those whom He appoints. There are no self-appointed prophets. God controls the office of prophet.

In Deuteronomy 13:1–5 God gave the people rules and principles to identify a true prophet from a false prophet within the kingdom. Just as the priests were accountable to God's laws to fulfill their duties properly, and just as the kings were accountable, so also the prophets were accountable to these laws. In those verses, the basic test of a prophet isn't just that what he predicts comes true, but whether his words line up and match with the law of God. True prophets reinforce and uphold the law of God. False prophets lead away from it. Prophets police the word of God, which is the covenant. Prophets remind the people of their commitments, their obligations, and the curses of God threatening those who are unfaithful.

This is an echo of Adam who was also charged with enforcing the Word of God in the garden of Eden. He failed to preserve the purity of God's Word, the purity of His law. Adam allowed Satan to question God's command and threat. The prophets were sent to Israel to reinforce the law of God to the people and to lead them back to obedience and repentance. Thus, the law controlled the identity and the message of its prophets. Anyone who was not appointed or anointed to that office was to be rejected and put to death for breaking God's law.

e. The covenant governs blessing and cursing

The previous points in many ways deal with governing the people as they interact with each other. The larger function of the covenant is to govern Israel's relationship not just within itself but with God, the great King of the kingdom. If Israel obeys, they will be blessed by God; if they disobey they will be cursed by God, as demonstrated by the curses covered above. This truth needs reinforcing, to emphasize that the covenant governed everything in the kingdom of Israel—the people's daily life and interactions, the structure of the kingdom itself, and their relationship with God.

This reality was powerfully instilled in the Israelites just before they entered Canaan when God commanded them to perform an interesting ceremony in which part of the Levites stood on one hill, and part of the Levites stood on an opposite hill. One group declared the curses that would fall on the people if they disobeyed; the other group declared the blessings that would fall on them if they obeyed. Introducing this ceremony, recorded in Deuteronomy 27:9–10, Moses and the Levites say "9 Keep silence and hear, O Israel: this day you have become the people of the LORD your God. 10 You shall therefore obey the voice of the LORD your God, keeping his commandments and his statutes, which I command you today." Verses 15 and following pronounce curses followed by the people responding with an "Amen" as an acknowledgment and agreement. The conclusion is in verse 26, "Cursed be anyone who does not confirm the words of this law by doing them. And all the people shall say, 'Amen.'"

One chapter later, the opposite is recorded in Deuteronomy 28:1–2. "1 And if you faithfully obey the voice of the LORD your God, being careful to do all his commandments that I command you today, the LORD your God will set you high above all the nations of the earth. 2 And all these blessings shall come upon you and overtake you, if you obey the voice of the LORD your God." What follows is an opposite set of blessings for the people proclaimed by the priests.

A similar event was programmed into Israel's ongoing life. The people of Israel were commanded in Deuteronomy 31:9–13 to read the law in the Feast of Booths every seven years "that they may hear and learn to fear the LORD your God, and be careful to do all the words of this law, and that their children, who have not known it, may hear and learn to fear the LORD your God, as long as you live in the land that you are going over the Jordan to possess."

Moses concluded and summarized the covenant in Deuteronomy 32:45–47.

> 45 And when Moses had finished speaking all these words to all Israel, 46 he said to them, "Take to heart all the words by which I am warning you today, that you may command them to your children, that they may be careful to do all the words of this law. 47 For it is no empty word for you, but your very life, and by this word you shall live long in the land that you are going over the Jordan to possess.

The sum is clear. If they obey, they will be blessed. If they disobey, they will be cursed. The function of the covenant is to rule the kingdom.

Conclusion

The Mosaic Covenant controls everything. It governs the people in its various kinds of laws; it governs the priests, the kings, and the prophets. Everyone lives by the law of God. If they do, they will be blessed. If they don't they will be cursed. As God had told Abraham that he and his descendants must keep the covenant or be cut off, so also the Mosaic Covenant expanded the very same relationship, controlling the enjoyment of the very same blessings. If the children of Abraham obey the law of Moses, they will enjoy the blessings of Abraham. If they disobey, they will lose them. The Abrahamic Covenant established the kingdom of Israel and lays out basic obligations. The Mosaic Covenant expanded and implemented covenantal government over the kingdom as it arose and flourished in Canaan.

Though this will be discussed in greater fullness later, the Mosaic Covenant advanced the mystery of Christ in monumental ways, the priesthood and the sacrifices being chief among all. The blessing for the nations will emerge not just within Canaan and the circumcised offspring of Abraham, but also within this complex of laws and statutes, within this system of priests and sacrifices, within this system of blessings and curses. Hebrews 10:1 declares that "the law has but a shadow of the good things to come." Its shadowy status was its great privilege. In the promise of a nations-blessing descendant, the Abrahamic body placed a body in the future, a body casting a shadow backward. The Mosaic Covenant began to delineate the lines of the Savior's silhouette. Without righteousness, there is no blessing. Without the spilling of blood, there is no remission of sins. Without the High Priest, there is no sacrifice. The Davidic Covenant focused this typological mystery into one very specific person.

8

The Davidic Covenant

Introduction

The Kingdom of Israel was established and ruled by covenants. The land was promised to Abraham's people in the Abrahamic Covenant. The Mosaic Covenant instituted the full complex of laws that God used to rule the people in that land. In the Davidic Covenant, the kingdom reaches consummation. As it was for the Mosaic covenant, so also in this case awareness of the context of the covenant is vital.

1. The Context of the Covenant

a. The promises of the Abrahamic Covenant

In Genesis 17:6 and 16, God promised Abraham and Sarah, and later to Isaac, that kings would come from them. This promise was narrowed down to the tribe of Judah when Jacob blessed his sons. The scepter would not depart from Judah. A covenant that establishes a kingship in Israel is therefore a fulfillment of God's promise to Abraham and a direct development of the kingdom of Israel.

b. The problems of the Mosaic Covenant

The Mosaic Covenant governed everything. And God told the Israelites that when they entered the land they could have a king over themselves, one of their own. Entering and settling in the land was not a quick or easy process, though God was faithful in fulfilling his promise. Under

Joshua and Caleb, and with the blessing and power of God, Israel entered Canaan and obtained its inheritance. The book of Joshua describes the complete conquest of the land as well as its apportioning to each tribe so that the entire people, the descendants of Abraham, could settle in the land. God kept His promises completely. The fullness of the land promise allotted by God was enjoyed.

The book of Joshua, in general, describes the fulfillment of God's promises to Abraham. The picture is generally positive, though at times Israel is disobedient and is therefore defeated, as at Ai. Problems soon arose in the land, however. Judges 2:10–11, 20–21 sets the scene.

> 10 And all that generation also were gathered to their fathers. And there arose another generation after them who did not know the LORD or the work that he had done for Israel. 11 And the people of Israel did what was evil in the sight of the LORD and served the Baals... 20 So the anger of the LORD was kindled against Israel, and he said, *"Because this people have transgressed my covenant* that I commanded their fathers and have not obeyed my voice, 21 I will no longer drive out before them any of the nations that Joshua left when he died."

Moses had painstakingly and thoroughly communicated the reality of God's promises and threats to the generation that invaded Canaan. They saw the death of their parents in the wilderness and chose life through obedience rather than death through disobedience. But a new generation arose that grew up in the land and didn't understand what it took to arrive where they were. The generation that grew up in the land was lazy and idolatrous.

Key to understanding the context, then, is that God punished Israel for transgressing the covenant. They disobeyed the law of the Mosaic Covenant therefore they cannot enjoy the blessings of Abrahamic Covenant. The rest of the book of Judges repeats this pattern. A tribe is disobedient, God permits a foreign power to oppress them, God raises up a deliverer, and that tribe is restored. It's a book of fragmented and partial rebellion and deliverance. There is no centrality, no leadership, no cohesion to the nation. And there is a very important statement in Judges, mentioned a few times throughout the book, including the very last verse of the entire book. "In those days there was no king in Israel. Everyone did what was right in his own eyes" (Judges 21:25).

This is precisely the context of the Davidic Covenant. Israel entered the land as promised to Abraham, but they disobeyed the law delivered by Moses. And as a result, they were afflicted and oppressed. There was no king in Israel. There was no obedience in Israel. The law was neglected, and the people suffered. What Israel needed was for someone to keep the law of Moses for the nation, bringing blessing and deliverance to all the children of Abraham.

c. The preference of the people

A discussion of the Davidic Covenant cannot overlook that David was not the first king of Israel. In 1 Samuel 8:7–9, the people of Israel were being threatened by the Ammonites and wanted a king to fight for them. They asked Samuel to appoint one, but Samuel did not want to. God told Samuel to permit it and to give the Israelites a taste of their own medicine.

> 7 And the LORD said to Samuel, "Obey the voice of the people in all that they say to you, for they have not rejected you, but they have rejected me from being king over them. 8 According to all the deeds that they have done, from the day I brought them up out of Egypt even to this day, forsaking me and serving other gods, so they are also doing to you. 9 Now then, obey their voice; only you shall solemnly warn them and show them the ways of the king who shall reign over them."

Israel was rejecting God by asking for a king. Samuel warned them that the king would take and take and take. It wouldn't be a beneficial relationship for them. They would lose, not gain, with a king. Despite the warning, the people insisted.

> 19 But the people refused to obey the voice of Samuel. And they said, "No! But there shall be a king over us, 20 that we also may be like all the nations, and that our king may judge us and go out before us and fight our battles." 21 And when Samuel had heard all the words of the people, he repeated them in the ears of the LORD. 22 And the LORD said to Samuel, "Obey their voice and make them a king."

Verse 20 explains why this is a rejection of God. The people don't just want a king. They want a king like all the nations have, one who will not just fight for them, but will judge them. In other words, they want new laws. They want new religion. They want new authority. They don't want a king to lead them under God. They want a king to lead them away from and apart from God. They want a king after their own heart.

Israel's first choice of kings was not according to God's choosing because Saul was not a man after God's own heart, nor was he a member of the tribe of Judah. Saul's kingship resulted in failure. It was set up by man and thus fell apart. Saul did give a measure of protection and success to the kingdom, but he was proud and selfish, erecting monuments to himself, making rash vows related to his pride, disobeying commands of sacrifice and warfare, and being extremely jealous of David's rise to prominence in his kingdom.

In God's timing, Saul and his line were killed and removed from the throne. This brings Israel's kingdom-history all the way from Abraham's promises, to Moses' precepts, to Israel's conquest, to the Judges' deliverance, to the people's preference, and Saul's failures. There is one more element, however, that completes a proper appreciation of the context of the Davidic Covenant.

d. The prospect of consummation

The Mosaic Covenant anticipated the Davidic Covenant, not only by laying out basic laws for the king, but also in its prospect of consummation. Deuteronomy 12:8–12 looked forward to a time when there would be a centralized location for sacrificial worship in the kingdom.

> 8 "You shall not do according to all that we are doing here today, everyone doing whatever is right in his own eyes, 9 for you have not as yet come to the rest and to the inheritance that the LORD your God is giving you. 10 But when you go over the Jordan and live in the land that the LORD your God is giving you to inherit, and *when he gives you rest from all your enemies around*, so that you live in safety, 11 then to *the place that the LORD your God will choose, to make his name dwell there*, there you shall bring all that I command you: your burnt offerings and your sacrifices, your tithes and the contribution that you present, and all your finest vow offerings that you vow to the LORD. 12 And you shall rejoice before the LORD your God, you and your sons and your daughters, your male servants and your female servants, and the Levite that is within your towns, since he has no portion or inheritance with you."

The Mosaic Covenant put before the eyes of the people a prospect of consummation. They would enter the land and experience rest from their enemies. That is the idyllic picture that the Abrahamic Covenant promises. But more importantly, what really brings the Israelite kingdom into its complete and consummated stage is when God makes His name to dwell in a particular place. In other words, when there is an established temple of God's presence and blessing in a particular place, *then* the kingdom will be consummated. The people of God in the land of God, with the presence and blessing of God, is what Israel is called to be through its covenants. All of this sets the stage for the covenant itself.

2. The Blessings of the Covenant

The Bible records the covenant God made with David in 2 Samuel 7:8–16.

> 8 "Now, therefore, thus you shall say to my servant David, 'Thus says the LORD of hosts, I took you from the pasture, from following the sheep, that you should be prince over my people Israel. 9 And I have been with you wherever you went and have cut off all your enemies from before you. And I will make for you a great name, like the name of the great ones of the earth. 10 And I will appoint a place for my people Israel and will plant them, so that they may dwell in their own place and be disturbed no more. And violent men shall afflict them no more, as formerly, 11 from the time that I appointed judges over my people Israel. And I will give you rest from all your enemies.
>
> Moreover, the LORD declares to you that the LORD will make you a house. 12 When your days are fulfilled and you lie down with your fathers, I will raise up your offspring after you, who shall come from your body, and I will establish his kingdom. 13 He shall build a house for my name, and I will establish the throne of his kingdom forever. 14 I will be to him a father, and he shall be to me a son. When he commits iniquity, I will discipline him with the rod of men, with the stripes of the sons of men, 15 but my steadfast love will not depart from him, as I took it from Saul, whom I put away from before you. 16 And your house and your kingdom shall be made sure forever before me. Your throne shall be established forever.'"

Its blessings can be summed up in three ways.

a. An established throne

Verse 16 states that David's house, kingdom, and throne will be established and made sure. The kingship of Israel is not founded on the people's desire to free themselves from God, as with Saul, but on God's commitment to establish the throne of David.[1] The stability of the throne of David

---

[1] Psalm 89 is a commentary on God's covenant with David and it repeats these ideas in verses 3–4. "3 You have said, 'I have made a covenant with my chosen one; I have sworn to David my servant: 4 I will establish your offspring forever, and build your throne for all generations.'" Psalm 132:11–12 declares the same, "11 The LORD swore to David a sure oath from which he will not turn back: 'One of the sons of your body I will set on your throne. 12 If your sons keep my covenant and my testimonies that I shall teach them, their sons also forever shall sit on your throne.'"

becomes the stability of the entire nation. They can look to the king and see God's appointed and anointed king, God's chosen one whose throne will be established by God Himself. It was God's promise, God's commitment.

b. Rest and prosperity in Canaan

Verses 10–11 promise rest and security for Israel. As referenced above, this had been promised through Moses, and it was partially fulfilled in the time of Joshua.[2] But that rest was problematic, partial, and incomplete. Now it will be fulfilled for the nation, not just for a tribe here and a tribe there as in the time of the Judges. When Solomon dedicated the temple, he declared this promise fulfilled in 1 Kings 8:56. "Blessed be the LORD who has given rest to his people Israel, according to all that he promised. Not one word has failed of all his good promise, which he spoke by Moses his servant."

Peace and rest will not simply be a state of affairs where Israel is never threatened or attacked, but rather God will bless the King's defense of the nation. As David said in Psalm 144:1–2, "1 Blessed be the LORD, my rock, who trains my hands for war, and my fingers for battle; 2 he is my steadfast love and my fortress, my stronghold and my deliverer, my shield and he in whom I take refuge, who subdues peoples under me." After the time of the judges and Saul, this is what Israel desperately needed.

c. The presence and protection of God

The Davidic Covenant is full of language of God's presence. In verse 9 God says that He has been with David. In verse 13 God says that one of David's descendants will build a house for God, a house of God's presence. And in verse 15 God promises that His steadfast love will not depart from David's descendants. God will be with David's line, and He will protect it.

At the heart of the Davidic Covenant is the temple. David was contemplating building a temple for God since the presence of God among the people was still mediated through the tabernacle. But God told David that he would not be the one to build the temple because he was a warrior. A man of peace would build the temple. The Davidic heir, Solomon, whose name means "man of peace," built the temple.

In 1 Kings 6:12–13 God said to Solomon, "12 Concerning this house that you are building, if you will walk in my statutes and obey my rules

---

[2] Joshua 21:44, "And the LORD gave them rest on every side just as he had sworn to their fathers."

and keep all my commandments and walk in them, then I will establish my word with you, which I spoke to David your father. 13 And I will dwell among the children of Israel and will not forsake my people Israel." God promised to dwell among the children of Israel through the temple. All of this is a part of the Davidic Covenant.

The glory of these statements must not be overlooked. The generation of Joshua and Caleb came out of Egypt and into Canaan. They died. Their children, the idolatrous generation, passed through the time of the Judges and died. At the tail end of the Judges was Samuel. He died in 1 Samuel 25. David is old and dies in 1 Kings 2. When one arrives at the period of the construction of the temple under Solomon, Israel is at last in their own land, filled with their own people, under their own king, with their God in their temple in their capital city. Under Solomon all the promises and blessings of God delivered to Abraham and Moses and David reach their zenith. Solomon's dedication of the temple is the high point of the entire Old Testament.[3]

Through the Davidic Covenant, God gave Israel an established throne, rest and prosperity in Canaan, and His own presence and protection. But, this is only the "I will" part of the covenant. The "you will" part of the covenant follows.

3. The Conditions of the Covenant

The Davidic Covenant was not comprised simply of God's promises to David, but also of God's commands to David and his descendants. And there were sanctions associated with whether David and his sons were faithful to these commands or conditions.

a. Guard God's sanctuary

In 2 Samuel 7:13, God says of David's son that "He shall build a house for my name." A house for God's name is not just a house named after God. God's name is His presence, thus it is the King's responsibility to construct a temple where God's presence will be manifested among His people, and where the people will worship their God.

In 1 Kings 8, the temple was completed by Solomon and the Israelites celebrated with a dedication service. Solomon offered up a prayer to God on this occasion.

---

[3] "In the Davidic covenant, God's purposes to redeem a people to himself reach their climactic stage of realization so far as the Old Testament is concerned. Under David the kingdom arrives." Robertson, *The Christ of the Covenants*, 229.

27 But will God indeed dwell on the earth? Behold, heaven and the highest heaven cannot contain you; how much less this house that I have
built! 28 Yet have regard to the prayer of your servant and to his plea, O
LORD my God, listening to the cry and to the prayer that your servant
prays before you this day, 29 that your eyes may be open night and day
toward this house, the place of which you have said, "My name shall be
there," that you may listen to the prayer that your servant offers toward
this place.

Solomon knew that the temple did not contain God, but it did mediate
His presence to the people because His name was there. Central to the
kingship and the Davidic Covenant was the temple and God's presence.

But as for the king, he must keep the worship of God pure. The purity
of the temple worship is his concern and responsibility. The history of the
kings from Solomon onward consistently makes this the tipping point of
whether a king did what was right in God's eyes. The question is always directed at whether they purified the land from idolatry and led the people in
holy worship. Building the temple was not the king's only concern. Guarding the temple of God was the key responsibility of the king. Israelite
kingship, therefore has a priestly function. The king was not a priest, but
the purity of God's worship and temple were of utmost concern to him.

b. Keep God's law

As discussed previously God gave laws to Israel's future kings in Deuteronomy 17. They were required to write a Levite-approved copy of the
law and to submit themselves to God's commands. This infuses the kingship with a prophetic function. Prophets preserve and deliver the word of
God to the people. In this case, the King is to copy the law of God and
to lead the kingdom in obeying it. He is not to add his own laws to God's
laws, nor to neglect God's word. The king does not create the law; the king
keeps the law. He is to be God's vice-regent, or under-king, to Israel.

God said in the Davidic Covenant that "When he commits iniquity,
I will discipline him with the rod of men." The opposite, then, is true, that
when the king keeps the law and practices righteousness, he will not be
disciplined. He will be blessed.

c. Represent God's people

Federal headship is an integral aspect of covenant-making in the Bible. God covenants with one person on behalf of many. In the Davidic
Covenant, David is the federal head of his sons. Only David's offspring
have a rightful claim to this covenant because only they fall under his fed-

eral headship. But David's federal headship over his sons is not the concern of this point. Rather, *the Davidic king is appointed as the federal head of the Mosaic Covenant.* The Mosaic Covenant had a Mediator, Moses, but not a federal head. God delivered the law through Moses, but descent from Moses or relation to Moses did not affect one's standing in the Mosaic Covenant. Moses' disobedience in striking the rock as opposed to speaking to it as commanded may have disinherited him from entrance into Canaan, but no one else suffered for his infraction. As the book of Judges stated so prominently, everyone did what was right in their own eyes, and there was no king in Israel.

The Davidic Covenant established the heirs of David as the representatives or federal heads of the kingdom. They are not just to lead the people as an example of righteousness and law-keeping. They are to *represent* the people in their law-keeping. This means that if the king is righteous, the people are blessed. If the king is wicked, the people are cursed. As goes the king, so goes the kingdom. This is the consistent testimony of the historical record of Kings and Chronicles. Righteous kings brought blessing on the land. Wicked kings brought curses on the land.[4]

4. The Sanctions of the Covenant

The Davidic king was a federal head or representative for the nation, whose obedience or disobedience determined the blessing or cursing of the people. These details become clearer when discussing the sanctions of the covenant.

a. The judgment of God himself

In the Davidic Covenant, God gave promises to David and his descendants and He obligated David and his descendants to obey certain laws. To make this a formal covenant, God threatened David's sons with discipline and punishment. In 2 Samuel 7:14 God said, "I will be to him a father, and he shall be to me a son. When he commits iniquity, I will discipline him with the rod of men, with the stripes of the sons of men."

The Davidic king and God have a very special Father-son relationship. God will protect and bless the king, watching over him. But when the king does not keep the law, God will discipline him and punish him. This is repeated in Psalm 132:11–12.

---

[4] "The Mosaic covenant at Sinai is… the basis for God's covenant with David. The king of Israel is the administrator and mediator of the Mosaic covenant, representing God's rule to the people and representing the people as a whole." Gentry and Wellum, *Kingdom through Covenant*, 295.

11 The LORD swore to David a sure oath from which he will not turn back: 'One of the sons of your body I will set on your throne. 12 *If your sons keep my covenant and my testimonies that I shall teach them*, their sons also forever shall sit on your throne.

If the sons keep the covenant, they will sit on the throne. They must do what is required of them, or they will be punished and disciplined. Solomon declared the same in 1 Kings 8:25–26.

25 Therefore, LORD God of Israel, now keep what You promised Your servant David my father, saying, 'You shall not fail to have a man sit before Me on the throne of Israel, *only if your sons take heed to their way, that they walk before Me as you have walked before Me.*' 26 And now I pray, O God of Israel, let Your word come true, which You have spoken to Your servant David my father.

Discipline and punishment may appear to be mild terms, but the covenantal threats, the sanctions, are more serious than that.

b. Expulsion from the land of Canaan

In the Davidic Covenant, the curses threatened in the Mosaic Covenant are now directed at the nation through the king. Discipline and punishment are not just slaps on the wrist, but a complete disinheritance from the blessings promised to Abraham. After the temple's completion and Solomon's coronation, God appeared to him and said in 1 Kings 9:4–9,

4 And as for you, *if you will walk before me, as David your father walked, with integrity of heart and uprightness, doing according to all that I have commanded you, and keeping my statutes and my rules*, 5 then I will establish your royal throne over Israel forever, as I promised David your father, saying, "You shall not lack a man on the throne of Israel." 6 But *if you turn aside from following me, you or your children, and do not keep my commandments and my statutes that I have set before you, but go and serve other gods and worship them, 7 then I will cut off Israel from the land that I have given them*, and the house that I have consecrated for my name I will cast out of my sight, and Israel will become a proverb and a byword among all peoples. 8 And this house will become a heap of ruins. Everyone passing by it will be astonished and will hiss, and they will say, "Why has the LORD done thus to this land and to this house?" 9 Then they will say, 'Because they abandoned the LORD their God who brought their fathers out of the land of Egypt and laid hold on other gods and worshiped them and served them. Therefore the LORD has brought all this disaster on them.

This passage confirms and unites the previous points. If Solomon and his sons obey God's law, the statutes and rules, they will be blessed. If they turn aside and do not keep the commandments, then Israel will be cut off from the land. God quoted from Deuteronomy 28 where Israel is threatened that it will become like a byword and proverb, "At least we're not like Israel."

1 Kings 11:11–13 provides additional confirmation. God kept his word and punished Solomon for his idolatry.

> 11 Therefore the LORD said to Solomon, *"Since this has been your practice and you have not kept my covenant and my statutes that I have commanded you*, I will surely tear the kingdom from you and will give it to your servant. 12 Yet for the sake of David your father I will not do it in your days, but I will tear it out of the hand of your son. 13 However, I will not tear away all the kingdom, but I will give one tribe to your son, for the sake of David my servant and for the sake of Jerusalem that I have chosen."

The Davidic Covenant is much like the Abrahamic Covenant. God made promises to Abraham that were sure to the whole nation, but individuals and groups could be cut off for unfaithfulness. So also, God's promises to David are sure to his line, but individual kings who are unfaithful will be cut off from those blessings.[5] God took the throne from Solomon because he did not keep the covenant. But He did not take it away entirely, for the sake of David.

This cycle repeats through many generations until the tipping point for Judah in 2 Kings 23:26–27. Israel was destroyed and exiled over 100 years earlier. But there came a time when Judah would no longer be allowed to stay in the land because of its wickedness and idolatry.

> 26 Still the LORD did not turn from the burning of his great wrath, by which his anger was kindled against Judah, because of all the provocations with which Manasseh had provoked him. 27 And the LORD said, "I will remove Judah also out of my sight, as I have removed Israel, and I will cast off this city that I have chosen, Jerusalem, and the house of which I said, My name shall be there."

Prior to this point, Judah was called to repent and return to their God. But from Manasseh onward, Judah's downfall was inevitable. And it came about because of the wickedness of the king. Wicked kings were cursed, culminating in complete expulsion and exile for Judah. As goes the king, so goes the kingdom. And the curse exacted on Israel is declared by God

---

[5] Cf. Schreiner, *Covenant and God's Purpose*, 78. "God will certainly fulfill his covenant, but the fulfillment will be realized only with an obedient king."

in the same terms it was proposed in the Davidic Covenant. The worst thing that can happen to Israel is for God to remove His presence from His temple.

This point makes a giant historical leap all the way from Solomon to the exile. But this span of time tells one very legible story because the proper foundation for comprehending God's relationship with Israel has been laid in the Davidic Covenant, which can be summed up in this way: Insofar as the Davidic king keeps the Mosaic Covenant, the kingdom enjoys the blessings of the Abrahamic Covenant. Insofar as the Davidic king fails to keep the Mosaic Covenant, the kingdom suffers the curses of the covenants.

Conclusion

With the Abrahamic, Mosaic, and Davidic Covenants put together we can clearly see the kingdom of Israel in full. It is what it is because of these covenants by which it was established and through which it was governed. They all have the same parties, precepts, promises, and penalties. They are all directed to Abraham's offspring in the land of Canaan. Abraham's federal headship continues to define the people in view in this kingdom. Abraham's inheritance of Canaan continues to determine the boundaries of the kingdom. The Mosaic Covenant simply expands on the obligations of the people in that land. And the Davidic Covenant focuses the kingdom into one person through whom obedience must be rendered, and through whom blessings and curses will fall on the nation. But the Mosaic and Davidic Covenants do not extend any further than the initial scope set down in the Abrahamic Covenant. In order to enjoy blessed life in Canaan, God's covenant must be kept.

This is why the Old Covenant includes the Abrahamic, Mosaic, and Davidic Covenants. Moses controls Abraham and David. The Mosaic Covenant is the most prominent covenant in the Old Testament because it controls whether you enjoy Abraham's covenant and it stands over the Davidic kings who must copy and keep the law. It is impossible to refer only to the Mosaic Covenant when speaking of the Old Covenant because it unavoidably brings along with it the other two covenants that it controls. This argument is clear when studying how various covenants combine and collaborate in order to establish and govern a particular kingdom. The kingdom that the Abrahamic Covenant established and governed is the same as that which was further established and governed by the Mosaic Covenant and the Davidic Covenant. In sum, the old covenant governs the kingdom of Israel. It includes the Abrahamic Covenant, the Mosaic Covenant, and the Davidic Covenant.

9

The Messiah
of the Old Covenant

Introduction

The primary concern of this chapter is the development of the central concept of the Messiah to the kingdom of Israel and its covenants. Tracing this development is the tracing of the progress of the mystery of Christ, especially when we remember that Messiah and Christ are the same word. If the hope of the Messiah is the central hope of Israel's kingdom and covenants, then the mystery of Christ is the central hope of Israel's kingdom and covenants.

1. The Messianic Purpose of the Old Covenant

From its inception in Genesis 12, the Israelite kingdom and its covenants contained the promise of a blessing-mediating descendant. All subsequent kingdom and covenant developments subserved this promise. They were the "covenants of promise" belonging to Israel according to the flesh (Romans 9:4; Ephesians 2:12). The purpose of the Old Covenant was to produce the New Covenant because the purpose of the Old Covenant was to provide the Messiah, the Christ, the Mediator of the New Covenant.

The progress of the old covenants from Abraham to Moses to David expanded the typology of this promise in a broad and narrow way. Broadly, the entire kingdom of Israel and its covenants were typical, as Hebrews 10:1 asserts. "The law has but a shadow of the good things to come instead of the true form of these realities." The land of Canaan was a shadow of a greater land. The sacrificial system was a shadow of a greater sacrifice.

The priestly lineage was a shadow of a greater High Priest. The victories and triumphs of David were a shadow of David's greater Son. The people of Abraham in their numerous tribes were a shadow of a transnational people. The exodus was a shadow of a greater deliverance from bondage. The Passover was a shadow of a greater passing over. Examples could be multiplied. The law, i.e., the kingdom of Israel, including the Abrahamic, Mosaic, and Davidic Covenants, was an earthly shadow, and not the true form of heavenly realities.

Narrowly, the progress of the covenants focuses the eyes of the children of Abraham on one person, the son of David, the Messiah. And the mission of the Messiah was legible because of the rich picture that had already been painted and promised concerning Him. The typology of the Old Covenant revealed the Messiah and His covenant and kingdom in general. But Israel's Messianic hopes were much more specific than a broad expectation of a child of Abraham who would bless the nations. Israel had specific hopes concerning a specific individual.

2. The Messianic Hope of the Old Covenant

The messianic hope of the Old Covenant derives directly from the Davidic Covenant. The Davidic Covenant focuses the kingdom of Israel into one person. As goes the king, so goes the kingdom. The hopes and confidence of the people were placed in the anointed king, because of the covenant God made with David and his sons. This produced great expectations for the kingship in the people's minds.

a. The present Messiah

The people of Israel's expectations relative to the king are seen in the Scriptures by paying attention to the word "anointed," which we know as "Messiah." To say "Messiah" is to say "The anointed one." It is important to equate "the anointed one" with the king. The Davidic king is the anointed one. The king is messiah.

The people's expectations of God's blessing on the Davidic king, the anointed one, are recorded in Psalm 18:50.

> Great salvation he brings to his *king*, and shows steadfast love to his *anointed, to David and his offspring forever.*

Their confidence stemmed from God's covenantal commitments to them through David in the Davidic Covenant.

For the same reason, the people were confident in the king as he went out to battle. God was on his side because of the Davidic Covenant. They did not trust in their military might or prowess, but in God's blessing on the anointed one, David and his offspring.

> 6 Now I know that the LORD *saves his anointed*; he will answer him from his holy heaven with the saving might of his right hand. 7 Some trust in chariots and some in horses, but we trust in the name of the LORD our God. 8 They collapse and fall, but we rise and stand upright. 9 O LORD, *save the king*! May he answer us when we call (Psalm 20:6–9).

The anointed one, the Messiah, is the Davidic king. The Psalms are full of this. The king and his relationship with Jehovah are at the heart and center of so many of the Psalms. That's how the Psalms begin. Psalm 1 sets out who the righteous and just man is, and Psalm 2 says that it's the king. The Davidic king is the anointed one. The Psalmist unites these concepts in Psalm 132:10–18.

> 10 For the sake of your servant David, do not turn away the face of your *anointed* one. 11 The LORD swore to David a sure oath from which he will not turn back: "One of the sons of your body I will set on your throne. 12 If your sons keep my covenant and my testimonies that I shall teach them, their sons also forever shall sit on your throne." 13 For the LORD has chosen Zion; he has desired it for his dwelling place: 14 "This is my resting place forever; here I will dwell, for I have desired it. 15 I will abundantly bless her provisions; I will satisfy her poor with bread. 16 Her priests I will clothe with salvation, and her saints will shout for joy. 17 There I will make a horn to sprout for David; I have prepared a lamp for my *anointed*. 18 His enemies I will clothe with shame, but on him his crown will shine."

It is important to see that the Psalms cited here do not contain a *future* hope in the anointed one, but a *present* hope. The origin of the Messianic concept was the present, current Davidic king reigning in Jerusalem.[1] The king is messiah, the anointed of the Lord, and rightly so, by virtue of the Davidic Covenant. The people's expectations of blessedness were wrapped up in the present king.

The king was at the front and center of the kingdom. He was the federal head of the people, the son of God, the blessed one, the anointed one, the one whom God will protect and preserve. And the people of the king-

---

[1] When Samuel was sent to anoint one of Jesse's sons to replace Saul as king, his explanation of why none of the sons present were to be king was that none of them was *meshiach*, "the anointed one."

dom invested their trust in the king to this degree because of the promises of the Davidic Covenant that gave protection and stability to their own lives. These were their kingly expectations.

This aspect of the kingship of Israel strongly echoes the garden of Eden. The king is the son of God in a new paradise, deeply connected to the temple and sanctuary of God's presence, standing in the place of the nation, called to keep the law and preserve the purity of God's Word and worship. Israel is a new Eden, and the king is a new son of God, a new Adam guarding a new temple. But the king had to be faithful, and few kings of the kingdom were.

b. The future Messiah

The higher you climb, the farther you fall. Israel's hopes climbed high, due to God's promises in the Abrahamic, Mosaic, and Davidic Covenants. But the enjoyment of those promises depended to a great degree on their obedience to God's law. Israel's obedience as a nation was never up to the level that it should have been. Like Adam, they were unfaithful to God's covenant, and they fell far, very far (Hosea 6:7).

The history of Kings and Chronicles identifies each king as either good or bad. Either they did what was right, or they did evil. All of the kings of the northern kingdom, the kingdom of Israel, were evil. In the southern kingdom, the kingdom of Judah, most of the kings were evil, but some of them were righteous. Blessings or curses follow the goodness and badness of each king.

The failures of the kings, placed against the backdrop of the promises of the Davidic Covenant caused a shift in perspective. God promised David that his descendants would sit on the throne, but He also threatened that He would punish the disobedient kings. The repeated failings of the kings and the lack of stability that this inevitably brought upon the nation shifted Judah's hope in the anointed king from *the present king*, to the idea of *a future king* who would be righteous and bring blessing to the land. God had not established the throne of *this* son of David, but He will establish the throne of *a* son of David.

Psalm 89:28–49 expresses the contrast between God's promises to David and his sons, and what Israel was experiencing. The first section lays out the foundation, God's promises.

> 28 My steadfast love I will keep for him forever, and my covenant will stand firm for him. 29 I will establish his offspring forever and his throne as the days of the heavens. 30 If his children forsake my law and do not walk according to my rules, 31 if they violate my statutes and do not keep

my commandments, 32 then I will punish their transgression with the
rod and their iniquity with stripes, 33 but I will not remove from him
my steadfast love or be false to my faithfulness. 34 I will not violate my
covenant or alter the word that went forth from my lips. 35 Once for all I
have sworn by my holiness; I will not lie to David. 36 His offspring shall
endure forever, his throne as long as the sun before me. 37 Like the moon
it shall be established forever, a faithful witness in the skies."

God promised an established throne, but this conflicted with Israel's present experience.

38 *But now you have cast off and rejected; you are full of wrath against your
anointed.* 39 *You have renounced the covenant* with your servant; you have
defiled his crown in the dust. 40 You have breached all his walls; you have
laid his strongholds in ruins. 41 All who pass by plunder him; he has become the scorn of his neighbors. 42 You have exalted the right hand of his
foes; you have made all his enemies rejoice. 43 You have also turned back
the edge of his sword, and you have not made him stand in battle. 44 You
have made his splendor to cease and cast his throne to the ground. 45 You
have cut short the days of his youth; you have covered him with shame.

Judah accused God of renouncing the covenant. It was the conclusion
they drew from witnessing and experiencing defeat and exile. They saw exile as God failing to fulfill His promises in the Davidic Covenant. Indeed,
it would seem so when Jerusalem is overrun, the temple is sacked, and the
walls of the city are razed. Zedekiah the king was taken to Babylon, and
his sons were killed in front of his eyes, then his eyes were gouged out. The
last thing he ever saw was the murder of his own sons. Israel could not
reconcile this with the Davidic Covenant.

46 How long, O LORD? Will you hide yourself forever? How long will
your wrath burn like fire? 47 Remember how short my time is! For what
vanity you have created all the children of man! 48 What man can live
and never see death? Who can deliver his soul from the power of Sheol?
49 Lord, where is your steadfast love of old, which by your faithfulness
you swore to David?

Judah was longing for the Lord to raise up His anointed one because
God had promised it. When the kingship showed its flaws and sinfulness, the hope of Israel in the anointed one, or the Messiah, became less
concrete and more abstract. It shifted from the present to the future. With
each flawed ruler, Israel looked to the next one, awaiting a truly righteous
king whose throne would be established. And once the exile came, the
question in Israel's mind was simply, "where is the Lord's anointed?"

When the promises of the Davidic Covenant are placed side by side with the events of Israel's history and the exile it automatically creates questions as to the identity of the Messiah. Where is the Messiah? Who will be the faithful son of God? Who will deliver us from our enemies? Who will restore us to our inheritance? Who will keep the law for us? Who will lead us in pure worship? Who will cleanse the temple? Who will give the pure Word of God to us?

It was in this context that the prophets gave words of encouragement to the people of Judah, promising the that the Lord would raise up a Davidic descendant in whom the promises of the covenant would be fulfilled. It is necessary to read this passage in light of the rich biblical data covered to this point, from Adam to Noah to Abraham to Moses to David, to all of the history, to all of the sin and failure, to all of the hopes and expectations based on God's promises.

> 14 Behold, the days are coming, declares the LORD, when I will fulfill the promise I made to the house of Israel and the house of Judah. 15 In those days and at that time I will cause a righteous Branch to spring up for David, and he shall execute justice and righteousness in the land. 16 In those days Judah will be saved, and Jerusalem will dwell securely. And this is the name by which it will be called: 'The LORD is our righteousness.' 17 For thus says the LORD: David shall never lack a man to sit on the throne of the house of Israel, 18 and the Levitical priests shall never lack a man in my presence to offer burnt offerings, to burn grain offerings, and to make sacrifices forever (Jeremiah 33:14–18).

The Lord will provide a Davidic descendant, a king who brings righteousness to the nation of Israel. He will do it. The days are coming. In the words of the prophets, the dawning light of Jesus Christ gleamed on the horizon. The prophets did not know Him, but Jesus Christ was the hope of the Israelites. He was promised to them. Isaiah 9:1–7 adds to this.

> 1 But there will be no gloom for her who was in anguish. In the former time he brought into contempt the land of Zebulun and the land of Naphtali, but in the latter time he has made glorious the way of the sea, the land beyond the Jordan, Galilee of the nations. 2 The people who walked in darkness have seen a great light; those who dwelt in a land of deep darkness, on them has light shone. 3 You have multiplied the nation; you have increased its joy; they rejoice before you as with joy at the harvest, as they are glad when they divide the spoil. 4 For the yoke of his burden, and the staff for his shoulder, the rod of his oppressor, you have broken as on the day of Midian. 5 For every boot of the tramping warrior in battle tumult and every garment rolled in blood will be burned as fuel for the fire. 6 For to us a child is born, to us a son is given; and

the government shall be upon his shoulder, and his name shall be called Wonderful Counselor, Mighty God, Everlasting Father, Prince of Peace. 7 Of the increase of his government and of peace there will be no end, *on the throne of David* and over his kingdom, to establish it and to uphold it with justice and with righteousness from this time forth and forevermore. The zeal of the LORD of hosts will do this.

There will be a king on the throne of David. His kingdom will not end. His government will increase without opposition. He shall be called "Wonderful Counselor, Mighty God, Everlasting Father, Prince of Peace." That would be healing for the spirit of a disillusioned and exiled Israelite. A faithful son of David runs throughout the prophets' words to Israel. There will be a future Messiah.

3. The Messianic Promise of a New Covenant

The imperfections of the Israelite kingdom and its covenants, combined with the promises of God, produced a longing for something other and greater than what Israel experienced. The exile heightened this tension to its maximum. Life could not get worse for a people who had been promised something so much better. And as the prophets received their word from God, God began to put in the minds of His people a New Covenant through a future Messiah, a covenant of peace with a new sanctuary of God's presence.

24 My servant David shall be king over them, and they shall all have one shepherd. They shall walk in my rules and be careful to obey my statutes. 25 They shall dwell in the land that I gave to my servant Jacob, where your fathers lived. They and their children and their children's children shall dwell there forever, and David my servant shall be their prince forever. 26 *I will make a covenant of peace with them. It shall be an everlasting covenant with them.* And I will set them in their land and multiply them, and will set my sanctuary in their midst forevermore. 27 My dwelling place shall be with them, and I will be their God, and they shall be my people. 28 Then the nations will know that I am the LORD who sanctifies Israel, when my sanctuary is in their midst forevermore. (Ezekiel 37:24–28)

Given the burden of the law of the Mosaic Covenant and the curses poured out from the Mosaic and Davidic Covenants, this would have been wonderful news. And it is in this context of exilic devastation and the failures of the Davidic line that a well-known passage sings a song sweeter than any other.

31 Behold, the days are coming, declares the LORD, when I will make a new covenant with the house of Israel and the house of Judah, 32 not like the covenant that I made with their fathers on the day when I took them by the hand to bring them out of the land of Egypt, my covenant that they broke, though I was their husband, declares the LORD. 33 For this is the covenant that I will make with the house of Israel after those days, declares the LORD: I will put my law within them, and I will write it on their hearts. And I will be their God, and they shall be my people. 34 And no longer shall each one teach his neighbor and each his brother, saying, 'Know the LORD,' for they shall all know me, from the least of them to the greatest, declares the LORD. For I will forgive their iniquity, and I will remember their sin no more (Jeremiah 31:31–34).

For those living under a covenant that is designed to remind its people of their sin on a repetitive basis, there would be nothing more soul-refreshing than to hear of a New Covenant whose fundamental promise is the forgiveness of iniquity and the casting of sin into oblivion. God is going to make a New Covenant *that isn't like the old one.* God is going to make a new covenant that forgives sins, a covenant that places the law inside of you as your guide, not outside of you as your taskmaster. After all of the sin from Adam to Noah to Abraham to Moses to David, at last this covenant will forgive sins. The Messianic hope of the Old Covenant, then, is nothing other than the New Covenant hope of the Old Covenant. When that future perfect Messiah comes, He will bring a new covenant with Him, and all the people of the Lord will know God.

4. The Messianic Inclusion of the Nations

In Genesis 12, God had promised that Abraham's line would produce a descendant through whom a blessing for the world would come. The descendant would provide that blessing, which is the New Covenant. The focusing of the Israelite kingdom and covenants into one person, the Davidic king, brought the silhouette of this figure into sharp focus, though it was the silhouette of a future Messiah, a future faithful son of David.

The prophets declared that the blessings of the Messiah would extend beyond the offspring of Abraham. The Messiah will gather the nations in a restored and perfected temple. First, it is promised that the nations will flow to the house of God.

1 It shall come to pass in the latter days that *the mountain of the house of the LORD shall be established as the highest of the mountains,* and it shall be lifted up above the hills; and *peoples shall flow to it,* 2 and *many nations shall come,* and say: "Come, let us go up to the mountain of the LORD, to

the house of the God of Jacob, that he may teach us his ways and that we may walk in his paths." For out of Zion shall go forth the law, and the word of the LORD from Jerusalem. 3 He shall judge between *many peoples*, and shall decide disputes for strong nations far away; and they shall beat their swords into plowshares, and their spears into pruning hooks; nation shall not lift up sword against nation, neither shall they learn war anymore; 4 but they shall sit every man under his vine and under his fig tree, and no one shall make them afraid, for the mouth of the LORD of hosts has spoken (Micah 4:1–4; cf. Isaiah 2:2–4; 56:6–8; Haggai 2:6–9).

Second, it is promised that the signal on God's mountain (i.e., temple) to which the nations are drawn is the Messiah, the son of David.

1 There shall come forth a shoot from the stump of Jesse, and a branch from his roots shall bear fruit. 2 And the Spirit of the LORD shall rest upon him, the Spirit of wisdom and understanding, the Spirit of counsel and might, the Spirit of knowledge and the fear of the LORD. 3 And his delight shall be in the fear of the LORD. He shall not judge by what his eyes see, or decide disputes by what his ears hear, 4 but with righteousness he shall judge the poor, and decide with equity for the meek of the earth; and he shall strike the earth with the rod of his mouth, and with the breath of his lips he shall kill the wicked. 5 Righteousness shall be the belt of his waist, and faithfulness the belt of his loins. 6 The wolf shall dwell with the lamb, and the leopard shall lie down with the young goat, and the calf and the lion and the fattened calf together; and a little child shall lead them. 7 The cow and the bear shall graze; their young shall lie down together; and the lion shall eat straw like the ox. 8 The nursing child shall play over the hole of the cobra, and the weaned child shall put his hand on the adder's den. 9 *They shall not hurt or destroy in all my holy mountain*; for the earth shall be full of the knowledge of the LORD as the waters cover the sea. 10 *In that day the root of Jesse, who shall stand as a signal for the peoples—of him shall the nations inquire*, and his resting place shall be glorious (Isaiah 11:1–10).

In the law, prophets, and writings, the mystery of Christ was made known. The Messiah of Israel, the son of David, will unite Israel and the nations in a new house of God through a new covenant of forgiveness and righteousness.

Many other passages in the prophets add to this, some of which will be discussed in the Covenant of Redemption. The Servant Songs of Isaiah say that the Servant of the Lord, the Lord's *anointed*, will speak Jehovah's word and will be given as a covenant to the people. He will die and suffer in their place, and by His wounds and death many will be made whole; many will be accounted righteous for His sake.

5. The Typological Nature of the Kingdom

The kingdom of Israel and its covenants were typical shadows of Christ, the substance. As types, they were their own entities serving their own purposes in their own contexts. Yet also as types, they pointed upward and onward to something greater than themselves. The promises of the prophets contributed a great deal to pushing the Israelite hopes beyond their present situation to something more ideal, something more perfect, something more permanent.

Yet, for all the quantity of revelation given to Israel, it was given through the mode of mystery and the medium of typology. The promises of the future kingdom and covenant of Messiah are all contained within the language of the typical realm. The revelation of the perfected future through the imperfect present, that is, the typological nature of the kingdom of Israel and its covenants, constituted the mystery of Christ. The Messianic hopes of the people under the Old Covenant, therefore, were commonly restricted to an idealized version of their present existence. They saw the Messiah bringing them victory over foreign powers, rebuilding their temple, and inviting the nations to become Jewish. What God had in store for them, and the world, was far better than they could have imagined. They failed to realize just how much the New Covenant would not be like the Old Covenant, and why that was such a blessed reality.

Israel's hopes rose and fell with restoration from exile and the rebuilding of the temple. But they never regained their former glory, nor did one of their kings sit on the throne. Soon after, the prophetic voice of the Spirit fell silent for centuries. Until one day…

> 26 In the sixth month the angel Gabriel was sent from God to a city of Galilee named Nazareth, 27 to a virgin betrothed to a man whose name was Joseph, *of the house of David*. And the virgin's name was Mary. 28 And he came to her and said, "Greetings, O favored one, the Lord is with you!" 29 But she was greatly troubled at the saying, and tried to discern what sort of greeting this might be. 30 And the angel said to her, "Do not be afraid, Mary, for you have found favor with God. 31 And behold, you will conceive in your womb and bear a son, and you shall call his name Jesus. 32 He will be great and will be called the Son of the Most High. *And the Lord God will give to him the throne of his father David, 33 and he will reign over the house of Jacob forever, and of his kingdom there will be no end*" (Luke 1:26–33).

That child was born, and shepherds and royal wise men were informed of the birth of the King of the Jews. Then a man named John declared the arrival of the Lord, one vastly greater than he, and "14 Jesus came into Galilee, proclaiming the gospel of God, 15 and saying, 'The time is fulfilled, and the kingdom of God is at hand; repent and believe in the gospel'" (Mark 1:14–15). Neighbors heard that a man named Jesus was healing diseases and casting out demons and preaching about the kingdom of God. And Andrew found his brother Simon (Peter) and said, "We have found the Messiah (which means Christ)" (John 1:41). At last, this is it. He's here.

Conclusion

In a world cursed through Adam and stabilized through Noah, a special kingdom was formed through covenants made with Abraham and his descendants in Canaan. In this kingdom and its covenants, a mystery took shape. This nation will bring a blessing to the nations. From Abraham to David, the mystery revealed that a Davidic son, a Messiah, would gather the nations in the house of God through a new covenant. This revelation of mystery, declared and gathered over centuries, was contained in typology. Present realities pointed to future realities greater and other than themselves. The Messiah ushered in the age of those new realities, those perfected realities, those eternal realities, in a new and eternal covenant granting an inheritance in a new and eternal kingdom.

Part Four

The Kingdom of Christ

The Kingdom of Creation was established and governed by the Covenant of Works and the Noahic Covenant. That kingdom is cursed and destined for destruction, but also preserved for the sake of salvation. The Kingdom of Israel was established and governed by the Abrahamic Covenant, the Mosaic Covenant, and the Davidic Covenant. God made invincible promises to Abraham but conditioned the enjoyment of those promises on obedience. Individuals and generations cut themselves off from enjoying those privileges through their disobedience. The Mosaic Covenant controlled everything through its laws, applying to everyone from the king to the commoner. And the Davidic covenant focused the kingdom into one person, a king who was commanded to keep the law on behalf of the nation. Righteous kings were blessed, and the nation was blessed with them. Wicked kings were cursed, and the nation was cursed with them. Israel was exiled for their wickedness, but God restored them for the sake of His unfulfilled promises to Abraham, in particular the promise of the offspring through whom the nations of the earth would blessed. That offspring was the Messiah, the Christ, whose blessing for the world was a new kingdom granted through a new covenant. This was not what Israel expected.

10

The Ministry of Christ

Introduction

Israel was longing and looking for a Davidic descendant whose throne would be established by God Himself in such a way that they would be freed from foreign powers and restored to the former glory of the kingdom. They expected the Messiah to perfect their present state. God sent that Son of David, Jesus Christ (Messiah), but the ministry of the Christ perplexed and perturbed the children of Abraham according to the flesh. He did not lead them to political supremacy or free them from foreign rule at all. He did not perfect their present state. In fact, He offered them something that seemed to them to be entirely *not* Jewish and of no real benefit to their current condition. The Jews stumbled over the unveiling of the mystery.

1. The Gospel of the Kingdom

From the beginning of the Christ's ministry, He declared good news (gospel). Jesus also declared that the response to this good news was repentance and faith.

> 14 Jesus came into Galilee, proclaiming the gospel of God, 15 and saying, "The time is fulfilled, and the kingdom of God is at hand; repent and believe in the gospel" (Mark 1:14–15).

Throughout His ministry, Jesus declared that this good news was for everyone. He was the Servant of the Lord proclaiming good news to the poor (Luke 4:18, 21), to the weary and heavy-laden (Matthew 11:28–30), to the sick (Matthew 9:11–12). He spoke to Samaritans, tax collectors, harlots, and declared good news to them all. But what was the good news? Were the benefits Jesus offered simply healing and freedom from demonic oppression (Mark 1:34)?

Jesus taught that the good news, the gospel, of the kingdom was that He was going to offer Himself up as a sacrifice, that He would rise from the dead, and that He would grant eternal life to all those who trusted in Him. He was the good Shepherd, David, who would gather a flock united to Himself and give life to all His sheep (John 10:14–18; Ezekiel 34:22–25; 37:24–28).

The gospel of the kingdom and the response of faith in the Messiah who proclaims that gospel are portrayed clearly in the profession of faith made by Martha.

> 25 Jesus said to her, "I am the resurrection and the life. Whoever believes in me, though he die, yet shall he live, 26 and everyone who lives and believes in me shall never die. Do you believe this?" 27 She said to him, "Yes, Lord; I believe that you are the Christ, the Son of God, who is coming into the world" (John 11:25–27).

From the inception of His ministry, therefore, the Messiah brought blessings, a reversal of the curse in Adam, the forgiveness of sins and everlasting life. Jesus was providing a life far beyond idealized existence in Canaan. This is evident not only by the good news that He preached, but also the way in which He spoke of the kingdom of God, or kingdom of heaven.

2. The Kingdom of Heaven

The kingdom proclaimed by the Christ is a kingdom not of this world (John 18:36). Though the full unveiling of the nature of this kingdom occurs in the apostolic writings, the ministry of Christ established all its fundamental features. It is a kingdom from above, a kingdom entered not by natural birth, but supernatural birth (John 3:3–6). It is a kingdom belonging not to those born of the flesh, but those born of the Spirit (Matthew 8:11–12). It is a kingdom belonging not to those born of Abraham's body, but his belief (John 8:39, 56). It is a kingdom whose localized assembly is based on faith in Christ and the exercise of His authority (Matthew 16:16–19). It is a kingdom of those who are humble and helpless like children (Matthew 18:1–4).

Many of the Jews, especially the religious leaders, were provoked by the non-Jewish character of this teaching. Jesus taught that the offspring of Abraham according to the flesh were tenant workers who could not claim a right in the kingdom apart from faith in Himself (the Christ).

They were the guardians of the arrival of the one who would bless, but had no automatic claim to the blessing He brought. The thought that a gentile, by faith, without circumcision or any Jewish connection, would inherit the kingdom while the very children of Abraham were excluded was enraging (Matthew 8:10–12; 21:33–45). They failed to understand, indeed they disbelieved, the Messiah's mission and message. They tripped over the stumbling block in Zion, the mystery of Christ. The kingdom of heaven preached by the Jewish Christ was a blessing for all nations irrespective of parentage or outward obedience to the Jewish laws.

The kingdom of heaven is everlasting life in a consummated creation (1 Corinthians 15). It is righteousness and resurrection. And it is for everyone who repents and believes the gospel, trusting in the Christ Himself.

3. The King of the Kingdom

The Christ, Jesus, claimed absolute authority in the kingdom of heaven. He is its king. He stood in the seat of Moses and interpreted, applied, and personified the law, establishing His kingdom as a kingdom of righteousness (Matthew 5:17–20). He is its Prophet who declares the pure word of God. He is its Priest who brings the people near to God through sacrifice.

Many in Israel wanted Jesus to be their king, and when He came to Jerusalem, they applied Psalm 118 to Him.

> And the crowds that went before him and that followed him were shouting, "Hosanna to the Son of David! Blessed is he who comes in the name of the Lord! Hosanna in the highest!" (Matthew 21:9)

Jesus was indeed son of David and king, but He had not come to vanquish Roman rule. He came to destroy the ancient foe of mankind, Satan. And He set His face to go to Jerusalem to lay down His life for His sheep. He was not just the king of Psalm 118, but also the festal sacrifice. And the night that He was betrayed, the night when the sequence of His crucifixion began, the Christ of Israel announced a new covenant of forgiveness in His own blood.

Conclusion

The ministry of Jesus Christ initiated the unveiling of the full and final plan of God. Jesus began to reveal the blessing for the nations—a new humanity in a new kingdom through a new covenant to be received by faith in Christ Himself.

11

The Covenant of Redemption

Introduction

The New Covenant announced by the Messiah was established on a preceding covenantal foundation. That covenantal foundation is the Covenant of Redemption. In 2 Timothy 1:9, Paul teaches that salvation is the result of a purpose given in Christ Jesus "before the ages began." In Titus 1:2, Paul says that eternal life was promised "before the ages began." Scripture presents that eternal purpose and promise of salvation to mankind metaphorically in the mode of a covenant transacted between the persons of the Trinity.[1]

---

[1] "The counsel of God is the Eternal purpose of his Will, called his Counsel because of the infinite Wisdom wherewith it is always accompanied. So that which is called the good pleasure which he had purposed in himself, Ephes. 1.9. is termed the Counsel of his Will, ver. 11. Counsel among men, is a rational deliberation about causes, means, effects, and ends according to the Nature of things advised about, and the proper Interests of them who do deliberate. In this sense Counsel, is not to be attributed unto God. For as the infinite Sovereign Wisdom of his Being admits not of his taking Counsel with any other; so the infinite simplicity of his Nature and Understanding comprehending all things in one single Act of his Mind, allows not of formal Counsel or Deliberation. The first therefore of these the Scripture explodes, Isa. 40.13. Rom. 11.34. and although in the latter way God be frequently introduced as one deliberating or taking Counsel with himself, it is not the manner of doing, but the effect, or the thing done is intended." Owen, *A Continuation of the Exposition*, 156.

1. The Parties of the Covenant

The parties of the covenant of redemption are the Father, the Son, and the Holy Spirit. This is evidenced by many passages in the Scriptures where God the Father, Son, and Holy Spirit make commitments to one another, with the promise of some kind of reward related to those commitments. The primary source of Biblical data is the Servant Songs in Isaiah, beginning with Isaiah 42.

> 1 Behold *my servant*, whom I uphold, my chosen, in whom my soul delights; I have put my Spirit upon him; he will bring forth justice to the nations. 2 He will not cry aloud or lift up his voice, or make it heard in the street; 3 a bruised reed he will not break, and a faintly burning wick he will not quench; he will faithfully bring forth justice. 4 He will not grow faint or be discouraged till he has established justice in the earth; and the coastlands wait for his law. 5 Thus says God, the LORD, who created the heavens and stretched them out, who spread out the earth and what comes from it, who gives breath to the people on it and spirit to those who walk in it: 6 "I am the LORD; I have called you in righteousness; I will take you by the hand and keep you; I will give you as a covenant for the people, a light for the nations, 7 to open the eyes that are blind, to bring out the prisoners from the dungeon, from the prison those who sit in darkness" (Isaiah 42:1–7; cf. Isaiah 49:8–9).

These verses describe the Servant of Jehovah, the Spirit of Jehovah, and Jehovah. Jehovah will give the Servant as a covenant for the people, a light for the nations. The Servant will accomplish a task. He has a mission.

In Isaiah 50:4–9, the Servant expresses His willingness to undertake the mission.

> 4 The Lord GOD has given me the tongue of those who are taught, that I may know how to sustain with a word him who is weary. Morning by morning he awakens; he awakens my ear to hear as those who are taught. 5 The Lord GOD has opened my ear, and I was not rebellious; I turned not backward. 6 I gave my back to those who strike, and my cheeks to those who pull out the beard; I hid not my face from disgrace and spitting. 7 But the Lord GOD helps me; therefore I have not been disgraced; therefore I have set my face like a flint, and I know that I shall not be put to shame. 8 He who vindicates me is near. Who will contend with me? Let us stand up together. Who is my adversary? Let him come near to me. 9 Behold, the Lord GOD helps me; who will declare me guilty? Behold, all of them will wear out like a garment; the moth will eat them up.

Jehovah has equipped the Servant for His task, and He has set Himself to fulfill it completely and perfectly because He knows Jehovah will sustain Him.

Jesus applied the Servant Songs to Himself in Luke 4:17–21.

> 17 And the scroll of the prophet Isaiah was given to him. He unrolled the scroll and found the place where it was written, 18 "The Spirit of the Lord is upon me, because he has anointed me to proclaim good news to the poor. He has sent me to proclaim liberty to the captives and recovering of sight to the blind, to set at liberty those who are oppressed, 19 to proclaim the year of the Lord's favor." 20 And he rolled up the scroll and gave it back to the attendant and sat down. And the eyes of all in the synagogue were fixed on him. 21 And he began to say to them, "Today this Scripture has been fulfilled in your hearing."

Gleaning from these passages, the Father and Son are presented as the primary parties of this covenant, but the Holy Spirit is everywhere present. Jehovah promises to supply His Spirit to the Servant to equip and sustain Him for His mission. The Servant declares that the Spirit of Jehovah is upon Him. The Scriptures portray, in the mode of covenant, an intra-trinitarian dialogue between the Father, the Son, and the Holy Spirit concerning the redemption of an elect people.

2. The Commitments of the Covenant

a. The Son's commitments

In the Servant Songs of Isaiah, God the Father gave a mission to His Servant. In fact, the very name "the Servant of Jehovah" is an indicator of this fact. The Father laid the Son under certain obligations or commitments. He commanded Him to become incarnate, to obey the law perfectly, and to offer Himself up as a substitutionary sacrifice for a special people. God the Father gave work to God the Son. The Covenant of Redemption was a covenant of works. God the Son had to fulfill commands to obtain the blessings of the covenant.

The mission of the Son and its effects will extend to a people represented by the Son. He is appointed a federal head in this covenant. Jesus Himself spoke of this in John 10:17–18. He said, "17 For this reason the Father loves me, because I lay down my life that I may take it up again. 18 No one takes it from me, but I lay it down of my own accord. I have authority to lay it down, and I have authority to take it up again. *This charge I have received from my Father.*" And later in the same chapter, in verses 27–29 Jesus said, "27 My sheep hear my voice, and I know them, and they follow me. 28 I give them eternal life, and they will never perish, and no one will snatch them out of my hand. 29 *My Father, who has given them to me,* is greater than all, and no one is able to snatch them out of the Father's hand." The Father gave a people to the Son. And the Son was commanded to lay down His life for that people as their federal head.

God the Son was sent to die for a people. But His mission included much more than simply His death. He was appointed by the Father to be a Mediator for His people, and as that Mediator to be the King, Priest, and Prophet of God's elect.

Psalm 2:6–9 describes the Son-King of God. "6 'As for me, I have set my King on Zion, my holy hill.' 7 I will tell of the decree: The LORD said to me, 'You are my Son; today I have begotten you. 8 Ask of me, and I will make the nations your heritage, and the ends of the earth your possession. 9 You shall break them with a rod of iron and dash them in pieces like a potter's vessel.'" The Son is appointed as a King by God the Father.

Psalm 110:4 describes the Lord appointing His servant as a priest. "The LORD has sworn and will not change his mind, 'You are a priest forever after the order of Melchizedek.'" The Servant King is *appointed* as a priest. The Son is *appointed* as a priest by God the Father. Where there is a change of priesthood, there must be a change in law. A new covenant appointed God the Son to this priesthood. That's why the word of oath comes after the law, as Hebrews 7:28 says. It's a new covenant-commission.

Isaiah 61:1–2, another Servant Song, describes the Servant of the Lord as the one who receives and delivers the Word of God. That is the basic qualification of a Prophet. It says, "1 The Spirit of the Lord GOD is upon me, because the LORD has anointed me to bring good news to the poor; he has sent me to bind up the brokenhearted, to proclaim liberty to the captives, and the opening of the prison to those who are bound; 2 to proclaim the year of the LORD's favor, and the day of vengeance of our God; to comfort all who mourn." The Servant of the Lord has a message for God's people. He is God's spokesman. He is God's mouthpiece. That is the office of a prophet. Jesus says the same of Himself in John 17:8. "For I have given them *the words that you gave me,* and they have received them and have come to know in truth that I came from you; and they have believed that you sent me." Jesus gave to His people the words the Father gave to Him.

In the gospels God the Father says of Jesus in the transfiguration, "Listen to him." Hebrews 1 declares that the prophets spoke of old, but God's final and definitive revelation came through His Son. God the Father appointed God the Son to be a faithful servant for a special people, and to be the prophet, priest, and king of that people.

b. The Father's commitments

In the Servant Songs, the Father lays the Servant under many commitments. But the Father likewise commits Himself to the Son. The Father not only promises to equip the Son for His mission, but also to help Him.

> I am the LORD; I have called you in righteousness; I will take you by the hand and keep you (Isaiah 42:6).

> Thus says the LORD: "In a time of favor I have answered you; in a day of salvation I have helped you" (Isaiah 49:8).

> 7 But the Lord GOD helps me… 9 Behold, the Lord GOD helps me (Isaiah 50:7, 9).

This is a contrast to the Davidic Covenant. The Davidic king was appointed as a federal head over the nation of Israel with a mission to protect and provide for them. And though God supplied His Holy Spirit to help the king, there was no guarantee of that assistance. David prayed that God would not remove His Holy Spirit from him as He did from Saul, which is not a reference to indwelling but to the Holy Spirit making the king fit for his tasks. In the covenant of redemption, God the Father engaged Himself to assure and secure the success and completion of the Servant's mission.

The Holy Spirit played a very important role in the Covenant of Redemption. The Father promised to sustain and uphold the Son in His mission, and He did this through the Holy Spirit. Jesus was fully conscious of this promise and quoted Isaiah 61 to say that the Holy Spirit of Jehovah was upon Him.

In Luke 1:35 Mary was told that the incarnation would take place by the power of the Holy Spirit. In Matthew 12:27–28, Jesus said that He cast out demons by the Spirit of God, that is by the power of the Holy Spirit. In John 3, Jesus said that He speaks the words of the One who sent Him because the One who sent Him gave Him the Spirit without measure. Hebrews 9:14 says that Jesus offered Himself up through the Eternal Spirit, that is through the Holy Spirit. So whether it's the incarnation, the miracles, the message, the ministry, or the sacrifice of Jesus Christ, there was no part of His mission in which the Holy Spirit was not helping Him and empowering Him in His human nature to fulfill His commitments and obligations in the Covenant of Redemption.

Covenants are commitments with attached rewards or blessings guarded by sanctions. The reward promised to the Son if He faithfully and perfectly completed the commitments and obligations of the covenant was *resurrection* and *exaltation*.

10 Yet it was the will of the LORD to crush him; he has put him to grief; when his soul makes an offering for guilt, he shall see his offspring; he shall prolong his days; the will of the LORD shall prosper in his hand. 11 Out of the anguish of his soul he shall see and be satisfied; by his knowledge shall the righteous one, my servant, make many to be accounted righteous, and he shall bear their iniquities. 12 Therefore I will divide him a portion with the many, and he shall divide the spoil with the strong, because he poured out his soul to death and was numbered with the transgressors; yet he bore the sin of many, and makes intercession for the transgressors (Isaiah 53:10–12).

The Son will suffer for a people, according to the will of the Father. But He shall see His offspring. He shall see the will of the Lord prosper. He shall see and be satisfied. Many will be accounted righteous because of Him. His days will be prolonged. And as a result, He will receive a great portion as a conquering victor. He will be rewarded and magnified.[2]

Paul declared in Philippians 2:8–11 that God did reward the Son for His obedience.

8 And being found in human form, he humbled himself by becoming obedient to the point of death, even death on a cross. 9 Therefore God has highly exalted him and bestowed on him the name that is above every name, 10 so that at the name of Jesus every knee should bow, in heaven and on earth and under the earth, 11 and every tongue confess that Jesus Christ is Lord, to the glory of God the Father.

The Covenant of Redemption is a wonderful and wondrous truth. The Father sent the Son on a mission as a federal head of an elect people, constituted Him a prophet, priest, and king, sustained Him in His work, and promised Him a reward of eternal resurrected glorified life for Himself and all His people in a new creation.

This covenant is a fuller explanation of God's promise that the seed of Eve would crush Satan's head. Adam's Covenant of Works was designed to bring man to a consummated creation in communion with God. God the Son's Covenant of Works was designed to rescue man from the ashes of Adam's broken Covenant of Works and elevate them to an eternal invin-

---

[2] In Psalm 16 God promises that His Holy One will not see corruption, a passage that Peter quoted in Acts 13:34–37 and applied to Jesus. John 17:4–5 expresses these truths. "4 I glorified you on earth, having accomplished the work that you gave me to do. 5 And now, Father, glorify me in your own presence with the glory that I had with you before the world existed." Jesus asks the Father to glorify Him based on the completion of His mission.

cible inheritance in a new creation. "The reason the Son of God appeared was to destroy the works of the devil" (1 John 3:8).

3. The Fulfillment of the Covenant

God the Son willingly took up the mission given to Him (Philippians 2:5–8; Isaiah 50:5–7). Even from an early age, Jesus told His parents that He must be about His Father's business. Jesus Himself spoke of this and the gospels describe Him as one who would not be deterred or distracted by any. Rather, He followed through with His mission to the bitter end despite the persecution and suffering, despite the abandonment of His disciples. No one took His life from Him. He laid it down. He willingly accepted the mission given to Him by the Father. And as Paul says, Jesus was "obedient to the point of death, even death on a cross." In so doing, He fulfilled the commitments of the Covenant of Redemption and earned the reward (Isaiah 53:10–12). He was raised from the dead and glorified.

> 32 This Jesus God raised up, and of that we all are witnesses. 33 Being therefore exalted at the right hand of God, and having received from the Father the promise of the Holy Spirit, he has poured out this that you yourselves are seeing and hearing (Acts 2:32–33).

> 12 But when Christ had offered for all time a single sacrifice for sins, he sat down at the right hand of God, 13 waiting from that time until his enemies should be made a footstool for his feet. 14 For by a single offering he has perfected for all time those who are being sanctified (Hebrews 10:12–14).

After successfully offering His sacrifice, the Son sat down at the right hand of God. That is exaltation and glory.

The angels and saints praise the ascended Christ in Revelation 5:12, "saying with a loud voice, 'Worthy is the Lamb *who was slain*, to receive power and wealth and wisdom and might and honor and glory and blessing!'" The Lamb entered heaven to loud praise. He was worthy because He was slain. He was glorified because He was successful. So then, it is evident that Jesus perfectly fulfilled the covenant because He received the reward in full.

Jesus' fulfillment of this covenant is amazing because Jesus fulfilled the covenant on at least three levels. First, the Son kept the law of nature. He perfectly obeyed the moral law. He was tempted by Satan and did not fall in temptation. Second, the Son kept the law of Moses to fulfill all righteousness. He was born as a son of Abraham, under the law of Moses. He kept the moral law, the ceremonial law, and the judicial law. He was never unclean and never had to offer sacrifices for His own sin. Hebrews says that other priests sacrificed for their own sins before offering the sacrifice on the day of atonement (Hebrews 5:3; 7:26–27). But Jesus was pure and undefiled. Third, Jesus kept the law of His own covenant, taking a creaturely nature upon Himself and giving up His life as a ransom for many.

The faithfulness and success of Jesus augment an appreciation for the mystery of Christ and the typology of the Old Covenant that made His mission legible to the world. Where there is failure, or partial fulfillment, or problematic fulfillment, or loss of blessings, or unfaithfulness, the Old Testament teaches us to expect One who is not like that, One who is obedient, faithful, just, and righteous.

The Son of God committed Himself to fulfill a covenant of works on behalf of an elect people. Jesus' perfect obedience brings His people into a consummated creation, into everlasting life, into perfect righteousness, into unending holiness and never-ceasing obedience to God. Jesus' covenant was the most difficult, indeed impossible, covenant of them all. And He fulfilled it willingly and perfectly on every level at every moment of every day of His life, a life that continues even now as He sits at the right hand of God the Father ever living to intercede for us. Praise the Son for His obedience.

Conclusion

The Covenant of Redemption is a wonderful doctrine. What the Father planned, the Son accomplished, and the Spirit applies. The result of the Father's commitments, the Son's commitments, and the Spirit's participation is nothing other than the eternal salvation of the people of Christ. And that salvation is mediated to the elect through the New Covenant of grace.

12

The New Covenant of Grace

Introduction

Jesus Christ is the son of Abraham and David, the one through whom the nations of the world are blessed (Matthew 1:1; Luke 1:68–75). He is also the Son of God who was commissioned to take many sons to glory, to bring a new humanity to a consummation Adam failed to reach. These two genealogies and purposes were united. Jesus Christ completed His heavenly mission in the context of the earthly covenants of Israel, born under the law to redeem those under the law (Galatians 4:4–5). And in the New Covenant he freely granted the salvation and new-creation inheritance he obtained in the Covenant of Redemption to all who received Him by faith.

1. The Establishment of the New Covenant

The writer to the Hebrews argues that the New Covenant is a better covenant than the Old because it was legally established (νενομοθέτηται) on superior promises to that of the old.

> But as it is, Christ has obtained a ministry that is as much more excellent than the old as the covenant he mediates is better, since it is enacted (νενομοθέτηται) on better promises (Hebrews 8:6).

One of the reasons for the New Covenant's superiority to the Old is that the death of Christ accomplished far more than the blood of the Old Covenant's sacrificial animal victims.

By means of animal blood, High Priests cleansed the nation once a year. But the people never drew near to the inner sanctuary of the tabernacle, the most holy Place, where the glory of God rested between the cherubim above the mercy seat set on the ark. Jesus' blood brings His people directly into the heavenly presence of God's glory and places them there by removing, once and for all, the sins the first covenant could not take away (Hebrews 9:11–15; Ephesians 2:16; Colossians 1:20–22). As the Old Covenant was inaugurated with ritual blood, so was the New. But the blood of Christ cleanses once for all (Hebrews 9:24–26). The benefits of this covenantal sacrifice were enjoyed throughout history, but the legal establishment of it took place "at the end of the ages" (Hebrews 9:25–26). The death of Christ establishes His people in the New Covenant on the basis of a perfect and permanent sacrifice.

The fullness of the benefits of the New Covenant extends beyond forgiveness to a complete restoration and transformation of the sinner.

2. The Blessings of the New Covenant

The New Covenant announced by Jesus Christ on the night of His betrayal is the New Covenant of Jeremiah 31.

> 31 Behold, the days are coming, declares the LORD, when I will make a new covenant with the house of Israel and the house of Judah, 32 not like the covenant that I made with their fathers on the day when I took them by the hand to bring them out of the land of Egypt, my covenant that they broke, though I was their husband, declares the LORD.
> 33 For this is the covenant that I will make with the house of Israel after those days, declares the LORD: I will put my law within them, and I will write it on their hearts. And I will be their God, and they shall be my people. 34 And no longer shall each one teach his neighbor and each his brother, saying, "Know the LORD," for they shall all know me, from the least of them to the greatest, declares the LORD. For I will forgive their iniquity, and I will remember their sin no more (Jeremiah 31:31–34; Hebrews 8:8–13).

The blessings of this covenant are numerous and include everything that flows from union with Jesus Christ the Mediator and federal head of the covenant. God declares that in this covenant He will grant everlasting forgiveness and righteousness. He will justify His people and save them from their sins.

a. Justification

Through one act of disobedience, Adam brought condemnation on all his people. Through one act of obedience, Christ brought justification on all His people (Romans 5:17–19). By offering Himself up as a pure and perfect sacrifice, Jesus justified His people. This justification includes the wiping away of their sins forever and the legal imputation of Jesus' perfect righteousness to his people.

With this promise of forgiveness, God through Christ undoes one of our greatest curses—condemnation in Adam. From the moment Adam plunged mankind into sin, and for millennia afterwards, the world longed for the fulfillment of the promise that enmity would be interposed between mankind and Satan, and that amity would be restored between God and man. At last, in the New Covenant, God provided the legal basis for forgiveness of sins and reconciliation between God and man.

This forgiveness is eternal. The writer to the Hebrews declares in Hebrews 10:14 that Christ's one offering perfected His people forever, once and for all. And later in verse 18 the writer teaches that the success and finality of Christ's offering is evidenced by the fact that there are no more offerings for sin. As the Psalmist says, "As far as the east is from the west, so far does he remove our transgressions from us" (Psalm 103:12). Isaiah 53:5 details the great exchange. The Servant suffers in covenant; His people are pardoned in covenant. By His wounds they are healed.

The fact that the New Covenant forgives sins, permanently, is one of the fundamental contrasts between itself and the Old Covenant. This forms the central argument of Hebrews 10:1–4.

> 1 For since the law has but a shadow of the good things to come instead of the true form of these realities, it can never, by the same sacrifices that are continually offered every year, make perfect those who draw near. 2 Otherwise, would they not have ceased to be offered, since the worshipers, having once been cleansed, would no longer have any consciousness of sins? 3 But in these sacrifices there is a reminder of sins every year. 4 For it is impossible for the blood of bulls and goats to take away sins.

The Old Covenant had a sacrificial system that forgave sins in the context of Canaan. But the Old Covenant could not forgive sins in the court of heaven. It purified the flesh, not the conscience. Hebrews 9:9–10, 13 explains this further.

> 9 According to this arrangement (i.e., under the Mosaic Covenant), gifts and sacrifices are offered that *cannot perfect the conscience of the worshiper,* 10 but deal only with food and drink and various washings, regulations for the body imposed until the time of reformation... 13 The blood of goats and bulls, and the sprinkling of defiled persons with the ashes of a heifer, sanctify for the purification of the flesh.

The blood of goats and bulls purified the flesh. They reconciled Israelites to the law of Moses so that they could keep living in Canaan. They did not cleanse the conscience. Rather than removing the sins of the Israelites, the sacrifices reminded the Israelites of their sins.

But the blood of the Son of God cleanses His covenant people from all unrighteousness. The author says, "13 For if the blood of goats and bulls, and the sprinkling of defiled persons with the ashes of a heifer, sanctify for the purification of the flesh, 14 how much more will the blood of Christ, who through the eternal Spirit offered himself without blemish to God, purify our conscience from dead works to serve the living God" (Hebrews 9:13–14). At last, God provided a perfect priest, a perfect sacrifice, and thus perfect forgiveness of sins. This is one of the chief reasons why the New Covenant is established on *better* promises than the Old. It forgives sins forever.[1] It is a perfect covenant.

Forgiveness of sins is only one half of justification. Isaiah 53:11 proclaims that the Servant's suffering will also cause many to be accounted righteous. They will be forgiven and declared positively righteous in God's eyes. Jesus' life of perfect obedience is attributed and legally (covenantally) imputed to all those whom He represents in covenant.

> 18 Therefore, as one trespass led to condemnation for all men, so one act of righteousness leads to justification and life for all men. 19 For as by the one man's disobedience the many were made sinners, so by the one man's obedience the many will be made righteous (Romans 5:18–19).

The many receive Christ's righteousness by faith, resting in His finished work. And all those who have believed in Jesus Christ are justified and freed from all condemnation and have peace with God (Romans 5:1–2; 8:1).[2] The Scriptures proclaim loudly and clearly that the New Covenant promise of forgiveness of sins is received fully and freely by faith in Jesus Christ.

---

[1] "The great benefit of this New Covenant in opposition to the Old, lyes in this, that in this New Covenant God doth not onely propound the tearmes, but ingages himselfe to perform the condition, whereas the Old Covenant set before you life and death, good and evill, but ingaged you to the performance of the good without assistance (for the Law was without you) or to the suffering of evill. But in the New Covenant, the Law is within, written in your hearts." Henry Lawrence, *A Plea for the Use of Gospell Ordinances*, (London: M.S., 1651), 22.

[2] The appropriate response to a free promise is an outstretched empty hand. To respond to a promise with anything other than an open hand implies disbelief. "The Gospel giveth freely and requires of us nothing else but to hold out our hands and to take that which is offered." Luther, *The Epistle of S. Paul to the Galathians*, fol. 97.

9 Because, if you confess with your mouth that Jesus is Lord and believe in your heart that God raised him from the dead, you will be saved. 10 For with the heart one believes and is justified, and with the mouth one confesses and is saved. 11 For the Scripture says, "Everyone who believes in him will not be put to shame." 12 For there is no distinction between Jew and Greek; for the same Lord is Lord of all, bestowing his riches on all who call on him. 13 For "everyone who calls on the name of the Lord will be saved" (Romans 10:9–13).

This was the message of Jesus Himself from the outset of His ministry. He cried out "Repent and believe in the gospel." Jesus was calling the world to repent and believe in Him. He was proclaiming the blessing of the New Covenant and the way in which to receive it.

b. Regeneration and Sanctification

The New Covenant is better than the Old, not only because it promises lasting, perfect, heavenly forgiveness through obedience rendered outside of and apart from the one receiving it, but also because it promises to perform an inward work of renewal in the people of God.

33 For this is the covenant that I will make with the house of Israel after those days, declares the LORD: I will put my law within them, and I will write it on their hearts. And I will be their God, and they shall be my people. 34 And no longer shall each one teach his neighbor and each his brother, saying, "Know the LORD," for they shall all know me, from the least of them to the greatest, declares the LORD (Jeremiah 31:33–34).

26 And I will give you a new heart, and a new spirit I will put within you. And I will remove the heart of stone from your flesh and give you a heart of flesh. 27 And I will put my Spirit within you, and cause you to walk in my statutes and be careful to obey my rules (Ezekiel 36:26–27).

The Israelites were criticized for the uncleanness of their hearts and commanded to circumcise their hearts (Deuteronomy 10:16; Jeremiah 4:4). But they were unable to do this, and their covenant did not provide such a blessing. God promised, however, that He would effect this change (Deuteronomy 30:6). And it is in the New Covenant that this blessing is granted.

The corruption and pollution of man's nature, inflicted by Adam's sin and the Covenant of Works, was untouched by the covenants of Israel. But this covenant does a definitive work of renewal followed by an ongoing work of renovation in the heart of God's people. These two blessings are regeneration and sanctification.

Regeneration is the birth of a child of God, the birth of the offspring of Christ, the birth of an inheritor of the new creation (John 3:3). It is the transfer of a member of the kingdom of darkness to the kingdom of the beloved Son (Colossians 1:12). It is a movement from Adam to Christ (1 Corinthians 15:48). It is an escape from the Covenant of Works and an implantation in the Covenant of Grace. It is the beginning of experiential blessings in the covenant. It is the application of new creation life to a sinner, an initial deposit of glory and holiness that will grow from that point onward.

And just as the curse of sin extended to all the parts and faculties of man, so also New Covenant salvation begins a complete inward renovation of Christ's people in regeneration. The mind that was darkened is enlightened (Ephesians 4:23; Colossians 3:10). The will that was enslaved is freed (Romans 6:17–18; 8:1–14; Ephesians 2:1–10).

Growing in a new creation regenerated nature is the process of sanctification. It is the putting to death of remaining sin, and the pursuing of holiness and obedience with joy and gratitude. It is a cultivation of the fruit of the Spirit. It is a continued growth in understanding, a continued growth in obedience. It is a putting off of the old man, Adam and a putting on of the new, Christ (Colossians 3).

The New Covenant promises this inward renewal. God will write the law on the heart of His New Covenant people, all of the New Covenant people will know the Lord, and He will cause them to walk in His ways. This is completely different from the Old Covenant, a contrast used by Paul in 2 Corinthians 3:5–9.

> 5 Not that we are sufficient in ourselves to claim anything as coming from us, but our sufficiency is from God, 6 who has made us sufficient to be *ministers of a new covenant*, not of the letter but of the Spirit. For the letter kills, but the Spirit gives life. 7 Now if the ministry of death, carved in letters on stone, came with such glory that the Israelites could not gaze at Moses' face because of its glory, which was being brought to an end, 8 will not the ministry of the Spirit have even more glory? 9 For if there was glory in the ministry of condemnation, the ministry of righteousness must far exceed it in glory.

Paul speaks of the law delivered by Moses as a ministry of death and condemnation because in the Old Covenant, the law was external to the covenant partner. It was written down on a tablet constantly testifying to one's compliance or noncompliance with the commands of the covenant (Romans 3:20). The law demanded loyalty in the covenant with a threat of disinheritance for failure to comply. The external law condemned Israelites to death for their sinfulness. Even the king had to write a copy of the law that commanded (and condemned) him. The law magnified mankind's sinfulness.

But the New Covenant puts the law in the hearts of its members. It makes its people the friends of the law because they are righteous. The law comforts and justifies them. It does not condemn them. The law leads them in righteousness.[3]

The New Covenant does not merely internalize the law as a path of grateful obedience for God's people, but it also provides the fuel that God's people need to obey it. God will *cause* His people to walk in His statutes and obey His rules. The people born of the Spirit will bear the fruit of the Spirit. It is from that perspective that we can see another reason why the New Covenant is not like the Old Covenant that was broken.

The inner renovation of Christ's people in the New Covenant is not merely a matter of what they do, but also what they know. In the New Covenant, all of God's people will know the Lord. The people of the Old Covenant were brought into being through natural generation within the confines of the offspring of Abraham. In the New Covenant, the people of the covenant are brought into being by supernatural generation, that is, re-generation. And these children know the Lord because their supernatural birth grants them faith in Christ through whom they have confidence and access to God (Romans 5:1–2).

The Prophets predicted this reality in the church through the language of Israel. Isaiah 54:13 says, "All your children shall be taught by the LORD, and great shall be the peace of your children." Jesus quoted this in John 6:45, "It is written in the Prophets, 'And they will all be taught by God.'" His application was that those who come to Christ, hear His message, and believe in Him are those who are taught by God. His words continue immediately after the quotation, "Everyone who has heard and learned from the Father comes to me— 46 not that anyone has seen the Father except he who is from God; he has seen the Father. 47 Truly, truly, I say to you, whoever believes has eternal life." Regeneration is a reality possessed and enjoyed by all true members of the new covenant. They are all taught by God because they have all come to God through Christ who speaks the words of the Father.

---

[3] This has been aptly put into verse by Ralph Erskine. "A rigid master was the law, demanding brick, denying straw, But when with gospel tongue it sings, it bids me fly and gives me wings" Ralph Erskine, *Gospel Sonnets, or Spiritual Songs* (London: E. Dilly, 1759), 224. A similar verse has been attributed to John Bunyan. "Run, John, run, the law commands, but gives us neither feet nor hands, Far better news the gospel brings: It bids us fly and gives us wings."

John assumes the reality of regeneration and knowing the Lord, alluding to Jeremiah 31:34 in 1 John 2:20–21.

> 20 But *you have been anointed by the Holy One*, and *you all have knowledge.*
> 21 I write to you, not because you do not know the truth, but because you know it, and because no lie is of the truth.

John treats the New Covenant church as a family born from heaven, some of which are newborn Christians (little children), some of which are growing in the faith (young men), and some of which have spent years in the Lord (fathers). Despite their varying levels of maturity and growth, they all have the anointing of the Holy One, and they all have knowledge. This is true because in the New Covenant, all will know the Lord, from the least to the greatest. And because this was true, John was able to expose false teachers' claims to secret knowledge. In the New Covenant, there are variations in quantity of knowledge, but not quality. The New Covenant does not grant secret knowledge necessary for salvation. There are varying levels of maturity and understanding, but none with greater privileges than others.

The Old Covenant was very different. The people of the Old Covenant are described in general terms as heard-hearted, stiff-necked, and wicked. Seeing the fruit of the Spirit was the exception, rather than the rule, of the Old Covenant. This is because the Old Covenant, in itself, did not grant the new birth, nor did it provide the indwelling of the Holy Spirit. The Old Covenant commanded and condemned through the external law, offering no help for obedience. The New Covenant reconciles its people to the law, gives them a new nature, and grants the Holy Spirit to help them know and obey God's Word.

The blessing of regeneration highlights the complete freeness of the New Covenant. Sinful mankind is justified by faith in Christ as offered in the New Covenant. But mankind does not have saving faith by nature. Man's mind and will are corrupted, suppressing the truth and delighting in sin. Man cannot summon faith in Christ thereby to be justified in Him. In regeneration, God acts powerfully to change the natures of the covenant people of Christ, granting them faith to believe in Jesus Christ.[4]

---

[4] The fact that God causes the people of the covenant to believe has led some to describe the New Covenant as unconditional. This can be an unhelpful way of speaking, albeit true. The New Covenant has conditions of connection, but not conditions of merit. In other words, God has ordained that the way to obtain the promised good of this covenant is through faith. There is a necessary required connection and sequence. Faith unlocks the treasure chest of forgiveness. But faith is not a condition of merit. It is not something that earns or equals or accrues

The Scriptures teach that this new birth, or regeneration, occurs ordinarily through the preaching of the gospel, which is the publishing of the New Covenant (Romans 10:17; James 1:18; 1 Peter 1:23). The New Covenant, which powerfully causes its children to be born again and gives them faith, thereby fulfills its own requirements in its own people. By God's own power, the new creation life that Jesus won for His people is applied to the children of God through the preaching of the gospel. God causes His children to be born again, writing the law on their hearts, causing them to believe. Even that which He requires of us He supplies to us.[5] The Old Covenant was not so.

c. Adoption and Preservation

The people of the New Covenant, the people of Christ, are the children of God (John 1:12–13). They are born from above and constitute a new humanity in a new and last Adam. They are the family of God, born of the Spirit. Regeneration is the birth of a child of God. But the fullness of adoption is the indwelling of the Holy Spirit of Adoption (Romans 8:15) by which the children of God enjoy all of the benefits of divine paternity (1 John 3:1–2). Apart from union with Christ and receiving His benefits, there is no adoption because this is a blessing of Christ's covenant. Adoption is therefore limited to the people of the New Covenant and the New Covenant alone. The children of God are the children of the new creation. They are the inheritors of the new heavens and new earth.

anything. It is simply the outstretched hand of a helpless sinner. It is a necessary condition in succession and connection, but not a condition of merit or reward. Cf. Owen, *A Continuation of the Exposition*, 269. "Unto a full and compleat interest in all the Promises of the Covenant, Faith on our part, from which Evangelical Repentance is inseparable, is required. But whereas these also are wrought in us by vertue of that Promise and Grace of the Covenant which are absolute, it is a meer strife about words to contend whether they may be called conditions or no. Let it be granted on the one hand, that we cannot have an actual participation of the relative grace of this Covenant in Adoration and Justification, without Faith or Believing; and on the other, that this Faith is wrought in us, given unto us, bestowed upon us, by that Grace of the Covenant which depends on no condition in us as unto its discriminating administration, And I shall not concern my self what men will call it."

[5] The Second London Baptist Confession expresses this well, "It pleased the Lord to make a covenant of grace wherein he freely offereth unto sinners, life and salvation by Jesus Christ, requiring of them faith in him, that they may be saved; and promising to give unto all those that are ordained unto eternal Life, his holy Spirit, to make them willing, and able to believe" (2LCF 7.2).

One of the benefits of having God as one's Father is the discipline and chastening of sonship (Hebrews 12:3–11). The Lord chastens those whom He loves. If one is not chastened, therefore, one is not loved. And God is not one's Father. This discipline is what preserves God's people. God removes the idols of His people's hearts and little by little weans them off the world, preparing them for heaven.

If in the New Covenant God is the One who will change His people's hearts and cause them to walk in His ways, then they will certainly be preserved. God promised in Jeremiah 32:40, "I will make with them an everlasting covenant, that I will not turn away from doing good to them. And I will put the fear of me in their hearts, that they may not turn from me." God's discipline of His children, therefore, is not condemnation but chastisement. It does not push away, but draws in and preserves. This is very different from the Old Covenant. The Old Covenant, in itself, exiled the unfaithful.[6] The everlasting covenant includes the promise of preservation and perseverance (2LCF 17.2).

d. Resurrection and Glorification

The Servant of Jehovah was promised in Isaiah 53 that if He poured out His life for His people, His days would be prolonged, He would see His offspring, and He would be exalted. The Holy One of God was promised that His flesh would not see corruption (Psalm 16:10). Because Jesus Christ was faithful in the Covenant of Redemption, He earned resurrected eternal new creation life for His people. His offspring are those people born from above, united to the one who died and rose again for their justification (Romans 4:25).

Jesus declared that His mission (the will of the Father) was to gather a people to be raised up on the last day (John 6:39–40, 44, 54). And He promised that He would accomplish this. He laid down His life, He was raised up, and Jesus is therefore the one who takes "many sons to glory" (Hebrews 2:10). He is the firstborn from among the dead, the one who went to the grave and emerged victorious (Colossians 1:18). He is the "life-giving spirit" that Adam never was (1 Corinthians 15:45). Christ's people have died and risen with Him in regeneration (Colossians 3:1–4), and after they die they will be raised again on the last day.

Death, therefore, does not lead to a curse for the child of God, the offspring of Christ. It is a release and homecoming. Death's sting has no ven-

---

[6] For those who were saved under the Old Covenant, but not by the Old Covenant, the benefits of liberty of conscience "were common also to Believers under the Law for the substance of them" (2LCF 21.1).

om, the law lays no claim, sin has no power, and Satan cannot but watch as he is bound and his captives are plundered (1 Corinthians 15:54–57; Mark 3:22–27). Resurrected life, however, is not yet experienced by the people of God. At death, their perfected souls go to be with Christ and they await the redemption of their bodies in full and final future glory.

The majesty and glory of the new creation inheritance of the saints in light (Colossians 1:12) is impossible to describe (Romans 8:18–25; 1 Corinthians 2:9; 2 Corinthians 4:13–18). Creation groans for it. God prepares His children for it. The people of Christ must wait patiently for it. And it will be glorious. One of its glories will be the glorification of Christ's people. They will be confirmed for eternity in their perfected natures and perfected bodies living in the image of Christ their Savior.

The supreme blessing of the consummated new heavens and earth, the pinnacle blessing of the covenant of Christ is seeing the glory of God in the face of Christ Himself (Revelation 22:4; 2 Corinthians 4:6). For what gift could be superior to the Giver, and what present is greater than the Presenter, and what promise is greater than the Promisor, and what satisfaction is there in any created thing that could rival or replace the supreme blessing of being in the presence of one's Creator (Psalm 73:23–28)? As the Psalmist says, "In your presence there is fullness of joy; at your right hand are pleasures forevermore" (Psalm 16:11).

3. The Foundation of the New Covenant

The Covenant of Redemption is the foundation of the New Covenant.[7] The covenant of redemption was a covenant of works from the Father to the Son. The Son had a mission, a work to complete, with a reward suspended on condition of His obedience. Jesus willingly and perfectly fulfilled that Covenant of Works. He Himself said that it is finished.

The New Covenant of grace mediates the blessings obtained in the Covenant of Redemption. In other words, the New Covenant is the fulfilled Covenant of Redemption mediated to those for whom the Son was appointed head in the Covenant of Redemption. The New Covenant is God the Father covenanting to sinners forgiveness of sins and eternal life

---

[7] "Still it does not remove the incongruity of Christ's being represented as at once a party and a mediator of the same covenant. There are in fact two covenants relating to the salvation of fallen man, the one between God and Christ, the other between God and his people. These covenants differ not only in their parties, but also in their promises and conditions…The latter, the covenant of grace, is founded on the former, the covenant of redemption. Of the one Christ is the mediator and surety; of the other He is one of the contracting parties." Hodge, *Systematic Theology*, II:357–358.

based on faith in God the Son, through whom they receive all the benefits. The eternal resurrected new creation life that Jesus obtained when He kept the Covenant of Redemption is offered to the world in Christ by the Father. The New Covenant is a kept Covenant of Works, mediated to the world. The Old Covenant longed for completion and fulfillment. It longed for faithfulness. The New Covenant is a covenant already completed, already kept, and delivered to Christ's people.[8] Jesus Christ is the Mediator of a "better covenant" established on "better promises" (Hebrews 7:22; 8:6; 12:24).

The New Testament regularly connects the ideas of inheritance and covenant in a way that indicates that Christ mediates to His people that which belongs to Him, or that which He obtained from the Father. Ephesians 1:11 says of Christ that, "In him we have obtained an inheritance, having been predestined according to the purpose of him who works all things according to the counsel of his will."[9] And Hebrews 9:15 teaches that Jesus "Is the mediator of a new covenant, so that those who are called may receive the promised eternal inheritance." Through Christ in the new covenant the eternal inheritance obtained in the Covenant of Redemption is mediated to the world.

The relationship between the Covenant of Redemption and the New Covenant establishes an obvious, but important, fact. Jesus Christ is the federal head of the New Covenant. This is so because he was appointed as a federal head in the Covenant of Redemption, particularly as a priest. What Christ obtained by virtue of His obedience in the Covenant of Redemption redounds upon all those whom He represents, namely His elect people. In the New Covenant, God the Father covenants with the elect through His Son.

Apart from union with Christ, the federal head of the New Covenant of grace, there is no participation in the blessings and benefits of Christ's covenant.[10] Paul is quite clear that "Anyone who does not have the Spirit

[8] "By fulfilling the conditions on which the promises of the covenant of redemption were suspended, the veracity and justice of God are pledged to secure the salvation of his people; and this secures the fidelity of his people. So that Christ answers both for God and man. His work renders certain the gifts of God's grace, and the perseverance of his people in faith and obedience. He is therefore, in every sense, our salvation." Hodge, *Systematic Theology*, II:364.

[9] Cf. 1 Peter 1:3–4 "Blessed be the God and Father of our Lord Jesus Christ! According to his great mercy, he has caused us to be born again to a living hope through the resurrection of Jesus Christ from the dead, 4 to an inheritance that is imperishable, undefiled, and unfading, kept in heaven for you."

[10] John Spilsbury said, "For God approves of none in covenant with him by his Word out of Christ, nor of any in Christ without faith. Nay, God denies his

of Christ does not belong to him" (Romans 8:9). This is consistent with all
other cases of federal headship in the covenants of Scripture. Apart from
Adam, none participate in the Covenant of Works. Apart from Abraham,
none participate in the Abrahamic Covenant. Apart from David, none
participate in the Davidic Covenant. Federal headship always defines and
delimits the extent of the blessings and benefits (or curses) of each covenant.

Because Christ's federal headship was established in the Covenant of
Redemption, and because the New Covenant mediates that covenant to its
inheritors, the extent of the blessings and benefits of the covenant is limited to those for whom Jesus Christ is High Priest in the New Covenant.
As summed up by John in 1 John 5:11–13. "11 And this is the testimony,
that God gave us eternal life, and this life is in his Son. 12 Whoever has the

approving of any in fellowship or communion with him, that doe not believe; as
John 3.5, 6. Heb. 11.6. Rom. 8.9." John Spilsbury, *A Treatise Concerning the Lawfull Subject of Baptisme* (London: n.p., 1643), 9. Thomas Patient contended that
the only way of being in the covenant was through "union or in-being in Christ
by faith." Patient, *The Doctrine of Baptism*, 83. Edward Hutchinson argued that
"there is no other way to partake of the promise but by faith in Christ." Hutchinson, *A Treatise Concerning the Covenant*, 27–28. Cf. Hutchinson, *A Treatise Concerning the Covenant*, 36. He said, "the promises running to Christ personally,
God makes him over for a Covenant to the Elect, and all the promises in him…
So that in *Christ* he is our God, and in *Christ*, he takes us to be his people. In
Christ, and a right to the promises; out of *Christ*, and strangers to the Covenants
of promise." Nehemiah Coxe said, "It is by Union to him that Believers obtain a
new-Covenant-interest." Coxe, *A Discourse of the Covenants*, 12. Later he added,
"all the Blessings of this Covenant redound upon Believers by means of their
Union and Communion with the Lord Jesus Christ, who is both the Head, and Root
of the New-Covenant." Coxe, *A Discourse of the Covenants*, 85. "It is by Union
to [Christ] as the Root of the New-Covenant, that *the free Gift comes upon them
to the Justification of Life*; and none can have Union to him but by the *indwelling
of his holy Spirit*." Coxe, *A Discourse of the Covenants*, 87. Benjamin Keach said,
"Now we have not actual Interest in it, and so personally it cannot be said to be
made with us, until we have actual Union with Christ, and do believe in him."
Benjamin Keach, *The Everlasting Covenant, A Sweet Cordial for a drooping Soul:
Or, The Excellent Nature of the Covenant of Grace Opened: In a Sermon Preached
January the 29th. At the Funeral of Mr. Henry Forty* (London: H. Barnard, 1693),
17. He added, "This Covenant stands firm, this Foundation of God is sure, it was
Established from all Eternity by an Eternal Act of God, that cannot be Repealed,
Altered or Changed: God is thine, Christ is thine, if thou hast Union with him,
all is thine; and the Oath of God, the Truth and Faithfulness of God is engaged
for the making good all the Blessings that are contained in this Covenant; God is
thine, and Christ is thine for ever." Keach, *The Everlasting Covenant*, 43.

Son has life; whoever does not have the Son of God does not have life. 13 I write these things to you *who believe in the name of the Son of God* that you may know that you have eternal life."

The writer to the Hebrews reinforces the perfection of the federal headship of Jesus Christ by pointing to oath-swearing. Covenants are sanctioned commitments, and oaths are forms of imposing sanctions. They are guarantees of promises and participation. The writer to the Hebrews offers parallel examples to emphasizes that, what God the Father swore to God the Son is the foundation of what the Son brings to His people. First, He points to God's oath to Abraham as an example of how God confirms His covenantal promises with oaths, for our benefit.

> 13 For when God made a promise to Abraham, since he had no one greater by whom to swear, *he swore by himself*, 14 saying, 'Surely I will bless you and multiply you.' 15 And thus Abraham, having patiently waited, obtained the promise. 16 For people swear by something greater than themselves, and in all their disputes *an oath is final for confirmation* (Hebrews 6:13–16).

Second, the author points out that Christ's priesthood is also confirmed by an oath, "You are a priest forever."

> 17 So when God desired to show more convincingly to the heirs of the promise the unchangeable character of his purpose, he guaranteed it with an oath, 18 so that by two unchangeable things, in which it is impossible for God to lie, we who have fled for refuge might have strong encouragement to hold fast to the hope set before us. 19 We have this as a sure and steadfast anchor of the soul, a hope that enters into the inner place behind the curtain, 20 where Jesus has gone as a forerunner on our behalf, having become a high priest forever after the order of Melchizedek (Hebrews 6:17–20).

The federal headship of Christ and the blessings that flow through Him in covenant to His people are grounded and founded, therefore, in God's oath to Christ.

This is developed further in Hebrews 7:15–22. The covenant of which Christ is the guarantor is a better covenant because it perfects its people. It perfects its people because its priest was appointed by an eternal oath. The Old Covenant priests had no such oath made to them and therefore the Old Covenant made nothing perfect.

> 15 This becomes even more evident when another priest arises in the likeness of Melchizedek, 16 who has become a priest, not on the basis of a legal requirement concerning bodily descent, but by the power of an

indestructible life. 17 For it is witnessed of him, 'You are a priest forever, after the order of Melchizedek.' 18 For on the one hand, a former commandment is set aside because of its weakness and uselessness 19 (for the law made nothing perfect); but on the other hand, a better hope is introduced, through which we draw near to God. 20 And it was not without an oath. For those who formerly became priests were made such without an oath, 21 but this one was made a priest with an oath by the one who said to him: 'The Lord has sworn and will not change his mind, You are a priest forever.' 22 This makes Jesus the guarantor of a better covenant.

In the context of Hebrews, to doubt or reject Christ's priesthood and sacrifice, and to return to Levitical priests and animal sacrifices, is therefore to reject the priesthood of Christ and to dispute the oath the Father swore to the Son.

Both the oath of consecration and the resulting benefits of Christ's priestly mediation are elements of the Covenant of Redemption. And the writer to the Hebrews tells us that these foundations make the covenant that Jesus guarantees and mediates infinitely superior to the Old Covenant. The covenant of Christ is as perfect and eternal as the oath (covenant) that stands behind Christ and His covenant.

The New Covenant is not like the Old Covenant that Israel broke (Jeremiah 31:32). The New Covenant is a Covenant of Works already kept and mediated in Christ to an elect people. This is what grants it the name the New Covenant of *grace*. Its blessings are freely and fully bestowed upon its people, without any merit or work on their part. The guaranteed fulfillment of the delivery of these blessings rests solely on the promisor, God. The blessings have been definitively obtained, and they are definitively distributed.

Matter:	Restipulation:	Sanction:	Form:
Law →	Obedience →	Covenant partner →	Covenant of Works
Promise →	Reception →	Covenant imposer →	Covenant of Grace

As mentioned above while discussing regeneration, the response of God's people to the New Covenant of grace is resting in and receiving Christ by faith. And even this is worked in their hearts by God.

8 For by grace you have been saved through faith. And this is not your own doing; it is the gift of God, 9 not a result of works, so that no one may boast (Ephesians 2:8–9).

The New Covenant is the Covenant of Grace. It unfailingly and infallibly blesses all of its children. They all know the Lord. They all enjoy the forgiveness of sins. The certainty of this covenant rests on the Covenant of Redemption. The priesthood of Christ rests on the oaths the Father swore to the Son. The oaths have been sworn by God Himself. He who promised is faithful. We rest and rejoice in His faithfulness.

4. The Kingdom of the New Covenant

Kingdom and covenant always go hand in hand. Here, no less than elsewhere in the Scriptures, these concepts are intimately united. In the Covenant of Redemption, the Father covenanted a kingdom to the Son, and in the New Covenant, that kingdom is covenanted to Christ's people.

The kingdom covenanted to the Son was a new creation kingdom of eternal resurrected life. As firstborn from the dead, Jesus is Lord of that creation (Colossians 1:18). And He fills that creation with His people. It is their inheritance through Him. When John the Baptist and Jesus began their ministries, the recurring theme of their preaching and teaching was the kingdom of God. And their message was that all mankind is now called to believe in the gospel of the kingdom. In other words, the kingdom of God is covenanted to the world through the New Covenant. Forgiveness of sins and eternal life, the promises of the New Covenant, are the promises of the kingdom of God. That is why as Jesus says in John 3 that you have to be born again, born of the Spirit, in order to see or enter into the kingdom of God, the kingdom of Christ.

Luke 22:29 enriches this even further. In the ESV it reads "And I assign to you, as my Father assigned to me, a kingdom." But this translation falls short of communicating the rich connection between kingdom and covenant contained in this verse. The word translated "assign" is the Greek word διατίθεμαι which is the verb used when one makes a covenant (διαθήκη) which is a nominal form of the same root word. The Septuagint regularly uses διατίθεσθαι διαθήκην to render כָּרַת בְּרִית which is the standard Hebrew phrase for "to make" or "to cut" a covenant.[11] So, while

---

[11] For examples in the Septuagint of διατίθεσθαι διαθήκην being used to render כָּרַת בְּרִית and other common Hebrew covenant-making phrases see Genesis 9:17; 15:18; 21:27, 32; 26:28; 31:44; Exodus 24:8; Deuteronomy 4:23; 5:2, 3; 7:2; 28:69; 29:11, 13, 24; 31:16; Joshua 7:11; 9:6, 7, 11, 15, 16; 24:25; Judges 2:2; 1 Samuel 11:1, 2; 22:8, 23:18; 2 Samuel 3:12, 13, 21; 5:3; 1 Kings 5:26; 8:9,

"assign" or "engage" or "appoint" are possible translations, the covenantal context of this passage, namely the Messiah's announcement of the New Covenant, justifies translating our Lord's words as "And I covenant unto you, as my Father *covenanted* unto me, a kingdom."[12]

The importance of this verse and its interpretation must not be overlooked. The reward for the Son in the Covenant of Redemption was not simply salvation for His people, but also a new realm, a consummated reality. This kingdom was covenanted to Christ by the Father, and He mediates it through covenant to His people.

21; 15:19; 21:34; 2 Kings 11:4, 17; 17:35, 38; 23:3; 1 Chronicles 11:3; 16:15–16; 2 Chronicles 6:11; 16:3; 21:7; 23:3, 16; 29:10; 34:31; Ezra 10:3; Nehemiah 9:8; Psalm 49:5; 82:6; 88:4; 104:8–9; Isaiah 55:3; 61:8; Jeremiah 11:10; 31:31–33; 32:40; Ezekiel 17:13; 34:25; 37:26; Hosea 2:20; 10:4; 12:2; Zechariah 11:10. In the New Testament, διατίθεσθαι διαθήκην is used in Acts 3:25; Hebrews 8:10; 9:16–17; 10:16.

[12] Were it not for the context, the mere presence of the word "διατίθεμαι" would not automatically include the idea of "covenant." We must be careful not to assume that simply because a particular word is used, a given referent or concept is intended. Contextually, however, the concept of covenant is indeed in the forefront. Kline comments, "It is interesting that the verb translated 'appointed' (*diatithemi*) is the verb to which *diatheke*, 'covenant,' relates. Indeed, this affirmation of Jesus stands in the context of his ordaining the sacramental seal of the new covenant, in association with his statement, 'This is my blood of the new covenant' (Matthew 26:28; Mark 14:24; Luke 22:20; 1 Corinthians 11:25). Hence, in this biblical passage we have the next thing to an actual application of the term 'covenant' to the arrangement between the Father and the Son. A justifiable rendering would be: 'My Father covenanted unto me a kingdom.' Kline, *Kingdom Prologue*, 139–140. Berkhof states, "Wherever we have the essential elements of a covenant, namely, contracting parties, a promise or promises, and a condition, there we have a covenant... The statement in Luke 22:29 is particularly significant: 'I appoint unto you a kingdom, even as my Father appointed unto me.' The verb used here is *diatithemi*, the word from which *diatheke* is derived, which means to appoint by will, testament, or covenant. Moreover, in John 17:5 Christ claims a reward, and in John 17:6, 9, 24 He refers to His people and His future glory as a reward given Him by the Father." Louis Berkhof, *Systematic Theology* (Grand Rapids, MI: Eerdmans, 1996), 266. For the same interpretation and argument from Luke 22:29 see also, G.R. Beasley-Murray, *Jesus and the Kingdom of God* (Grand Rapids, MI: Eerdmans, 1986), 276–277; Berkhof, *Systematic Theology*, 282; Meredith G. Kline, *Glory in our Midst* (Overland Park, KS: Two Age Press, 2001), 106, 222; Turretin, *Institutes of Elenctic Theology*, II:668; Herman Witsius, *The Economy of the Covenants Between God and Man* (Phillipsburg, NJ: P&R, 1990), I:166; William Bucanus, *A Body of Divinity, Or: Institutions of Christian Religion* (trans. Robert Hill; London: Daniel Pakeman, 1659), 242.

The kingdom of God is the covenantal inheritance of the children of Christ and it comes to them through Him by covenant, the New Covenant. This meant that the Lord's Supper was not a celebration of the Passover and a deliverance from Egypt into Canaan, but a celebration of the death of the firstborn Son of God and a deliverance from the domain of darkness into the kingdom of the beloved Son. The body and blood of their Savior represented their covenantal right and title to heaven, the kingdom of God. And all those who joined them in that table professed a right to the same.

And when we grasp this, we also understand why Jesus said that He wouldn't drink of the fruit of the vine until that day when He would drink it anew in the kingdom of God. The Lord's Supper and the New Covenant look forward to the full assembly of God's people in the new creation, a consummated cosmos with a perfect harmony between Creator and creature. There the entire creation will be a temple of God's presence, because there will be no separation, no holy as opposed to unholy place. All will be perfect, and it will be perfect eternally.

So then, the kingdom of God is that new creation of perfection, obtained by the Son in the Covenant of Redemption and granted to the elect through the New Covenant. Those two covenants establish and govern the kingdom of God, defining its members and privileges.

5. The People of the New Covenant

The membership of a given covenant is always determined by the federal head of that covenant. In this case, Jesus Christ is the federal head of the New Covenant, the One through whom its blessings flow. And His federal headship was determined in the Covenant of Redemption. His sheep are those given to Him by the Father. The people of the New Covenant are the elect of God. They are those people whom Paul loves to say are "in Christ." They are those for whom the Father sent the Son. They are those for whom the Son died. They are those to whom the benefits of the Son of God's death are applied by the Holy Spirit. They are a new humanity in a new, and last, Adam.

There is no condemnation for those who are in Christ Jesus (Romans 8:1). Their sins are forgiven. They are not "in the flesh" but "in the Spirit" because the Spirit of God has regenerated them and dwells in them (Romans 8:9). All of these Spirit-bred and Spirit-led individuals are the "sons of God" to whom the Spirit Himself bears witness of their identity (Romans 8:14, 16). As the sons of God, they are co-heirs with Christ and will partake of His glory (Romans 8:17). These were predestined to this inheritance, called to this inheritance, justified and thus qualified for this inheritance, and will be glorified just as Jesus is already glorified (Romans 8:29–30). God will give the sons of God "all things" that were given to the Son (Romans 8:31). No one can accuse or condemn the sons of God, nor can anyone separate them from "the love of God in Christ Jesus our Lord" (Romans 8:33–39). These are they who give thanks to the Father who qualified them "to share in the inheritance of the saints in light" by delivering them "from the domain of darkness" and transferring them "to the kingdom of his beloved Son" in whom they have "redemption, the forgiveness of sins" (Colossians 1:12–14). Membership in the New Covenant, therefore, is defined and delineated exclusively by relation to the federal head of the covenant, Jesus Christ. And as Romans 8:9 states, "Anyone who does not have the Spirit of Christ does not belong to him."

Conclusion

The New Covenant of grace, established in the blood of Christ, founded in the Covenant of Redemption, and preached to the world in the gospel, is God's master plan. It is free salvation for the world through the Jewish Messiah, the Christ of Israel. It completely reverses the corruption and condemnation of the Covenant of Works and provides an eternal life of glory in perfect communion with God. This covenant establishes a kingdom, the kingdom of Christ, the kingdom of God. And the recipients of its blessings, all flowing from Christ the head, constitute the membership of that kingdom.

13

The Mystery of Christ

Introduction

From "before" creation, salvation in Christ for all nations had been planned (2 Timothy 1:9; Titus 1:2). This salvation was announced in the garden to Adam in the Seed of the woman. Abraham received the supreme blessing of fathering the nation from which the nation-blessing Seed would be born. And now that Jesus had come and completed His mission, He commissioned His apostles to go out into the nations and gather together a new humanity through the preaching and power of the gospel (Matthews 28:18-20; Romans 1:16).

However, after Jesus' resurrection the Apostles still thought that the growth of Jesus' kingdom would take shape as a Jewish kingdom (Acts 1:6). Despite their misunderstandings, Jesus taught the apostles concerning the kingdom of God during the forty days between His resurrection and ascension. And after Jesus ascended on high, He poured out His Spirit in a greater measure on His apostles at Pentecost which resulted in their arrival at a fuller apprehension and comprehension of what Jesus had been teaching throughout His ministry before and after His death and resurrection.

From that moment onward, the gospel went forth from Jerusalem to Samaria to Asia minor and on to the ends of the earth. And though questions of the relationship of Israel to the church continued to disturb the body of Christ, they were consistently answered through an appeal to the mystery of Christ. This final plan had been revealed antecedently, though as a mystery. God's plans had not changed, and He had not failed to fulfill His promises to Israel. Israel had failed to understand God's purposes and believe His promises.

179

1. The Unity of God's Plan

God has only ever had one plan, and history played out according to God's design. As Paul states in Ephesians 1:9–10, that "will," "purpose," and "plan" was to bring all things to unity and consummation in Christ

> 9 making known to us the mystery of his will, according to his purpose, which he set forth in Christ 10 as a plan for the fullness of time, to unite all things in him, things in heaven and things on earth (Ephesians 1:9–10).

The full and final plan of God was to bless the whole world through the Jewish Christ.

At Pentecost, Peter declared the absolute freeness of the blessings of the Christ evidenced by the fulfillment of Joel's prophecy that the Spirit would be poured out on all flesh. This blessing was for everyone, beginning in Jerusalem and spreading to the world.

> 38 And Peter said to them, "Repent and be baptized every one of you in the name of Jesus Christ for the forgiveness of your sins, and you will receive the gift of the Holy Spirit. 39 For the promise is for you and for your children and for all who are far off, everyone whom the Lord our God calls to himself" (Acts 2:38–39).

Peter's sermon announces the unveiling of the blessing for the nations. That promised blessing was poured out through the preaching of the gospel in Israel first in the Southern Kingdom (Jerusalem), then the Northern Kingdom (Samaria), then on to the ends of the earth.[1] Those who responded to this gospel by faith became a new humanity, baptized into a new family, the children of God indwelt by His Spirit, united to His Son and awaiting His return.

Paul expressed to the Colossians this same united plan to bless the world through the imparting of the Spirit of Christ freely. The mystery of Christ was "Christ in you," that is, Christ among the Gentiles. Paul was commissioned,

> 25... to make the word of God fully known, 26 the mystery hidden for ages and generations but now revealed to his saints. 27 To them God chose to make known how great among the Gentiles are the riches of the glory of this mystery, which is Christ in you, the hope of glory. 28 Him we proclaim, warning everyone and teaching everyone with all wisdom, that we may present everyone mature in Christ (Colossians 1:25–28).

[1] Cf. Schreiner, *Covenant and God's Purpose for the World*, 106–107.

Paul's self-conscious ministry was to explain in full something that had been understood in part for ages. The Jewish kingdom and covenants were preparatory, and Paul exhorted the Colossians not to submit themselves to the Jewish laws, the shadows of Christ, but to cling to the Substance, Christ (Colossians 2:4–23). Christ and the freedom He brings was the plan all along, and no reversion should be permitted to take root in the church.

Paul describes the same mystery in Ephesians 3:1–6.

1 For this reason I, Paul, a prisoner for Christ Jesus on behalf of you Gentiles— 2 assuming that you have heard of the stewardship of God's grace that was given to me for you, 3 how the mystery was made known to me by revelation, as I have written briefly. 4 When you read this, you can perceive my insight into the mystery of Christ, 5 which was not made known to the sons of men in other generations as it has now been revealed to his holy apostles and prophets by the Spirit. 6 This mystery is that the Gentiles are fellow heirs, members of the same body, and partakers of the promise in Christ Jesus through the gospel.

A few verses later, Paul described the mystery as "the plan of the mystery hidden for ages… according to the eternal purpose."

Peter likewise taught that there was one plan all along, and that the prophets understood it partially.

10 Concerning this salvation, the prophets who prophesied about the grace that was to be yours searched and inquired carefully, 11 inquiring what person or time the Spirit of Christ in them was indicating when he predicted the sufferings of Christ and the subsequent glories. 12 It was revealed to them that they were serving not themselves but you, in the things that have now been announced to you through those who preached the good news to you by the Holy Spirit sent from heaven, things into which angels long to look (1 Peter 1:10–12).

The prophets knew that there was something greater in their own words than even they themselves comprehended. But they did not know exactly what that would be. Jesus' identity and the fullness of His mission were revealed in the Old Testament, though as a mystery.

The law, prophets, and writings testify of one singular plan, a united eternal purpose revealed initially as a mystery and unveiled fully by Christ and His apostles.

2. Israel, Christ, and the Church

The kingdom and covenant of Christ declared by Jesus Himself during His ministry were neither defined nor determined by Jewish ancestry and obedience to Jewish laws. How was it that a kingdom and covenant inherited through supernatural birth and received by faith was the natural successor to a kingdom and covenants inherited through natural birth and maintained by the works of the law? To many Jews, this was a betrayal of the highest order. And they resisted the idea that the Christ of Israel would establish a kingdom and covenant irrespective of what defined them as Jews.

The apostles replied that this kind of thinking failed to understand what being Jewish was all about. They reasoned with the Jews that Christ's transnational kingdom and covenant were the natural and proper successor of the national kingdom and covenants of Israel and that this movement was the natural movement of God's singular redemptive plan. Acts 28:23 describes Paul doing this.

> When they had appointed a day for him, they came to him at his lodging in greater numbers. From morning till evening he expounded to them, testifying to the kingdom of God and trying to convince them about Jesus both from the Law of Moses and from the Prophets.

And in Acts 19:8–9 we find the same.

> 8 And he entered the synagogue and for three months spoke boldly, reasoning and persuading them about the kingdom of God. 9 But when some became stubborn and continued in unbelief, speaking evil of the Way before the congregation, he withdrew from them and took the disciples with him, reasoning daily in the hall of Tyrannus.

How, then, was the church the natural successor of Israel, and what was the relationship between the two? The apostles used a variety of parallels to explain the relationship, and connected them in the Christ. In these explanations, they showed that the Old Covenant was a means to an end, not an end in itself.

Israel	Church
The earthly covenants of promise	The heavenly covenant
The children of Abraham's flesh	The children of Abraham's faith
Those circumcised in the flesh	Those circumcised in heart
Those born according to the flesh	Those born according to the Spirit
The outward Jew	The inward Jew

a. Israel

Israel is the natural offspring of Abraham. Paul calls this group "God's people" in Romans 11:1 and places himself within that group, adding that they are "Israelites" and "descendants of Abraham." In Romans 4:1, Paul refers to Abraham as "our forefather according to the flesh." And in 2 Corinthians 11:22 Paul equates three terms: "Hebrews", "Israelites", and "offspring of Abraham." These descriptions concur plainly with the identity of Israel in the Old Testament. They are the natural offspring of Abraham.

The Scriptures attribute a plurality of covenants to Israel according to the flesh, the natural offspring of Abraham. After Pentecost, Peter spoke to a crowd of Jews and called them the sons of the covenant made in Genesis 12.

> 25 You are the sons of the prophets and of the covenant that God made with your fathers, saying to Abraham, 'And in your offspring shall all the families of the earth be blessed.' 26 God, having raised up his servant, sent him to you first, to bless you by turning every one of you from your wickedness (Acts 3:25–26).

Peter points to Abraham the federal head and his natural offspring as the parties of this covenant. And he notes that it was their great privilege to be the womb of the Messiah, as well as the first recipients of His mission and message.

In Romans 9:3–5, Paul speaks of his "kinsmen according to the flesh" and he declares that a plurality of "covenants" belongs to them.

> 3 For I could wish that I myself were accursed and cut off from Christ for the sake of my brothers, my kinsmen according to the flesh. 4 They are Israelites, and to them belong the adoption, the glory, the covenants, the giving of the law, the worship, and the promises. 5 To them belong the patriarchs, and from their race, according to the flesh, is the Christ, who is God over all, blessed forever. Amen (Romans 9:3–5).

Paul refers to these "covenants" in Ephesians 2:12 as the "covenants of promise." These covenants are the Abrahamic, Mosaic, and Davidic Covenants, as the previous parts of this book have asserted.

The apostles argued that the covenants of promise made with Abraham and his natural offspring, Israel according to the flesh, had a special purpose. They contained the full and final plan of God as a mystery. The apostles used this to teach a natural connection between Israel and the church because Israel according to the flesh was always designed to bring forth the Messiah, according to the flesh. As Paul said above, "from their race, according to the flesh, is the Christ." The Old Covenant provided the Messiah. The natural connection is that the Messiah provided the New Covenant. And because Israel's purpose as a covenant nation from its inception (Genesis 12) was to bring forth the Messiah who would bless the nations, a claim of authentic "Jewishness" that did not include an acceptance and belief in the Messiah bringing a blessing to the nations failed to understand the most fundamental reason for Israel's very existence. Free righteousness for all who believe in Jesus Christ was the *telos*, the destination, not the detour, of the Israelite kingdom and covenants (Romans 10:4).

In Romans 4:9–17, Paul argued that the sequence of events in God's dealings with Abraham was significant. The Scriptures record his faith and justification *prior* to circumcision so that his children according to the flesh, and the whole world, would know that salvation in the promised offspring is granted freely and received by faith.

> The purpose was to make him the father of all who believe without being circumcised, so that righteousness would be counted to them as well, 12 and to make him the father of the circumcised who are not merely circumcised but who also walk in the footsteps of the faith that our father Abraham had before he was circumcised (Romans 4:11b–12; cf. 4:16).

Abraham had a dual paternity, therefore. He is "the father of all who believe" and "the father of the circumcised." This means that Abraham has a dual offspring: "all who believe" and "the circumcised." There are the children of his body, and the children of his belief. There are those who share his blood, and there are those who "walk in the footsteps of his faith." Jesus spoke in the same way to the Jews in John 8:37, 39. First, Jesus told them "37 I know that you are offspring of Abraham" (John 8:37). Then he said, "If you were Abraham's children, you would be doing the works Abraham did" (John 8:39). In Romans 9:8, Paul sorts these as the "children of the flesh" and the "children of the promise" or "children of God."

> This means that it is not the children of the flesh who are the children of God, but the children of the promise are counted as offspring (Romans 9:8).

Some of Abraham's natural children fell under both categories. They were "the circumcised who are not merely circumcised but who also walk in the footsteps of [Abraham's] faith" (Romans 4:12). Paul argued that the declaration of Abraham's faith and justification prior to the giving of circumcision was designed to prevent the children of his flesh from opposing the children of his faith.

The addition of circumcision subsequent to this statement of faith and justification was a confirmation to Abraham that what he believed would indeed take place (Romans 4:11a).[2] God promised Abraham that from his offspring would come one who will bless the nations. God added circumcision to confirm this promise outwardly. Those who are circumcised are the people of the one who will bless the nations. Circumcision and Jewish identity, therefore, can never be used to oppose the idea of a blessing for all the nations received by faith, mediated through the Jewish Christ because circumcision was given to confirm that this would take place.

Paul made a similar argument in Galatians 3, pointing back to Genesis 12. As in Romans 4:12 and 9:8, he utilized the dual paternity of Abraham and called believers "the sons of Abraham."

> Know then that it is those of faith who are the sons of Abraham (Galatians 3:7).

Paul also argued that the free nature of the New Covenant and its inclusion of the Gentiles were definitively declared to Abraham far before the full complex of Jewish laws were instituted.

---

[2] The designation of circumcision as a seal has often been misused to make a systematic point when Paul is making a historical one. In the Greek text of Romans 4:11a, the words "circumcision" and "seal" form a double accusative, which can be translated in an abstract or concrete way. It could be translated to say that circumcision is "the seal" (concrete) or "a seal" (abstract). Paul's concern is the meaning of the timing of God's dealings with Abraham. The timing of circumcision subsequent to the promise of the birth of the one who blesses and the declaration of Abraham's justification is what serves as a confirmation to Abraham. There are additional difficulties of translation that must be addressed. Paul calls circumcision a seal "of the righteousness of faith that in the uncircumcision" (τῆς δικαιοσύνης τῆς πίστεως τῆς ἐν τῇ ἀκροβυστίᾳ). Some translations fill in the ambiguous blanks by referring to "the righteousness of faith *that Abraham had while* still uncircumcised." Given the context of Paul's argument regarding timing, this can be translated differently as looking forward to "the righteousness of faith *which was to be* in the uncircumcision." Paul's meaning, then, is that God gave circumcision to confirm to Abraham that he would indeed have a child who would bless the nations with the same righteousness obtained by faith that Abraham himself enjoyed. This interpretation was advanced by John Lightfoot and endorsed by the Particular Baptists in the appendix to their Confession of Faith. Cf. John Lightfoot, *Horæ Hebraicæ et Talmudicæ Impensæ in Epistolam Primam S. Pauli ad Corinthios* (Cambridge: Joan. Field, 1664), 47–49. Cf. also *A Confession of Faith Put Forth by the Elders and Brethren of Many Congregations of Christians (Baptized Upon Profession of their Faith) in London and the Country* (London: Benjamin Harris, 1677), 119–125.

16 Now the promises were made to Abraham and to his offspring. It does not say, "And to offsprings," referring to many, but referring to one, "And to your offspring," who is Christ. 17 This is what I mean: the law, which came 430 years afterward, does not annul a covenant previously ratified by God, so as to make the promise void (Galatians 3:16–17).

Paul points out that the promised blessings are restricted to Christ. The blessing does not belong to all of Abraham's children, but to one particular descendant of Abraham, through whom the nations of the world will be blessed. But, the descendant would be a child of Abraham. So, as we have said many times, the descendant will belong to the children of Abraham according to the flesh, but the blessing He provides will not belong to them on the same terms.

In verse 17, Paul says that the terms of a covenant were definitively declared in Genesis 12. When people make agreements and state the terms, the terms remain as stated (Galatians 3:15). If God declared that a descendant of Abraham, Christ, would bless the nations freely, then nothing subsequent could alter that. The covenant whose terms were declared in Genesis 12 is the New Covenant, carried within the covenants of promise. The Israelite covenants offered earthly blessings to Abraham's descendants and disinherited those who were disobedient. But they carried the promise of another covenant, the New Covenant, in that they promised the One who would bless freely, and the blessing He brought was the New Covenant. And Paul argues that once the terms of the New Covenant were set definitively, and once Israel was commissioned to bring forth the one who would bless according to those terms, no subsequent development in redemptive history would subvert that. Rather, the law subserved God's eternal plan and purpose (Galatians 3:19–22).

So, whether one consider Paul's argument in Romans 4 regarding the timing of Genesis 15 (faith and justification) relative to Genesis 17 (circumcision) or Paul's argument in Galatians 3 regarding the timing of Genesis 12 (the blessing in Christ) relative to Exodus (the law), the result is the same. Israel was commissioned to bring forth the Messiah, the nature of whose mission was revealed as a mystery, yet sufficiently so that any opposition to the idea of the Messiah including all the world in free salvation through a new covenant, irrespective of Jewish descent or obedience, was nothing other than unbelief and a rejection of the God of Israel.

In Galatians 4:21–31, Paul sums up the covenants of promise and the New Covenant allegorically by contrasting two covenants—an earthly covenant that produces bondage children from below with a heavenly covenant that produces free children from above. And he analogizes Ishmael's persecution against Isaac with the persecution of Israel according to the flesh against Israel according to the Spirit. Jews who regard the Old Covenant as an end in itself oppose the true end of the Old Covenant, the New Covenant. To an unbelieving Jew, it would have been a high insult to be told that you are Ishmael, and believing gentiles are Isaac.

Paul made a similar analogy in Romans 9, stating that unbelieving Israel is Esau, and believers are Jacob. According to Paul, unbelieving Israel is the reprobated vessel prepared for destruction. And the children merely of Abraham's body cannot fault God for predestining them to stumble over the Christ. God is free to do as he pleases with his own creatures. God gave them every advantage. And even now, they will be saved if they believe.

For unbelieving Jews, being told that they are Ishmael and Esau was infuriating. Paul explains their disbelief of the unveiled mystery in 2 Corinthians 3:14–16. "14 But their minds were hardened. For to this day, when they read the old covenant, that same veil remains unlifted, because only through Christ is it taken away. 15 Yes, to this day whenever Moses is read a veil lies over their hearts. 16 But when one turns to the Lord, the veil is removed."

The idea that the Old Covenant was a means to an end and not the end in itself provoked the question of what value it had. If the covenants of promise granted a relationship to the Messiah only according to the flesh, and if this were insufficient for inclusion in the unveiled kingdom and covenant of Christ, what real value was there in them? Paul answered that because God made the gospel known through typology and entrusted the Messiah to Israel according to the flesh, those who did not believe have only themselves to blame. What more could they ask for? Who else possessed such privileges?

> 1 Then what advantage has the Jew? Or what is the value of circumcision? 2 Much in every way. To begin with, the Jews were entrusted with the oracles of God. 3 What if some were unfaithful? Does their faithlessness nullify the faithfulness of God? 4 By no means! Let God be true though every one were a liar, as it is written, "That you may be justified in your words, and prevail when you are judged" (Romans 3:1–4).

The kingdom of Israel and its covenants were scaffolding around the kingdom of Christ and His covenant. Scaffolding and tarps give a general idea of something being built, but not necessarily a specific idea. They are not the final product, but they do contribute to that final product. When the kingdom of Christ was unveiled, and the world was invited to join, the Jews became enraged thinking that it belonged to them alone. They didn't realize that the purpose of what they were building was always designed for everyone.

Many construction projects put up "coming soon" signs and conceptual art of what the final product will look like. The Kingdom of Israel was one giant "Coming Soon" sign concerning the Messiah. From their land to their temple to their own genealogy to their sacrifices, they were a picture of the Messiah and his kingdom. Israel, chosen in Abraham, redeemed through Moses in the Exodus, under David's kingly rule, sacrificing lambs and goats while living in blessed life in Canaan was a tapestry of typology, the threads of the Mystery of Christ.

God gave Israel the supreme privilege of being the temporary tenants and construction workers of the Messiah's kingdom. But scaffolding, concept art, and sketches are not needed when the building is completed. The benefit for Israel was that though they were tenant workers in the Son's vineyard, and though their kingdom and covenants were dismantled, they were still invited to take their place along with the rest of the world on the same free and gracious terms (Matthew 20:1–16; 21:33–46). In fact, they were privileged to be its first recipients. Sadly, however, when the owner of the vineyard came to reap the fruits of what he had sowed, "He came to his own, and his own people did not receive him" (John 1:11).

Israel was the nation that descended from Abraham within the kingdom and covenants that God granted to them. The mystery of Christ was given to them in that they were a typical picture of the future realities, but above all in that one of their blood-brothers would bless the nations. No one else enjoyed such privileges.

b. The Christ

God's faithfulness to Israel is demonstrated above all in Jesus Christ. Descended from Abraham and David, Jesus Christ was born (Matthew 1:1). Jesus spent the entirety of His Messianic ministry in Israel. The great privilege of the children of Abraham according to the flesh was not just to say that Jesus was their brother, but to be the first recipients of His ministry and message, and to receive the same from Jesus' apostles (Romans 1:16). The gospel was preached first to the Jew, then the Greek.

God established the throne of David's faithful Son, Jesus Christ, and as King he called his people according to the flesh to join Him, and the world, in a new kingdom through a new covenant. But the Israelites wanted an idealized version of their present earthly kingdom, not the heavenly non-Jewish kingdom promised in the gospel.

The Jews' unbelief led to Paul's question in Romans 11:1. "I ask, then, has God rejected His people?" The language is significant. Israel according to the flesh is "His people," God's people. Paul includes himself among in this group. He is an "Israelite, a descendant of Abraham" (cf. Romans

4:1; 2 Corinthians 11:22). Paul argues that God has been faithful to Israel because He did not utterly cast them all off when they rejected Christ, but preserved a remnant among them, a portion who believed in the Christ and joined His kingdom by embracing His covenant (Romans 11:1–10). And even now, any and all of them can join the Christ by faith (Romans 11:23). The Christ blessed Israel according to the flesh *first*. And the blessing He offers remains available to them. It will always be their birthright, though they reject it in unbelief.

Jesus is the connection between Israel, the Christ, and the church. He is the source of the natural flow from the first to the second, according to God's eternal purpose. And no Israelite could argue unfaithfulness on God's part. They were called to faith then, and they are called to faith now. The brothers of Christ are called to become brothers in Christ among the people that the Christ gathered to Himself and in Himself, the people of the New Covenant, a people from all nations, the church.

c. The Church

The apostles used Psalm 118:22–23 to describe the transition from Israel to the church, centered around Jesus Christ. Jesus unveiled and established something new, and many Jews rejected Him for it.

> 22 The stone that the builders rejected has become the cornerstone.
> 23 This is the LORD's doing; it is marvelous in our eyes (Psalm 118:22–23).

Peter and Paul both applied this Psalm to describe the church. Paul said in Ephesians 2:19–22,

> 19 So then you are no longer strangers and aliens, but you are fellow citizens with the saints and members of the household of God, 20 built on the foundation of the apostles and prophets, Christ Jesus himself being the cornerstone, 21 in whom the whole structure, being joined together, grows into a holy temple in the Lord. 22 In him you also are being built together into a dwelling place for God by the Spirit.

And Peter said in 1 Peter 2:4–10,

> 4 As you come to him, a living stone rejected by men but in the sight of God chosen and precious, 5 you yourselves like living stones are being built up as a spiritual house, to be a holy priesthood, to offer spiritual sacrifices acceptable to God through Jesus Christ. 6 For it stands in Scripture: 'Behold, I am laying in Zion a stone, a cornerstone chosen and precious, and whoever believes in him will not be put to shame.'

7 So the honor is for you who believe, but for those who do not believe,
'The stone that the builders rejected has become the cornerstone,' 8 and
'A stone of stumbling, and a rock of offense.' They stumble because they
disobey the word, as they were destined to do. 9 But you are a chosen race,
a royal priesthood, a holy nation, a people for his own possession, that
you may proclaim the excellencies of him who called you out of darkness
into his marvelous light. 10 Once you were not a people, but now you
are God's people; once you had not received mercy, but now you have
received mercy.

In this language, Paul and Peter describe the church as the antitype of
Israel, and therefore its successor. And they likewise explain the transition
from Israel to the church. The cornerstone was unveiled in Israel to the
children of Abraham according to the flesh. But rather than being built
upon that foundation, many Israelites rejected it.[3]

With Christ as the cornerstone of a special house, those who believe in
him enjoy the honor of being God's household, God's people.

12 But to all who did receive him, who believed in his name, he gave the
right to become children of God, 13 who were born, not of blood nor of
the will of the flesh nor of the will of man, but of God (John 1:12–13).

These children of God are what Israel was not, and what Israel was invited
to be. And it all centers on Christ. As Paul said in Philippians 3:3,

For we are the circumcision, who worship by the Spirit of God and glory
in Christ Jesus and put no confidence in the flesh.

The building built on Christ, comprised of living spiritual stones, is
the church. It is the body of Christ, consisting of all those united to Christ
the head.

And he is the head of the body, the church. He is the beginning, the
firstborn from the dead (Colossians 1:18).

This means that inwardly, or invisibly, the church began as far back
as Eden after the fall. The body of Christ, the company of those united
to Jesus and enjoying the benefits of His salvific work, did not appear or

---

[3] From the beginning, it was a part of God's plan that some of the Israelites
would reject the Messiah, and that God would use their rejection as a means of
accomplishing the Messiah's mission as well as a means of extending the Messiah's mission to the world. Cf. Isaiah 5:1–7; 27:1–13; Matthew 21:33–46; Romans 11:11–15.

begin subsequent to Christ's appearance. Without regard to time, tribe, or tongue, those who embrace Christ by faith are one in Him (Galatians 3:26–28). Those who reject Christ are excluded.

The unity of God's purpose and the centrality of Christ to a people connected to Him by faith as well as a people connected to Him by blood are wonderfully illustrated by Paul in the olive tree analogy of Romans 11:16–24. The people according to the flesh served a purpose for a time—the purpose of bringing forth the Christ. When Christ emerged from Israel, only a relationship by faith would legitimize placement in His kingdom and covenant. Jews who disbelieve do not enter into His kingdom. The Gentiles, who had no connection at all to Christ, gain a connection by faith and are included in His kingdom. And Jews who arrive at faith in Christ are once more incorporated.

Paul describes the salvation of the fullness of Jews and Gentiles as "All Israel" paralleling his description of Christ's people as "the Israel of God" in Galatians 6:16. The church is the antitype of Israel, the final stage, the result of God's eternal purpose and the mystery of Christ. And the people of the church, the body of Christ, are the children and heirs of the age to come.

> 16 From now on, therefore, we regard no one according to the flesh. Even though we once regarded Christ according to the flesh, we regard him thus no longer. 17 Therefore, if anyone is in Christ, he is a new creation. The old has passed away; behold, the new has come. (2 Corinthians 5:16–17)

The apostles taught that with the arrival of the kingdom of Christ and His covenant, the Israelite kingdom and covenants were now abrogated and annulled. In Galatians 3:24 Paul stated that the law was a Guardian *until* Christ. The writer to the Hebrews states that the establishment of the New Covenant annuls the old.[4]

---

[4] "Here, precisely as in the rending of the veil for the ceremonials of Judaism, the exclusive bond for the people was broken at the center: Christ's very mother and brothers were to have no precedence over others, nor any distinctive position in His kingdom; spiritual relations alone should prevail there, and the one bond of connection with it for all alike, was to be the believing reception of the gospel and obedience to it…So far, therefore, as regards Israel's typical character, their removed and isolated position is plainly at an end: all tribes and nations are on a footing as to the kingdom of God—members and fellow-citizens if they are believers in Christ, aliens if they are not." Fairbairn, *Prophecy*, 256–257.

> In speaking of a new covenant, he makes the first one obsolete. And what is becoming obsolete and growing old is ready to vanish away (Hebrews 8:13).

The substance has come. The shadows must disappear.

3. The Continuity of the Law and the Gospel

Salvation for the nations was promised to Abraham and his descendants. It was foretold by the prophets. One of the wonderful truths declared by the apostles was that those who trust in Christ and receive His benefits did not begin with themselves. Rather, there were many prior to Christ who trusted in Him through the mystery that made Him known and thus received all of the blessings that Jesus secured in His life, death, and resurrection. They believed in the gospel, the good news, and were the children of the New Covenant (John 8:56; Romans 4:6–8; 1 Corinthians 10:1–4; Galatians 3:8; Hebrews 11). The writer to the Hebrews asserted that the benefits of the New Covenant in Christ's blood were enjoyed "from the foundation of the world" and all throughout history, though its legal establishment occurred "at the end of the ages" (Hebrews 9:25–26).

The book of Hebrews teaches that only the New Covenant can cleanse the conscience. Animal sacrifices cannot accomplish this. These truths are evident in the Psalms. In Psalm 51, David appealed to God's mercy for the cleansing of his conscience, noting that animal sacrifices would be insufficient (v. 16). In Psalm 32:1, David rejoiced in the forgiveness of his sins. Paul quoted this in Romans 4:7–8 and declared that David's words represent the joy of one who was justified by faith. These passages teach us that the conscience-cleansing benefits of Christ's blood offered in the New Covenant were experienced and enjoyed by many long before Christ's earthly ministry.

In this way, the church may have begun outwardly after the death of Christ, above all at Pentecost. But inwardly, its people began long before. The church existed before Israel. The church existed in Israel. The church emerged out of Israel. As the womb of the Christ, Israel was the womb of the Church. The gospel was continuous throughout them all.

Another question of continuity that naturally arose from a consideration of the mystery of Christ pertained to the law. The apostles rejected the Israelite laws of circumcision, foods, and more. But the moral law is reinforced for the people of Christ's covenant and kingdom (Matthew 5:20–24). Paul affirms that there is a continuity of law that transcends the covenants. The law written by nature on the hearts of the Gentiles was written down for Israel (Romans 2:14–15) and later Paul quotes the Ten

Commandments as a reference for believers' obedience (Romans 13:8–10).[5] John strongly argues that the children of God keep the commandments of God (1 John 5:1–3). All of this is consistent with God's promise in the New Covenant to write "His" law upon the hearts of His people and to cause them to walk in His ways (Jeremiah 31:33). That law is "His" law, the moral law, written on tablets of stone by the finger (Spirit) of God in the Old Covenant, and written on tablets of flesh by the Spirit of God in the New Covenant.

The law and the gospel permeate the entirety of redemptive history, before, during, and after Israel. And they find their home in the New Covenant and kingdom of Christ among the children of God.

Conclusion

Paul prayed for wisdom to explain the mystery of Christ (Colossians 4:3–4), the connection of the people of God according to the flesh and the people of God according to the Spirit with the Christ at the center. This mystery is God's united and eternal purpose. To understand and explain it is not only to bring balance and unity to our comprehension of God's Word and will, but also to swim in the depths of God's mind. Let all students of such a subject pause and praise God, acknowledging that whatever they have learned is but a glimpse, a sliver, a partial and imperfect finite grasp of an infinite glory.

> 33 Oh, the depth of the riches and wisdom and knowledge of God! How unsearchable are his judgments and how inscrutable his ways! 34 "For who has known the mind of the Lord, or who has been his counselor?" 35 "Or who has given a gift to him that he might be repaid?" 36 For from him and through him and to him are all things. To him be glory forever. Amen (Romans 11:33–36).

[5] See Richard C. Barcellos, *In Defense of the Decalogue: A Critique of New Covenant Theology* (Enumclaw, WA: Winepress Publishing, 2001), 71–83. On the transcendence and continuity of the Sabbath in particular, see Barcellos, *Getting the Garden Right*, 81–269.

14

The Eschatological Nature of the Kingdom

Introduction

The kingdom that Adam should have built, but failed to build, and the kingdom that Israel was designed to prefigure and prepare, that kingdom was the Kingdom of Heaven, the Kingdom of God, the Kingdom of Christ. The protology of the creation kingdom and the typology of the Israelite kingdom are fulfilled in the eschatology of the Christ's kingdom. The kingdom of Christ is the unveiled end-times final plan of God, the eternal resurrected-life kingdom of the Son of God. It is the kingdom of the Son who fulfilled the Covenant of Redemption and covenants His kingdom to His people through the New Covenant.

That kingdom is not a purely future reality. Christ established a visible present manifestation of His kingdom in the present age, His church. Just as the kingdom of creation and the kingdom of Israel were what they were by virtue of their covenants, and not by nature of creation, so also the church is what it is by virtue of the dominion delegated to the Son by the Father in covenant, and the Son's rule over His people by covenant.

1. The Kingdom Inaugurated

The church is the kingdom of Christ in the present age.[1] Thus the church is established and governed by the New Covenant and the Covenant of Redemption. Jesus' ministry, and the later ministry of the apostles

---

[1] "It must be possible, this much we may confidently affirm, to call the church the kingdom." Vos, *The Teaching of Jesus Concerning the Kingdom of God and the*

194

and the entire Christian church involved teaching the good news of the kingdom, reasoning such things from the Old Testament. And those who received the word of the kingdom were gathered together into the church. The church is therefore the visible manifestation of the kingdom of God. The fact that the church is the visible manifestation of the kingdom of Christ through the covenant of Christ imbues and charges the church with an eschatological character.

Herman Ridderbos expresses this well.

> Just as the idea of the messianic people naturally results from the messianic character of Jesus' appearance and activity, so in the same way the no less essential basic motif of the covenant and of the people of God just as naturally leads to the appearance of the *ekklesia*. The connection between the messianic aspect and that of the covenant is expressed by the words "*my ekklesia*." The people of God are the people of the Messiah. And conversely, those who confess Jesus to be the Messiah are the new Israel. Thus the *ekklesia* is the community of those who, as the true people of God, receive the gifts of the kingdom of heaven provisionally now already since the Messiah has come, and one day in the state of perfection at the parousia of the Son of Man. In our opinion this is the irrefutable result of further reflection upon the general tenor of Jesus' preaching of the kingdom. On the basis of what has been said above it is possible in our opinion to summarize our view of the relation between *basileia* and the *ekklesia*. There can be no uncertainty about either the connection or the difference between these two fundamental notions: *The basileia is the great divine work of salvation in its fulfillment and consummation in Christ; the ekklesia is the people elected and called by God and sharing in the bliss of the basileia.*[2]

Church (NY: American Tract Society, 1903), 150. "This 'kingdom of the Son of man' agrees with the 'church of Jesus,' in that both phrases make the kingdom a body of men placed under the Messiah as their ruler." Vos, *The Teaching of Jesus*, 152. "Christ is already a king with his kingdom, but for now this realm is visible chiefly in the public ministry of Word, sacrament, and discipline, and also in the fellowship of the saints as they share their spiritual and material gifts in the body of Christ." Michael Horton, *The Christian Faith* (Grand Rapids, MI: Zondervan, 2011), 525.

[2] Herman Ridderbos, *The Coming of the Kingdom* (Philadelphia, PA: P&R, 1962), 354. (Emphasis in the original). "The *ekklesia* in all this is the people who in this great drama have been placed on the side of God in Christ by virtue of the divine election and covenant. They have been given the divine promise, have been brought to manifestation and gathered together by the preaching of the gospel, and will inherit the redemption of the kingdom now and in the great future… So there is no question of *basileia* and *ekklesia* as being identical." Ridderbos, *The Coming of the Kingdom*, 354–355.

Because the covenantal kingdom inheritance of Christ's people is the new creation, the church is therefore where the new-creation offspring of Christ are born anew with the down payment and firstfruits of new-creation spiritual life. The Holy Spirit regenerates the elect through the preaching of the gospel, which is the New Covenant. This takes place in the church, primarily, where the official sent-out ministers of Christ speak the words of Christ to the people of Christ (Romans 10:14–15; 2 Corinthians 5:20).

The connection of the church to the new creation infuses the church with a deeply eschatological identity closely associated with the Holy Spirit. A true church has the presence and power of the Holy Spirit (Revelation 2:5). A true child of God has the Holy Spirit (John 1; 3; Romans 8:9, 14). A true child of God bears the fruit of the Spirit (Galatians 5). This is a stark contrast from the Kingdom of Israel, and its source is the promises of the New Covenant won by Christ in the Covenant of Redemption.

As the nursery of the children of the new creation, the church takes on an already-not yet character. It is much like enrolling for a trip and waiting for the plane to depart. You have a ticket. You have a seat on the vehicle to a new place. But you have not yet departed. So also, the church is a waiting terminal. The church is where we enroll in the new creation kingdom of Christ.

Geerhardus Vos said,

> The present kingdom in Our Lord's teaching is one in essence with the final kingdom; according to the discourses in John eternal life is in principle realized here; with Paul there has been a prelude to the last judgment and resurrection in the death and resurrection of Christ, and the life in the Spirit is the first-fruits of the heavenly state to come. The eschatological state has arrived and the one great incision in history has already been made (Heb. 2:3, 5; 9:11; 10:1; 12:22–24).[3]

Indeed, "the great eschatological state has arrived" in the inauguration of the kingdom of Christ.

The people of the church, therefore, are the people of the new creation. They are a new humanity in the second and last Adam. Vos says,

> The church is a form which the kingdom assumes in result of the new stage upon which the Messiahship of Jesus enters with his death and resurrection. So far as extent of membership is concerned, Jesus plainly

---

[3] Geerhardus Vos, *Redemptive History and Biblical Interpretation* (Phillipsburg, NJ: P&R, 1980), 26.

leads us to identify the invisible church and the kingdom. It is impossible to be in the one without being in the other. We have our Lord's explicit declaration in John 3:3,5, to the effect that nothing less than the new birth can enable a man to see the kingdom or enter into it. The kingdom, therefore, as truly as the invisible church is constituted by the regenerate; the regenerate alone experience in themselves its power, cultivate its righteousness, enjoy its blessings.[4]

Vos is correct. The eschatological nature of the kingdom means that the membership of the kingdom and the elect are identical circles.

The concept of the new creation Kingdom of Christ and the New Covenant by which it is granted form the foundational content of our conception of the church. This means that we should strive to prevent cultural barriers or social distinctives from taking root in the church, lest they replace the proper definition and identity of the church with a man-made social gathering. There are no such distinctions in the kingdom of Christ. The people of the church-kingdom are all alike sinners and saints. The kingdom is open to Jews and Greeks, slaves and free, males and females, pharisees and tax collectors. The same Lord is Lord of all. As Bavinck says, "Entrance into that kingdom occurs, not by Pharisaic observance of the law, but by repentance, faith, rebirth, and for that reason is open above all to the poor, the lost, publicans, and sinners."[5]

Those who are united to the Christ by faith and by His Spirit are the family of God, the children of the new creation, the heirs of the consummation, who have begun to experience the powers of the future age and await the fullness of their inheritance. They are gathered together visibly in the church, the kingdom of Christ in the present age.

2. The Keys of the Kingdom

Because the church is the future in the present, the final kingdom already inaugurated, the value and meaning of joining and leaving the visible kingdom take on equal, but opposite, values.

---

[4] Vos, *The Teaching of Jesus*, 158–159. "The kingdom, as well as the church, is circumscribed by the line of regeneration, and the invisible church itself is that which determines its inner essence, its relation to God and Christ, a true kingdom, since it consists of those over whom the Messiah rules as the representative of God." Vos, *The Teaching of Jesus*, 160.

[5] Herman Bavinck, *Reformed Dogmatics* (Grand Rapids, MI: Baker, 2007), III:246.

a. Joining the kingdom through the covenant

Given that the church is the Kingdom of Christ, and given that the Covenant of Redemption and the New Covenant of grace govern the kingdom, and given that one can only participate in any covenant by virtue of union with the federal head, and given that Jesus Christ is the federal head of the New Covenant, and given that Jesus Christ is the head of his body, the church, and given that Jesus Christ is the King over His kingdom, how can one join His kingdom, and what does it mean to do so?

Inwardly, only God can regenerate the heart and give the faith by which one instrumentally takes hold of Christ and His benefits. On the other hand, that regenerated person can, and must, profess his or her faith in the context of the local visible church. In other words, to join the kingdom one must demonstrate a valid claim to the covenant. If the church is the body of Christ, the people of the Messiah, and those people are connected to Christ through His covenant, one must demonstrate a valid claim to Christ in order to take a place in His body. A valid claim to the covenant is a claim that regeneration has taken place and that one trusts in Jesus Christ alone, resting in Him and receiving His righteousness, for their salvation. The New Testament pattern is one of charity. Those who profess faith, unless a blatant contradiction indicates otherwise, are to be baptized. In the book of Acts, those who received the word of the apostles were baptized.

When the church is constituted on these grounds, new birth and faith in Christ according to the New Covenant, the contrasts of the New Testament fit perfectly. In Acts, there are those who confess Christ in Baptism and those who hate and persecute the church. There are those who repent and believe, and those who reject the gospel.

In Paul's epistles, there are those who are in Adam or in Christ, those who are justified by faith and those who are condemned by the law. There are those who belong to the domain of darkness and those who have been transferred into the kingdom of the beloved Son, there are those who have been given life and those who are dead in sins and trespasses.

In John's books, there are those who are born from above and those who are born from below. There are the children of God and the children of Satan. There are those who keep God's commandments, love their neighbor, and confess Christ, and those who disobey, hate, and deny.

And in Peter's thought, there are those who have been born again through the Word of God by the power of the resurrection and are being built into a spiritual house alongside of those who do not believe and are a people "living in sensuality, passions, drunkenness, orgies, drinking parties, and lawless idolatry" (1 Peter 4:3). We must draw the same lines concerning the kingdom of God on earth, the church of Jesus Christ.

Because the church is the kingdom of the new creation, a kingdom circumscribed by regeneration, to join the church is to place one's self on the side of Christ and to enroll in the new creation. To join the church is to profess that Jesus is Lord, and to believe that God raised Him from the dead (Romans 10:9). To join the church is to claim that the new birth has been experienced, and to express the fruits of that birth in a profession of faith and a life of thankful obedience. To join the church is a claim to Christ, to His covenant, and to His kingdom. The visible church, therefore, is to be comprised only of those who can make a valid claim to such.[6]

And it should be a great comfort and encouragement to professing believers when the gathered local church affirms their profession of faith and welcomes them into their membership. This is the church exercising the keys of the kingdom, and it is a statement that according to biblical criteria and human judgment, such an individual is a child of God, a member of the covenant, an heir of "the promised eternal inheritance" (Hebrews 9:15).

b. Guarding the kingdom through the covenant

The kingdom's existence in the world subjects it to difficulties. As Jesus taught in the parable of the wheat and tares, a sinful world will have an effect on the kingdom as it is visibly manifested.[7] Nevertheless, as Vos says, "This truth, however, in no wise interferes with the possibility nor absolves from the duty of church discipline."[8] Rather, it ought only to increase our vigilance and diligence.

As no unclean thing was to be admitted to Eden, nor any unclean thing to be permitted in the temple in Jerusalem, so also the church must not allow any unclean thing into God's sanctuary. Consequently, sin has no place in the New Covenant kingdom of Christ. Believers are to put to death their sin as they are renewed in the inner man (Colossians 3).

---

[6] "Because the kingdom is in its very essence a kingdom of righteousness, therefore it is impossible for any one to be truly in it without having previously repented. Because the kingdom intrinsically consists in the exercise of the divine saving grace and power, therefore it requires in every one who is to share its benefits that responsive and receptive attitude towards these divine attributes which is called faith." Vos, *The Kingdom*, 91. Vos' thought on this point prompted some wrestling on his part with the relationship of election, covenant, and baptism. See, for example, his correspondence with B.B. Warfield on this issue. http://www.opc.org/os.html?article_id=587.

[7] "During the present age the kingdom must partake of the limitations and imperfections to which a sinful environment exposes it." Vos, *The Kingdom*, 90.

[8] Vos, *The Kingdom*, 90.

Believers are to pursue righteousness and to bear the fruits of the vineyard workers who belong to the Messiah's vineyard.

But when a professing believer does not simply fall into sin, but practices sin (1 John 1:10; 3:8–10), an inconsistency exists between that person's public profession and their public actions. As a result, in the case of a lack of repentance, the church is to call such a person to flee from their sin and to pursue the holiness without which no one will see the Lord (Hebrews 12:14).[9] If that person will not heed the church's exhortation to repent, and if sufficient evidence and time have amounted to properly demonstrate the invalidity of an individual's profession of faith, such a person is to be removed from the church by excommunication. As joining the church declared them to be a child of God and heir of Heaven according to human judgment, so they are to be declared a child of Satan and heir of Hell according to human judgment.

No unregenerate person is welcome in the kingdom of Christ. No one without a wedding garment is welcome at the wedding feast. Insofar as these realities are evident in the present, we are to deal with people as such. The purpose of this discipline is "the self-preservation of the church in the state of holiness which befits her profession, and would be destroyed by the exercise of religious fellowship with such as remain unrepentant in the face of open sin."[10]

To the extent that is humanly possible, the visible kingdom should correspond to the invisible kingdom. That is, the visible church should correspond to the invisible church. Unbelief is a heinous sin, one of the central accusations of Christ against His hearers (John 3:18), and as such, the visible church, the visible kingdom, should accept no "religious fellowship" with any who do not profess faith in Jesus Christ, because they are living in unrepentant sin. Additionally, if there are those whose profession is suspect for legitimate reason, church discipline's necessary purpose is either to bring them to gospel repentance and reconciliation or to manifest their unbelief and openly expose their hypocrisy. Such individuals are, in Vos' words "simulating [the kingdom's] outward appearance," but they "do not belong to it in the inner spiritual reality."[11]

Church discipline thus restores Christ's sheep, and reveals Satan's goats. Nehemiah Coxe said, "That all are warned (and that very frequently) in the Scriptures to take heed of falling, is granted; and that these warnings

[9] Because of the close relationship between kingdom membership and repentance, barring unrepentant members from the Lord's Supper, the sacramental meal of the New Covenant, is an appropriate manner of exercising church discipline and a meaningful message to the unrepentant member.

[10] Vos, *The Kingdom*, 90.

[11] Vos, *The Kingdom*, 90.

are sanctified and made effectual by God for the preservation of his own Elect from final Apostacy, is pleaded."[12]

Church discipline guards the purity of the church. When members err, they are corrected and brought back into ordering their ways rightly according to God's Word. Sometimes that happens privately between brothers, sometimes that happens privately between members and elders, and sometimes that restoration happens through more public cases of discipline. The goal is always to restore the individual. But when someone persists in unrepentance, refusing to acknowledge sin and change their ways, the church must remove them from their midst.

And what does it mean when the gathered church of Jesus Christ declares that according to biblical criteria and collective human judgment, such an individual is not a believer in Jesus Christ? That's a very serious statement. Thus, joining and leaving the church have an identical proleptic value relative to eternal life in the new creation.[13] To depart from the covenant-kingdom of Christ is to depart from the kingdom covenanted by Christ.

c. Traitors of the kingdom

How, then, are we to view apostates, those who fully and finally reject the kingdom? Were they members of the covenant? Were they members

---

[12] Nehemiah Coxe, *Vindiciae Veritatis, Or a Confutation of the Heresies and Gross Errours Asserted by Thomas Collier in his Additional Word to his Body of Divinity* (London: Nath. Ponder, 1677), 96. "By Gospel-believers I presume he intends those that are members of the visible Church of Christ; such as profess Faith in him, and Obedience to him, and do not at present contradict their profession by a contrary practice in the light of men, My answer is, If we respect any particular person or persons among these, we are bound to hope so of them; because Charity always inclineth to the better part: But if we respect the whole bulk of professors together, we are not to believe that they are all regenerate persons; because the Scripture telleth us, there are foolish as well as wise Virgins, Hypocrites, as well as sincere Believers in the visible Church, though who they be we know not, till their works discover it; and when their Hypocrisie is discovered, we are not to think that they once were new Creatures, and are fallen from that state, but the quite contrary, I *Joh*. 2:19. So then though many Professors fall away, even such as have past under some common work of the Spirit; this doth not at all infer, That those who are truly born again, not of corruptible Seed, but incorruptible by the word of God that liveth and abideth for ever; may do so in like manner." Coxe, *Vindiciae Veritatis*, 94–95.

[13] In both of these actions of the local church, however, the church declares one to be a believer, or to be an unbeliever. The church does not make one a believer or an unbeliever.

of the kingdom? Because kingdoms are established and governed by covenant, and because the kingdom of Christ is visibly manifested on earth in the church, it is possible to encounter the kingdom on earth, to witness the kingdom on earth, and to falsely make a claim to membership in the kingdom on earth. This can be accomplished simply through feigned satisfaction of the criteria of the covenant, in a word, feigned repentance and faith, the fruits of regeneration. The way to think of such persons is quite simple. John says that they went out from us because they were not of us (1 John 2:19).

A friend of my son can come and visit my house, but while he visits he is not my son. And if one day I were to awake and find this friend sleeping in my guest room, claiming to be my son, his presence in my house and claim to my name does not make him my son. Unless I legally adopt him, he cannot force his way into my family. If someone shows up at my door claiming to be a long-lost relative, I may believe their story for a time, but eventually the truth will be revealed.

In the kingdom of Christ on earth, people make false professions, invisible to the eyes of fallible humans, and enroll in the wedding feast without a wedding garment. They are granted access to the sacraments of the kingdom and taste the powers of the age to come, but they remain illegal aliens in the kingdom. Their treachery is all too real. The apostate was not in covenant, but regarded as such (Acts 8:13; 2 Peter 2:1). The apostate was not a member of the kingdom, but regarded as such. But the apostate is legally accountable and liable to the supreme King and Lord of the covenant-kingdom.

Apostates are to be treated as true traitors of the kingdom by their violation of the covenant and their treason against the King. They are fully liable to a greater punishment for knowing so much about the gospel and the Son of God, for professing to trust in Him, and yet turning their back on Him (Hebrews 6:4–6; 10:29–30). If unbelief is severely condemned in the gospels in light of Christ's miracles, and contrasted as worse than Sodom and Gomorrah, then how much more condemnation accrues to someone who does not merely refuse to side with Christ, but actually names Christ's name and yet departs from Him?

A true covenant member is chastened and returned to his place, but a wolf is excommunicated, dismembered, and placed under a sure curse of death and judgment apart from repentance.[14] We can invoke Psalm 50:16

---

[14] Responding to the objection that "all that were Baptized by the Apostles themselves, were not saved," Andrew Ritor replied "I answere, and grant, that all Baptized by the Apostles, were not saved, and yet deny the consequence, by distinguishing betweene the rule by which they are to be Baptized, (which is in-

against such a person, "But to the wicked God says: 'What right have you to recite my statutes or take my covenant on your lips?'"

In sum, we must be equally willing to accept Simon Magus' profession of faith, and equally willing to excommunicate him. The criteria for each decision are equal, and their meaning is symmetrically opposite. To join the kingdom is to be placed on the side of Christ and to unite with the children of God and heirs of the new creation. To abandon or be removed from the kingdom is to be unmasked and placed on the side of Satan with his hell-bound children.

3. The Sacraments of the Kingdom

Christ has given His church visible tangible means of participating in His promises. These have been called sacraments, because a sacrament is a visible word. Amandus Polanus described them in this way, "Look what is propounded or promised by the word, the same is signified and sealed by the sacraments. Therefore the sacrament is called a visible word."[15] He

fallible) and the judgements of men who are fallible, and may be deceived in applying this rule;…This fayling then here, is not in the rule but in their judgments, who are but men; and can judge only in the outward appearance." Ritor, *The Second Part of the Vanity*, 7. Isaac Backus was charged with "Not distinguishing between a soul's being internally united to Christ, and a person's being in visible covenant relation." He replied that "This charge is very unjust, for we are well sensible of that distinction, and the dispute is not whether some may not, through man's imperfection, be admitted as true believers who are not so; but it is, whether the rule gives us warrant to baptize any without personal profession of their being such or not?" He goes on to cite various examples in Acts where baptism was granted upon profession of faith, even when certain professions were proved false. Then he concludes "Here this distinction is plain; they were received to baptism as true believers, and were rejected when they discovered that they were not such. The same may be observed in *Rom.* 11. Compared with *John* 15. Christ is the *Vine*, his members are *graffed* in, and *stand by faith* in him; but if any are received as branches of him who is the Head of his church, that prove fruitless, they will be *broken off*, and *taken away*, while living branches *are purged* that they may bring forth *more fruit*… At the same time *Arminians* draw an argument from hence for their doctrine of falling from grace; and the sense given above is, the best guard against both of these abuses of the apostles discourse." Isaac Backus, *A Short Description Of the difference between the Bond-woman and the Free; As they are the two Covenants, with the Character and Conditions of each of their Children* (Boston: Edes and Gill, 1770), 55–56.

[15] Amandus Polanus, *The Substance of Christian Religion* (London: Arn Hatfield, 1600), 295. Cf. also, William Perkins, *A Commentarie or Exposition, upon the five first Chapters of the Epistle to the Galatians* (Cambridge, UK: John Legat, 1604), 254. "Every sacrament is the word of God made visible to the eye."

added, "The sacraments of the covenant of grace show the same things to the eyes that the word of the Gospel declares to the ears. Hence it is, that the sacraments are called the visible Gospel."[16] Sacraments are words in a visible mode.

In the Covenant of Works, the trees made promises of life and death visible. In the Noahic Covenant, the Rainbow makes the promise of preservation visible. In the Abrahamic Covenant, circumcision makes the promise of Canaan and the threat of punishment visible. In the Mosaic Covenant, the Passover and sacrifices made the promises of God visible. In the New Covenant, baptism and the Lord's Supper make the promises of the covenant visible.

Sacraments are not just God's Word to His people, but also His people's participation in the very promise made visible. John Calvin defined a sacrament as "a testimony of God's favor towards us confirmed by an outward sign, with a mutual testifying of our godliness toward him."[17] In the Lord's Supper, for example, God reminds us of His promise to forgive our sins through the sacrifice of Christ. And we remember and proclaim that death until He comes.

a. Baptism

Baptism is a visible word, a representation, of new creation life through death. In the Scriptures, from Genesis 1 to the flood in Genesis 7 to the parting of the Red Sea in Exodus 14, water is consistently a symbol of new creation and death. These types teach us that to go into the waters is to go into judgment. To pass through the waters is to experience the salvation of God. Baptism is thus a two-way declaration. On the one hand, it is God's visible promise that all who are in His Son are new creations by virtue of their union with Christ in His death and resurrection (Romans 6:3–5). And on the other hand, it is the individual's profession of faith in those very promises (1 Peter 3:31–22).[18]

[16] Polanus, *The Substance of Christian Religion*, 304.

[17] Calvin, *The Institvtion of Christian Religion*, fol. 90v. (IV. 13. 1). Cf. also fols. 94v–95r. (IV. 13. 13–14). Cf. also Perkins, *A Commentarie*, 249. "Baptism serves to be a pledge unto us in respect of our weakness, of all the graces and mercies of God, and especially of our union with Christ, of remission of sins, and of mortification. Secondly, it serves to be a sign of Christian profession before the world, and therefore it is called 'the stipulation or interrogation of a good conscience,' 1 Pet. 3:21."

[18] Interestingly, the Westminster Assembly debated the role of a profession of faith in baptism and decided that the parent must make a profession of faith when bringing their child to baptism. The vote for this decision was 28–16. See

In light of the eschatological nature of the church as the visible kingdom of Christ constituted and governed by his covenant, baptism is the perfect symbol for one's entrance into the covenant and for Christ's children to name his name publicly before the world and the church. In fact, because of the visible nature of the church, when a church collectively agrees to baptize an individual based on their profession of faith, that baptism publicly places the name "brother" on that person. And they bear that name until the church removes it (1 Corinthians 5:11).[19]

As regeneration is the invisible initiation into the kingdom of Christ, the first blessing of the application of salvation to Christ's people, so the symbol of regeneration and union with Christ, baptism, is the visible initiation into the kingdom of Christ, the first blessing of integration into the local gathered kingdom of the saints. It is God's visible promise to His people, and the people's declaration of participation and trust in that promise.

b. The Lord's Supper

The bread and wine of the Lord's Supper are visible words of Christ's New Covenant pledges to His people. Because His death has occurred, our debts have been paid to the law. Because His death has occurred, the new creation has been won for us. Because His death has occurred, eternal life is our right, inheritance, privilege, blessing. It belongs to Christ's people by birthright from their federal head. It is theirs by covenant. Because God is just, there is never any question about whether those who partake of Christ's body and blood will enter everlasting life. The covenant guarantees it. The body and blood of Christ testify to it. There is no one to condemn. God is the one who justifies (Rom 8:33–34).

The Lord's Supper has two sides, like Baptism. On the one hand it is God's declaration of forgiveness of sins to His people in covenant. It is His visible word to them. On the other hand, it is the people's pledge of faith and participation in those promises. We do not simply contemplate the sacraments. We celebrate and enjoy the sacraments. Given that the Lord's Supper, like baptism, involves active faith in the promises signified by the symbol, it takes on a special character because the church collectively professes its faith in the Lord's Supper.

George Gillespie, *Notes of Debates and Proceedings of The Assembly of Divines and Other Commissioners at Westminster* (Edinburgh: Robert Ogle and Oliver and Boyd, 1846), 88–91.

[19] The Greek text says, "ἐάν τις ἀδελφὸς ὀνομαζόμενος," "If one 'brother' is named." This is not an active concept of making a profession, but being one publicly marked as a brother by the church.

206 of Part 4: The Kingdom of Christ

The sacraments of the kingdom of Christ demonstrate its eschatological character. Baptism signifies new creation life. And the Lord's Supper signifies our right to that new creation and ongoing nourishment until we reach it. Even more so, however, the Lord's Supper is the rehearsal dinner of the great marriage feast of Christ and His bride. Partaking in the one is an anticipation and foretaste of the other. And just as wedding garments are needed for that final feast, they are needed for the initial feast. You cannot make a claim on the present kingdom, the kingdom of grace, without making a claim on the final kingdom, the kingdom of glory.[20]

The Israelites celebrated the Passover dressed as those ready to leave. So also, we proclaim the Lord's death only until He comes. When He arrives, there will be no more need for sacraments. We will experience the fullness of what these signs provide in foretastes. This means that the Lord's Supper is the church's collective confession of its hope that Jesus is returning, and that we want every celebration of the Lord's Supper to be our last. Consequently, the kingdom of Christ locally assembled ought to proclaim the Lord's death in this sacrament with a frequency that reflects their desire to be reminded of God's covenant promises and their hopeful expectation of Christ's return.

The blessed promises of the Lord's Supper and the communal nature of the church's participation in it make absence from the church and its common confession in the Lord's Supper unthinkable, as the writer to the Hebrews said,

> 23 Let us hold fast the confession of our hope without wavering, for he who promised is faithful. 24 And let us consider how to stir up one another to love and good works, 25 not neglecting to meet together, as is the habit of some, but encouraging one another, and all the more as you see the Day drawing near (Hebrews 10:23–25).

The sacraments of the kingdom make the promises of the covenant visible to the people of the covenant and remind them of their present salvation and future inheritance in the new creation.

4. The Kingdom Consummated

We proclaim the Lord's death until He comes. When Jesus Christ returns, He will bring all things to consummation. He came first as Savior; He comes second as Judge. God the Father appointed the Son to be Judge

---

[20] This is again why barring unrepentant members from the table is an appropriate form of discipline because it bars them from the reassurance of their salvation, which is only due to them upon repentance.

of the world and "has fixed a day on which he will judge the world in righteousness by a man whom he has appointed; and of this he has given assurance to all by raising him from the dead" (Acts 17:31). Jesus endured the wrath of God for His sheep, but He will mete out the wrath of God on the goats.

When the gospel of the kingdom is preached, the King of the universe is calling "all people everywhere to repent" (Acts 17:30). There is a high price to be paid for those who do not kiss the Son in the acceptable day (Psalm 2:12). The world must know its self-inflicted peril. We live in a time of peace and patience, but when that trumpet blast is sounded, the last of Christ's sheep will have been gathered into the fold, and judgment day will have come (2 Peter 3:15). The power of the kingdom to save will be matched by the power of the kingdom to judge, conquer, and destroy (2 Thessalonians 1:4–10; Hebrews 9:27–28).

For now, the citizens of that kingdom wander as strangers and sojourners in a strange and foreign land, fed and nourished in the church. But there will come a time when Christ returns, the dead will be raised, mankind will be judged, and some will enter everlasting blessedness while others are cast into everlasting cursedness (Matthew 25:31–46; Revelation 20:15).

Then Jesus will deliver the kingdom to the Father (1 Corinthians 15:24) and the children of God, the children of the covenant and kingdom of Jesus Christ, will enjoy a consummated creation freed from the chaos of sin and wrapped in a cosmos of glory. Saints will arrive at their inheritance, the new creation, the temple of God, and they will dwell forever in the city of God (Revelation 21:1–7, 22–27). The fullness of the Jews are there (Revelation 21:12). The blessed nations are there (Revelation 21:26). The tree of life is there (Revelation 22:2). But above all, the Lamb is there, the bridegroom, the Christ, Jesus our God and Savior. His glory is the brightness of the new creation (Revelation 21:23; 22:5). His name is the song of the saints (Revelation 5:9–10). His presence is the consolation of God's children (Revelation 21:3–4). The glory that the first Adam failed to reach will shine in the face of the last Adam, in the face of Jesus Christ, and the children of eternity will enjoy His infinite majesty forever and ever (Revelation 22:4).

And that Jesus Christ, in whom all the promises of God are "yea and amen" comforts His covenant-kingdom in the present age with the certainty of His return.

16 "I, Jesus, have sent my angel to testify to you about these things for the churches. I am the root and the descendant of David, the bright morning star." 17 The Spirit and the Bride say, "Come." And let the one who hears say, "Come." And let the one who is thirsty come; let the one who desires

take the water of life without price.... 20 He who testifies to these things says, "Surely I am coming soon." Amen. Come, Lord Jesus! 21 The grace of the Lord Jesus be with all. Amen (Revelation 22:16–18, 20–21).

Conclusion

The kingdom of Christ is an inaugurated manifestation of the eschatological kingdom of God. It is where the future meets the present, and where the present enrolls in the future. The boundaries of its membership align with this eschatological character, and thus its keys admit and remit members based on their relationship to Christ as judged by fallible men and women based on infallible rules set down in God's Word.

Those who belong to the kingdom through the covenant and thus claim Christ as their own and a place among His body enjoy the visible tokens of His promises to them. Baptism is a picture of God's promises of salvation to those united to Christ in His death and resurrection as well as that person's declaration of faith and participation in those very promises. Likewise, the Lord's Supper is a picture of God's promise of salvation to those united to Christ in His death and resurrection and the church's communal profession of faith and participation in those promises. Those who profess faith in Christ and later renounce and reject their profession go out from the covenant and kingdom because they were not of it. Yet they are liable for their lies and culpable of greater judgment for sinning against light, grace, and the King Himself.

The King will return to raise and judge mankind, sending His sheep to everlasting glory in the new creation, and the goats to everlasting punishment in Hell. And the fullness of the blessings of the New Covenant and the kingdom of God will be enjoyed eternally, the supreme blessing being the bridegroom himself, Jesus Christ "who is God over all, blessed forever. Amen" (Romans 9:5).

Conclusion

God covenanted a kingdom to Adam, and Adam set it on fire. God put out that fire with a flood. God covenanted a kingdom to Abraham, enclosing within its boundaries a blessing that the entire world needed— free, full, and final salvation. God covenanted a kingdom to His Son, Jesus Christ. And Jesus Christ mediated that kingdom to the world through the New Covenant, providing the promised blessing. That kingdom exists presently in the church. The church consists of a people awaiting their arrival at a home they have not seen. They know that this inheritance is theirs because it belongs to their Head, their Lord, their Savior, Jesus Christ. And they belong to Him. They have His Spirit. And if God has given them the greatest of all things, His Son, how could he not give them all other things as well (Romans 8:32). Jesus has died. He has risen. He has ascended. He has sat down. He will return. So, they wait, knowing that all things contribute ultimately to their good and God's glory. And one day the waters of Jordan will part, the Canaanites will disappear, and the Israel of God will enter the promised eternal inheritance.

As stated at the outset of this work, the study of the mystery of Christ, His covenant, and His kingdom is a devotional experience. It is a way of wonderment, a path of praise. It is a balm, a salve, a nepenthe, a panacea, a cordial, a precious remedy, a sweet medicine, "a sure and steadfast anchor for the soul" (Hebrews 6:19). The mystery is free everlasting salvation in Christ, and it is for everyone.

> 11 For the Scripture says, "Everyone who believes in him will not be put to shame." 12 For there is no distinction between Jew and Greek; for the same Lord is Lord of all, bestowing his riches on all who call on him. 13 For "everyone who calls on the name of the Lord will be saved" (Romans 10:11–13).

14 For this reason I bow my knees before the Father, 15 from whom every family in heaven and on earth is named, 16 that according to the riches of his glory he may grant you to be strengthened with power through his Spirit in your inner being, 17 so that Christ may dwell in your hearts through faith—that you, being rooted and grounded in love, 18 may have strength to comprehend with all the saints what is the breadth and length and height and depth, 19 and to know the love of Christ that surpasses knowledge, that you may be filled with all the fullness of God.

20 Now to him who is able to do far more abundantly than all that we ask or think, according to the power at work within us, 21 to him be glory in the church and in Christ Jesus throughout all generations, forever and ever. Amen (Ephesians 3:14–21).

Bibliography

Ames, William. *The Marrow of Sacred Divinity*. London: Edward Griffin, 1642.

Backus, Isaac. *A Short Description Of the difference between the Bond-woman and the Free; As they are the two Covenants, with the Character and Conditions of each of their Children*. Boston: Edes and Gill, 1770. 2nd edition.

Barcellos, Richard C. *The Covenant of Works*. Palmdale, CA: RBAP, 2016.

_____. *In Defense of the Decalogue: A Critique of New Covenant Theology*. Enumclaw, WA: Winepress Publishing, 2001.

_____. *Getting the Garden Right: Adam's Work and God's Rest in Light of Christ*. Cape Coral, FL: Founders Press, 2017.

Barret, John. *God's Love to Man, and Man's Duty towards God: Manifested in several Discourses on the Covenants of Works and Grace. Wherein divers Propositions are laid down, and sundry Cases resolved*. London: Jonathan Robinson, 1678.

Bauer, W., Danker, F. W., Arndt, W. F., and Gingrich, F. W. *Greek-English Lexicon of the New Testament and Other Early Christian Literature*. 3rd ed. Chicago, IL: University of Chicago Press, 2000.

Bavinck, Herman. *Reformed Dogmatics*. John Bolt, general editor and John Vriend, translator. Grand Rapids, MI: Baker Academic, 2007. 4 vols.

Beale, G. K. *Handbook on the New Testament Use of the Old Testament.* Grand Rapids, MI: Baker Academic, 2012.

Beale, G. K. and Gladd, Benjamin L. *Hidden But Now Revealed: A Biblical Theology of Mystery.* Downers Grove, Il: InterVarsity Press, 2014.

Beasley-Murray, G. R. *Jesus and the Kingdom of God.* Grand Rapids, MI: Eerdmans, 1986.

Berkhof, Louis. *Systematic Theology.* Grand Rapids, MI: Eerdmans, 1996.

Binning, Hugh. *The Common Principles of Christian Religion.* London: R.S., 1666.

Bucanus, William. *A Body of Divinity, Or: Institutions of Christian Religion.* trans. Robert Hill; London: Daniel Pakeman, 1659.

Bullinger, Heinrich. *Common places of Christian Religion.* trans. Iohn Stockwood; London: Tho. East and H. Middleton, 1572.

_____. *Fiftie Godlie and Learned Sermons, Divided Into Five Decades, Containing The chiefe and principall points of Christian Religion, written in three seuerall Tomes or Sections.* trans. H. I.; London: Ralph Newberie, 1587.

Burgess, Anthony. *Vindiciae Legis: Or, A Vindication of the Morall Law and the Covenants, From the Errours of Papists, Arminians, Socinians, and more especially, Antinomians. In XXIX. Lectures, preached at Laurence-Jury, London.* London: James Young, 1646.

Calvin, John. *The Institvtion of Christian Religion.* London: Reinolde Wolfe and Richard Harrison, 1561.

Casselli, Stephen J. *Divine Rule Maintained: Anthony Burgess, Covenant Theology, and the Place of the Law in Reformed Scholasticism.* Grand Rapids, MI: Reformation Heritage Books, 2016.

Cheare, Abraham and Steed, Robert. *A Plain Discovery Of The Unrighteous Judge and False Accuser.* London: Henry Mortlock, 1658.

Collins, Hercules. *The Marrow of Gospel History.* London: n.p., 1696.

_____. *The Sandy Foundation of Infant Baptism Shaken*. London: n.p., 1695.

A Confession of Faith Put Forth by the Elders and Brethren of Many Congregations of Christians (Baptized Upon Profession of their Faith) in London and the Country. London: Benjamin Harris, 1677.

Coxe, Benjamin, Knollys, Hanserd, and Kiffin, William. *A Declaration Concerning The Publike Dispute Which Should have been in the Publike Meeting-House of Alderman-Bury, the 3d of this instant Moneth of December; Concerning Infants-Baptisme. Together with some of the Arguments which should have been propounded and urged by some of those that are falsly called Anabaptists, which should then have been disputed*. London: n.p., 1645.

Coxe, Nehemiah. *A Discourse of the Covenants That God made with Men before the Law. Wherein, The Covenant of Circumcision is more largely handled, and the Invalidity of the Plea for Paedobaptism taken from thence discovered*. London: J.D., 1681.

_____. *Vindiciae Veritatis, Or a Confutation of the Heresies and Gross Errours Asserted by Thomas Collier in his Additional Word to his Body of Divinity*. London: Nath. Ponder, 1677.

Coxe, Nehemiah and Owen, John. *Covenant Theology: From Adam to Christ*. eds., Ronald D. Miller, James M. Renihan, and Francisco Orozco; Palmdale, CA: Reformed Baptist Academic Press, 2005.

Delaune, Thomas. *Truth Defended, Or a Triple Answer to the late Triumvirates Opposition in their Three Pamphlets*. London: n.p., 1677.

Dolezal, James. *All That Is in God*. Grand Rapids, MI: Reformation Heritage Books, 2017.

Erskine, Ralph. *Gospel Sonnets, or Spiritual Songs*. London: E. Dilly, 1759.

Fairbairn, Patrick. *The Typology of Scripture*. Grand Rapids, MI: Zondervan, 1965.

Fesko, J. V. *Last Things First*. Scotland, UK: Christian Focus Publications, 2007.

Fisher, Edward. *The Marrow of Modern Divinity*. London: R. Leybourn, 1646.

Flavel, John. *Planelogia. A Succinct and Seasonable Discourse of the Occasions, Causes, Nature, Rise, Growth, and Remedies of Mental Errors*. London: R. Roberts, 1691.

Foulkes, Francis. "The Acts of God," in *The Right Doctrine from the Wrong Texts?* ed. G.K. Beale; Grand Rapids, MI: Baker, 1994.

Gentry, Peter J. and Wellum, Stephen J. *Kingdom through Covenant: A Biblical-Theological Understanding of the Covenants*. Wheaton, IL: Crossway, 2012.

Gillespie, George. *Notes of Debates and Proceedings of The Assembly of Divines and Other Commissioners at Westminster*. Edinburgh: Robert Ogle and Oliver and Boyd, 1846.

Gillespie, Patrick. *The Ark of the Testament Opened, Or, The secret of the Lords Covenant unsealed, In A Treatise of the Covenant of Grace*. London: R.C., 1661.

Golding, Peter. *Covenant Theology*. Scotland, UK: Mentor, 2008.

Goppelt, Leonhard. Typos: *The Typological Interpretation of the Old Testament in the New*. Grand Rapids, MI: Eerdmans, 1982.

Hamilton, James M. Jr., "The Typology of David's Rise to Power: Messianic Patterns in the Book of Samuel." *SBJT* 16.2 (2012): 4–25.

Hodge, Charles. *Systematic Theology*. Peabody, MA: Hendrickson, 2008. 2 vols.

Horton, Michael. *The Christian Faith*. Grand Rapids, MI: Zondervan, 2011.

Hughes, John J. "Hebrews IX 15ff. And Galatians III 15ff. A Study in Covenant Practice and Procedure" in *Novum Testamentm*. Vol. XXI, no. 1 January (1979): 27–96.

Hutchinson, Edward. *A Treatise Concerning the Covenant and Baptism Dialogue-wise, between a Baptist & a Poedo-Baptist, Wherein is shewed, That Believers only are the Spirituall Seed of Abraham; Fully discovering The Fallacy of the Argument drawn from the Birth Priviledge.* London: Francis Smith, 1676.

Johnson, Dennis. *Him We Proclaim: Preaching Christ From All The Scriptures.* Phillipsburg, NJ: P&R, 2007.

Keach, Benjamin. *The Everlasting Covenant, A Sweet Cordial for a drooping Soul: Or, The Excellent Nature of the Covenant of Grace Opened: In a Sermon Preached January the 29th. At the Funeral of Mr. Henry Forty.* London: H. Barnard, 1693.

Kline, Meredith G. *Glory in our Midst.* Overland Park, KS: Two Age Press, 2001.

_____. *Kingdom Prologue: Genesis Foundations for a Covenantal Worldview.* Overland Park, KS: Two Ages Press, 2000.

Lawrence, Henry. *Of Baptisme.* Rotterdam: n.p., 1646.

_____. *A Plea for the Use of Gospell Ordinances.* London: M. S., 1651.

Lightfoot, John. *Horæ Hebraicæ et Talmudicæ Impensæ in Epistolam Primam S. Pauli ad Corinthios.* Cambridge: Joan. Field, 1664.

Luther, Martin. *A Commentarie of M. Doctor Martin Lvther Vpon The Epistle of S. Paul to the Galathians.* London: Thomas Vautroullier, 1575.

Manton, Thomas. *A Practical Commentary, or an Exposition with Notes on the Epistle of James.* London: J. Macock, 1651.

Norton, John. *The Orthodox Evangelist.* London: John Macock, 1654.

Owen, John. *A Continuation of the Exposition of the Epistle of Paul the Apostle to the Hebrews.* London: Nathaniel Ponder, 1680.

_____. *Exercitations Concerning the Name, Original, Nature, Use, and Continuance of a Day of Sacred Rest.* London: R.W., 1671.

_____. *Exercitations on the Epistle to the Hebrews Concerning the Priesthood of Christ… With a Continuation of the Exposition on the Third, Fourth, and Fifth Chapters*. London: John Darby, 1674.

Patient, Thomas. *The Doctrine of Baptism, And the Distinction of the Covenants*. London: Henry Hills, 1654.

Perkins, William. *A Commentarie or Exposition, upon the five first Chapters of the Epistle to the Galatians*. Cambridge, UK: John Legat, 1604.

Polanus, Amandus. *The Substance of Christian Religion*. London: Arn Hatfield, 1600.

Purnell, Robert. *A Little Cabinet Richly Stored*. London: R. W., 1657.

_____. *The Weavers Shuttle Displayed*. London: Giles Calvert, 1652.

Renihan, Samuel D. *From Shadow to Substance: The Federal Theology of the English Particular Baptists* (1642–1704). Oxford: Regent's Park College, 2018.

Ridderbos, Herman. *The Coming of the Kingdom*. Philadelphia, PA: P&R, 1962.

Ritor, Andrew. *The Second Part of the Vanity & Childishnes of Infants Baptisme*. London: n.p., 1642.

Robertson, O. Palmer. *The Christ of the Covenants*. Phillipsburg, NJ: P&R, 1980.

_____. *The Israel of God*. Phillipsburg, NJ: P&R, 2000.

Schreiner, Thomas R. *Covenant and God's Purpose for the World*. Wheaton, IL: Crossway, 2017.

Spilsbury, John. *A Treatise Concerning The Lawfull Subject of Baptisme*. London: n.p., 1643.

_____. *Truth Vindicated in Several Branches*. London: n.p., 1695.

Turretin, Francis. *Institutes of Elenctic Theology*. Phillipsburg, NJ: P&R, 1994. 3 vols.

Vos, Geerhardus. *Biblical Theology*. Banner of Truth: Carlisle, PA: 2007.

_____. *Redemptive History and Biblical Interpretation*. Phillipsburg, NJ: P&R, 1980.

_____. *The Teaching of Jesus Concerning the Kingdom of God and the Church*. NY: American Tract Society, 1903.

Witsius, Herman. *The Economy of the Covenants Between God and Man*. Phillipsburg, NJ: P&R, 1990. 2 vols.

Woolsey, Andrew A. *Unity and Continuity in Covenantal Thought*. Grand Rapids, MI: Reformation Heritage Books, 2012.

Made in the USA
Las Vegas, NV
08 February 2024

85482906R00128